Birgit Abegg, Michael Benford

Short Course Communication for Business

Kurzlehrgang englische Handelskorrespondenz und Bürokommunikation

Max Hueber Verlag

To Rosalind, Rebecca, Jake and David
Für Peter, Pete und Gabi

Acknowledgements
The authors and publishers are grateful to the following copyright owners for permission to reproduce documents. It has not been possible to identify the sources of all the material used and in such cases the publishers would welcome information from copyright owners.
The names of persons and companies used in the book are fictitious. Any similarities to existing persons are purely unintentional.
The letterheads and logos may not be copied or used otherwise.

p. 204 H. & E. Brunswick GmbH & Co., Hamburg, Germany
pp. 205, 207, 208, 210 SITPRO, London, UK
p. 206 British Airways, London, UK
p. 209 Lloyd's, London, UK

5. 4. 3. | Die letzten Ziffern
2008 07 06 05 04 | bezeichnen Zahl und Jahr des Druckes.
Alle Drucke dieser Auflage können, da unverändert,
nebeneinander benutzt werden.
1. Auflage

Verlagsredaktion: Heike Lenz, Frankfurt
Umschlaggestaltung, Layout und Herstellung: Christiane Gerstung, München
Zeichnungen: Reinhard Blumenschein, München
Druck: Appl Firmengruppe, Wemding
Bindung: Ludwig Auer GmbH, Donauwörth
Printed in Germany
ISBN 3-19-002695-5

Vorwort

Communication for Business – Short Course ist für Lernende konzipiert, die sich mit wenigen Unterichtsstunden pro Woche möglichst schnell die Grundlagen der Handelskorrepondenz aneignen wollen. Diese Kurzfassung ist sowohl in Schulen (z. B. Höhere Handelsschule) als auch in Betrieben einsetzbar.

Auf komplizierte Sachverhalte wurde bewusst verzichtet, damit die Lernenden problemlos und ohne langes Suchen alle im Lehrwerk enthaltenen Aufgaben mit Hilfe der *Standard Expressions* (Satzbausteine) und der *Phraseology* lösen können. Jede Unit besteht aus:

- Letter Plan(s)
- Specimen Letter
- Specimen Fax bzw. E-mail
- Standard Expressions
- Phraseology
- Exercises
- Stichwortaufgaben.

Der Aufgabenapparat (*Exercises*) beinhaltet unter anderem Kreuzworträtsel, Anagramme und Suchaufgaben. Er wird von dem Brettspiel *Contract* ergänzt, das von zwei bis etwa sechs Personen gespielt werden kann. Somit haben Lernende die Möglichkeit, bereits eingeführte Inhalte auf spielerische Art und Weise zu festigen. Die englisch-deutsche *Phraseology* am Ende jeder Unit eignet sich in der Länge zum Auswendiglernen und bildet somit die Grundlage für das von der Lehrkraft bevorzugte Prüfverfahren (z. B. Tests, Klassenarbeiten u. ä.).

Die sechs *Secretarial Activities*, zu denen jeweils Tonaufnahmen vorliegen, beinhalten je nach Aufgabentyp eine Kombination folgender Elemente:

- Musterausdrücke
- Hörverständnisaufgabe(n)
- Satzbausteine
- englisch- oder deutschsprachige Aufgaben.

Auch hier sollen Lernende ihre schriftliche und mündliche Arbeit jeweils mit Hilfe von *Standard Expressions* (Satzbausteinen) strukturieren und fehlerfrei gestalten können.

Last but certainly not least hoffen wir, dass Sie bei der Arbeit mit diesem Lehrwerk viel Spaß und Erfolg haben werden.

Birgit Abegg, Michael Benford
Mai 2000

Inhalt

Unit 1
Layouts

Introduction

English is the most widely-used language in business communication in the world. As it is used in so many different countries, it is impossible to lay down firm rules about the way a letter, fax, e-mail or memo should be set out. For this reason only the most frequently found formats used in written business communication are reproduced here.

Business Letters

British Layout (Fig. 1)

Here the main points to remember are:

- Block form (flush-left) with open punctuation (i. e. no commas) is recommended for everything apart from the letterhead, for which there is no set layout.
- The reference initials are *before* the date.
- In the date the month should be written as a word (e. g. 21 January ..) because an all-figure date (e. g. 9 / 10 / ..) means 9 October in Britain and September 10 in the USA.
- The name of the British town or city in the inside address is written in capitals on one line and the postcode is written in capital letters on the next line (see **Fig. 4** "Private Letter").
- There is an important link between the salutation and the complimentary close (see **Table "T"**).
- The subject line is *after* the salutation.
- The paragraphs in the body of the letter are separated by a free line.
- The signatory's name and position must be written clearly after the signature.

American Layout (Fig. 3)

Here the important things to remember are:

- Except in the letterhead, for which there is no set layout, block form (flush-left) with standard punctuation is recommended, i. e.
  - a comma in the date before the year
  - a comma before the ZIP code in the inside address
  - a colon after the salutation
  - a comma after the complimentary close (AE: complimentary closing)
- In the date, the month should be written as a word (e. g. January 21, ..) because an all-figure date (e. g. 9 / 10 / ..) means 9 October in Britain and September 10 in the USA.
- The subject line is *before* the salutation and is *not* underlined, in capital letters or in bold type.
- Try to write to a named person if possible. If this is not possible, use the salutation "Ladies and Gentlemen:".
- The paragraphs in the body of the letter are separated by a free line.
- The reference initials (signatory's and typist's initials) are typed after the signatory's position.

British Layout

Block form / open punctuation. This is the most common form of layout.

Green Wrap Ltd

21 Fullwell Rd
PRESTON
PN2 5AJ
England
Tel. +44 (0)17 72 5 62 23
Fax +44 (0)17 72 5 62 25
E-mail: Johnson@greenwrap.co.uk
http://www.greenwrap.co.uk

• *(One free line – optional)*
MB/TT
10 September ..
• *(one free line)*
URGENT
•
Messrs Smith & Co
12604 Prince Street
Buda, TX 78610
USA
•
For the attention of Mr Lewis, Despatch Section
•
Dear Mr Lewis
•
<u>Your Order of 3 September .. for Packaging Material</u>
•
Many thanks for the above-mentioned order, which will be processed by our Despatch Department within the next ten days.
•
We trust the goods will arrive punctually and in good condition and look forward to the pleasure of serving you again in the near future.
•
Yours sincerely
GreenWrap Ltd
•
Margaret Brown
•
Margaret Brown (Ms)
Managing Director
•
•
Enc
•
•
cc: T. Johnson, Sales Manager

1. Letterhead with logo, postcode (UK), telephone, fax and e-mail numbers and Internet address. The "+" sign stands for the international access code.
2. Reference initials. "MB" stands for the signatory (Margaret Brown). "TT" (or "tt") stands for the typist, e.g. Triona Taylor.
3. Date. Write the month as a word.
4. Special markings (e.g. "AIR MAIL", "REGISTERED", "CONFIDENTIAL").
5. Inside address. "Messrs." is the plural of "Mr". "TX" stands for "Texas" and 78610 is the ZIP code.
6. Attention line.
7. Salutation. See table (**Table "T"**) for link with complimentary close.
8. Subject line. This is underlined and the important words are capitalised.
9. Body of the letter. The first word has a capital letter.
10. Complimentary close with the signature, name (followed by preferred title in brackets in the case of a woman) and position of the signatory clearly written. See table (**Table "T"**) for link with salutation.
11. Enclosure (Enc), Enclosures (Encs). These may be listed below.
12. Carbon copy for T. Johnson, the sales manager.

Fig. 1

Links between the Salutation and the Complimentary Close

British Forms

	Salutation	Complimentary Close
1	Dear Sir / Madam Dear Sir or Madam Dear Sir Dear Sirs	Yours faithfully
2	Dear Mr Brown Dear Ms Brown Dear Miss Brown Dear Mrs Brown Dear Customer	Yours sincerely
3	Dear John Dear Susan	Yours sincerely or: With best regards or: Best regards or: Regards

American Forms

	Salutation	Complimentary Close
4	Ladies and Gentlemen: Dear Mr. Brown, Dear Mr. Brown: Dear Ms. Brown, Dear Ms. Brown: Dear Miss Brown, Dear Miss Brown: Dear Mrs. Brown, Dear Mrs. Brown: Dear Customer, Dear Customer:	Sincerely, or: Sincerely yours,
5	Dear John, Dear John: Dear Carol, Dear Carol:	Cordially, or: Sincerely,

Table "T"

Continuation Pages

These have the page number, the date and the recipient's name blocked at the left margin at the top of the next page.

2
•
28 June ..
•
Mr James Brown
•
Text text text text text text text text text text text text text text text text text text text text text text text text text text text text text text text text …

Fig. 2

American Layout

Green Wrap Ltd *488 East Prince Street* *Reno, NV 89509* *USA* *Tel. +1 (9 16) 2 72-8 94 99* *Fax +1 (9 16) 2 72-9 14 88* *E-mail: gwinc@greenwrap.com* *http://www.greenwrap.com*	**1.** Letterhead with logo, ZIP code (Nevada), telephone, fax and e-mail numbers and Internet address.
• *(one free line)* September 10, ..	**2.** Date (month-day-year)
• Carl T. Lewis, Vice President Smith Shipping Corp. 12604 Prince Street Buda, TX 78610 USA	**3.** Inside address with ZIP code.
• Re: Your Order of September 3, ..	**4.** Subject line before the salutation.
• Dear Mr. Lewis:	**5.** Salutation followed by a colon.
• Many thanks for the above-mentioned order, which will be processed by our Despatch Department within the next ten days. • We trust the goods will arrive punctually and in good condition and look forward to the pleasure of serving you again in the near future.	**6.** Body of the letter. The first word has a capital letter.
• Sincerely, • • *Michael Brown* • • Michael Brown President	**7.** Complimentary close (AE: complimentary closing) followed by a comma, the signature and the name and position of the signatory clearly written.
• MB:tt	**8.** Signatory's and typist's initials, separated by a colon.
• Enclosure: Catalog	**9.** Enclosure(s)
• Copies: Trent Johnson, Sales Manager Alicia Montara, Export Division	**10.** Copies for Trent Johnson and Alicia Montara.

Fig. 3

Private Letter

Heinrich-Gustav-Str. 99
69121 Heidelberg
Germany

Your ref. ESC/kw 20 January ..

Ms Kate Williams
Human Resources Officer
PowerGen Plc
90–100 Coronation Street
LANCASTER
LA1 4GH
England

Dear Ms Williams

Your Advertisement on the Internet for the Post of European Sales Clerk

I am writing with reference to the above-mentioned advertisement and am most interested in applying for the post you offer.

I am currently employed as a business administration clerk at Neckarstahl AG in Heidelberg and have held this post for five years. Even though I am successful in my current position I would like to work for a firm at which I would be able to put my knowledge of English to good use.

I enclose my CV and copies of my qualifications. Should you require a reference, Frau Wiebke Pütz, who teaches business administration theory and English at Heidelberg Vocational Training College, will be pleased to provide you with any information you may need.

I look forward to hearing from you at your earliest convenience.

Yours sincerely

Rita Räumschüssel

Rita Räumschüssel (Ms)

Encs:
CV
Certificates

Fig. 4

Notes:

1. The sender's address is written in the top right-hand corner. The sender's name is *not* normally written at the top of the page.
2. The date can be written under the sender's address or above the inside address.
3. "Your ref." can be included above the inside address on the same level as the date.
4. The sender's name (Rita Räumschüssel) is clearly written after the signature. A woman can add how she wishes to be addressed by adding (Miss), (Mrs) or (Ms) after her name.

Fax Layout

There is no set layout for a fax (facsimile). The following example contains all the necessary information. "FAO" stands for "For the attention of".

Fax cover sheet

FAO:	Ms Heike Maybaum Export Sales Department Damen-Mode GmbH Gelsenkirchen Germany
Fax No:	00 49 (2 09) 5 56 17
From:	Tim Wright Purchasing Department Green Wrap Ltd 21 Fullwell Road PRESTON PN2 5AJ England Tel +44 (17 72) 5 62 23 Fax +44 (17 72) 5 62 25 E-mail: greenwrap@greenwrap.co.uk
Date:	28 December ..
Subject:	Birmingham
Total Pages:	1

Dear Heike

Sorry about the delay in replying. We've now got transport arranged for the equipment so there shouldn't be any hitches.

Please contact me if you have any queries.

Kind regards

Tim

Fig. 5

E-mail

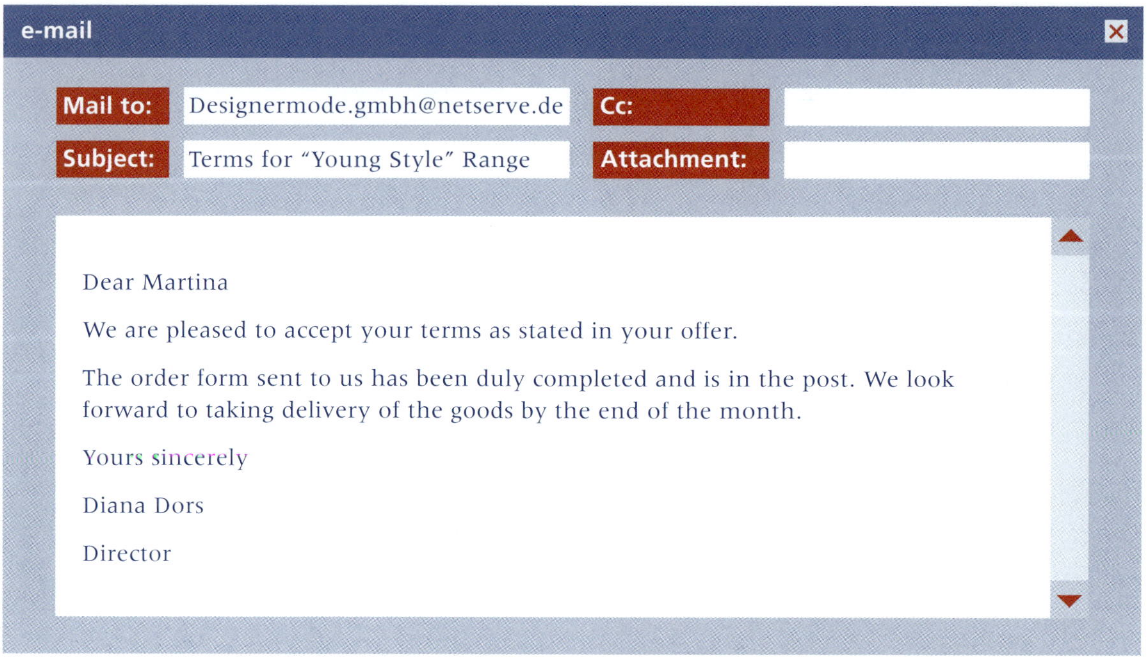
e-mail

Mail to: Designermode.gmbh@netserve.de

Cc:

Subject: Terms for "Young Style" Range

Attachment:

Dear Martina

We are pleased to accept your terms as stated in your offer.

The order form sent to us has been duly completed and is in the post. We look forward to taking delivery of the goods by the end of the month.

Yours sincerely

Diana Dors

Director

Fig. 6

E-mails are written on-screen and pre-structured by the computer program used. The five boxes in which entries can be made are as follows:

Mail to:
The e-mail subscriber's e-mail address is written here.

Cc:
This stands for "carbon copy" (see page 7, point 12 "British Layout"). Copies of the e-mail can be sent automatically to any number of other subscribers listed in the e-mail program's address list.

Subject:
Here the content of the e-mail should be summarised in 8–10 words.

Attachment:
Here a file can be sent with the e-mail.

The message
Here the normal rules of business letter writing are used. The style of an e-mail is normally informal (short forms, first names, uncomplicated language) and there is no signature.

Exercises

Exercise 1: The date

How would the following dates be written in a business letter?

USA

1. 10 / 11 / 2001
2. 1 / 10 / 2004
3. 12 / 7 / 2000
4. 4 / 5 / 2001
5. 2 / 3 / 2003
6. 3 / 4 / 2005

UK

7. 9 / 8 / 2003
8. 7 / 9 / 2002
9. 5 / 2 / 2006
10. 21 / 6 / 2000
11. 10 / 11 / 2001
12. 2 / 1 / 2003

Exercise 2: Salutation / complimentary close

What would (1) the salutation and (2) the complimentary close be in the following cases?

2.1 You write a letter to a lady called Ramona Sanchez at an American company. You are not on first name terms with her.

2.2 You write a letter to the manager of a British bank. You have had no contact with the bank before.

2.3 A German business woman writes to the managing director of Sinclair plc in England. His name is J. Kenton.

2.4 An American businessman writes to a German businessman called Frank Stallmann, who is the sales director at his company. They are on friendly terms.

Layout exercises

Business Letters

Exercise 3: British Layout

Use **Fig. 1** as your model.

Thorsten Strauch, who works in the export section of Behr Glaskunst, Rotkäppchenstr. 23 in 81739 Munich, Germany, dictates a letter to his secretary, Tina Törner. The letter is to Smith & Pettit Ltd at 21 Highbury Road, Sheffield SH1 4WW, England. Herr Strauch wants Ms Ramona Stone to receive the letter, which is about article no. 445-A. He encloses photographs with the letter. The date is 6 / 7 / 20 .. .

Exercise 4: American Layout

Use **Fig. 3** as your model.

Klaus Teymann is an environmental technology consultant at Umwelttechnik GmbH, Harpener Hellweg 78, 44805 Bochum. He sends an air mail letter to Ms. Tricia O'Neil at Hudson Environmental Consulting Inc.,114 East 32nd Street, New York, NY 10010, USA. He dictates the letter to his secretary Tamara Wehrheim (today's date) and tells her to include a brochure with it. The letter is about Umwelttechnik's stand at the Chicago Environmental Convention next month.

Exercise 5: British Layout

Use **Fig. 1** as your model.
Terence Peabody, the general manager of Howitt and Tomkin Ltd, at 42 King Street, Nottingham NO3 4AA, England, dictates a letter to his secretary Fiona Ramsbottom and tells her to make sure Charles Stapleton, the Finance Controller, gets a copy. The letter is to Kuhn Baustoffgroßhandel, Sachsenstr. 27, 45128 Essen, about article no. 74/B. Mr Peabody signs the letter and encloses an order form. The date is 10 / 4 / .. .

Exercise 6: British or American Layout

Use **Fig. 1** or **Fig. 3** as your model.
Angela Klein is head of export sales at DTT Wärmesysteme GmbH, Reuterstr. 80, 90408 Nürnberg, Germany. Her secretary, Barbara Braun, sends a letter (today's date), dictated by Frau Klein and two leaflets to Nancy Shriver, the chief executive officer at Omega Air Conditioning Inc., 140 North Avenue, Hartland, WI 53029, USA. The letter is about Omega's offer dated the first of last month.

Exercise 7: Fax Layout

Use **Fig. 5** as your model and include a salutation and a complimentary close as in a business letter.
Tamara Terhoven, who is the European Sales Director at Haverkamp Design AG, Im Teich 24, 41258 Essen, fax +49 (2 01) 22 88 66, tells her secretary, Michaela Förster, to send a fax (today's date) to Mr Humphrey Hill, the Export Manager at Sterling Interiors Ltd, 99 Victoria Promenade, Eastbourne EF6 9KL, England, fax +44 (1323) 9 87 66. The fax is in reply to Humphrey Hill's recent letter (ref. HH/BK). She also tells her secretary to include four more pages of information with the fax. Tamara Terhoven is on friendly terms with Humphrey Hill.

Exercise 8: E-mail Layout

Use **Fig. 6** as your model.
You work in the European Division of a freight forwarding agency in Hamburg. You receive an e-mail from Carola Montez, who works for a firm in New York, e-mail: delmont@gnn.com. You know Carola from previous correspondence and phone calls. You now reply to this e-mail with a special offer for transport in eastern Europe. Use an American salutation and complimentary close. You send a file called "tarif.ost" with your e-mail.

Vocabulary List

able, to be ~ to	*können*
above-mentioned	*oben erwähnt*
add	*hinzufügen*
addressed, to be ~ (person)	*angeschrieben bzw. angesprochen werden*
advertisement	*Anzeige*
air conditioning	*Klimaanlage*
AIR MAIL	*Mit Luftpost*
all-figure date, an ~	*ein Datum, das nur aus Zahlen besteht*
apart from	*außer*
apply, to ~ for	*sich bewerben um / auf*
arrange	*hier: bestellen, organisieren*
as stated	*wie angegeben*
attachment	*Anlage*
attention, for the ~ of	*zu Händen*
avoid	*vermeiden*
below	*hier: darunter*
body of the letter	*Brieftext*
bold type, in ~	*fettgedruckt*
brackets , in ~	*in Klammern*
brochure	*Prospekt, Broschüre*
business administration clerk	*Industriekaufmann/ -frau*
business administration theory	*Betriebswirtschaftslehre*
by, ~ the end of the month	*bis Ende des Monats*
capitalised	*in Großbuchstaben geschrieben*
capitals, in ~	*in Großbuchstaben*
carbon copy	*hier: Verteilervermerk (wörtlich: Durchschlag)*
case, in the ~ of	*im Falle*
chief executive officer	*Vorstandsvorsitzende/r, Generaldirektor/in, Hauptgeschäfts-leiter/in*
clearly	*deutlich*
colon	*Doppelpunkt*
common	*häufig, weitverbreitet*
complete, to ~ (form)	*ausfüllen (Formular)*
complimentary close	*Schlussformel*
condition, in good ~	*in gutem Zustand*
CONFIDENTIAL	*vertraulich*
contain	*beinhalten*
contents, the ~	*Inhalt*
Continuation Page(s)	*Folgeseite(n)*
convenience, at your earliest ~	*so bald wie möglich*
Cordially	*Herzliche Grüße*
currently	*gegenwärtig*
CV	*Lebenslauf*
delay, the ~	*Verzögerung*
despatch section	*Versandabteilung*
different	*verschieden*
division	*Abteilung*
duly	*ordnungsgemäß*
e-mail subscriber	*E-Mail-Teilnehmer/in*
employ, to ~	*beschäftigen*
enclose	*beifügen*
entries, an entry	*Eintrag(ungen)*
envelope, window ~	*Fensterumschlag*
environmental convention	*Umwelttagung*
environmental technology consultant	*Berater/in für Umwelttechnik*
equipment	*Ausrüstung*
European sales clerk	*Verkaufssachbe-arbeiter/in für den europäischen Markt*
even though	*obwohl*
except	*außer*
extra practice	*zusätzliche Übungen*
file, a ~	*Datei*
firm	*fest*
flush-left	*linksbündig*
freight forwarding agency	*Spedition*
frequently	*häufig*
hitch, a ~	*Panne*
hold, to ~ (a post)	*(eine Stelle) innehaben*
human resources officer	*Personalleiter/in*
important	*wichtig*
impossible	*unmöglich*
in the top right-hand corner	*hier: oben rechts*
inside address	*Empfängeranschrift*
interiors	*hier: Inneneinrichtung*
international access code	*internationale Vor-wahlnummer (bei Auslandsgesprächen)*
knowledge of English	*Englischkenntnisse*
language	*Sprache*
lay down, to ~	*festlegen*
leaflet	*Faltblatt*
letterhead	*Briefkopf*
level, on the same ~	*auf der gleichen Höhe (wie das Datum)*

link, a ~	*Verbindung*
list, to ~	*auflisten*
look, to ~ forward to	*sich freuen auf*
managing director	*Geschäftsführer/in*
margin	*Rand*
memo	*Memorandum, innerbetriebliche Mitteilung*
message	*Nachricht*
Messrs	*(die) Herren*
misunderstanding	*Missverständnis*
named person, a ~	*eine namentlich genannte Person*
necessary	*notwendig*
need, to ~	*benötigen*
on-screen	*auf dem Bildschirm*
order form	*Bestellformular*
paragraph	*Absatz*
post, a ~	*hier: Stelle*
postcode	*Postleitzahl (britisch)*
preferred title	*bevorzugte Anrede*
pre-structured	*vorstrukturiert*
previous correspondence	*vorheriger Schriftverkehr*
process, to ~	*bearbeiten*
provide with, to ~ (a reference)	*geben (eine Referenz)*
punctually	*pünktlich*
punctuation	*Interpunktion*
purchasing director	*Einkaufsleiter/in*
put to good use	*gut einbringen, gut verwerten*
qualifications	*Befähigungsnachweise*
query, a	*Frage*
range	*Sortiment*
reason, for this ~	*aus diesem Grund*
receive	*erhalten*
recent letter	*hier: letzter Brief*
recipient	*Empfänger*
recommend	*empfehlen*
reference initials	*Bezugsinitialen*
reference, with ~ to	*mit Bezug auf*
Regards	*hier: Grüße*
REGISTERED	*Einschreiben*
reproduce	*wiedergeben*
require	*benötigen*
rule, a ~	*Regel*
sales manager	*Verkaufsleiter/in*
salutation	*Anrede*
separate, to ~	*trennen*
serve, to ~	*(be)dienen*
set, no ~ layout	*kein festgelegtes Layout*
set out, to ~	*hier: gestalten, formatieren*
should you …	*sollten Sie …*
signatory	*Unterzeichner/in*
signature	*Unterschrift*
special marking	*besondere Markierung*
special offer	*Sonderangebot*
subject line	*Betreff*
successful	*erfolgreich*
summarise	*zusammenfassen*
take delivery of, to ~	*in Empfang nehmen*
terms	*Bedingungen*
terms, on first name ~	*per Du*
terms, on friendly ~	*per Du*
trust, to ~	*davon ausgehen, dass*
typist	*Schreibkraft*
underline	*unterstreichen*
use, to ~	*verwenden*
vocational training college	*Berufsschule*
widely-used, most ~	*am häufigsten verwendet*
within	*innerhalb*
ZIP code	*Postleitzahl (amerikanisch)*

Unit 2
Enquiries

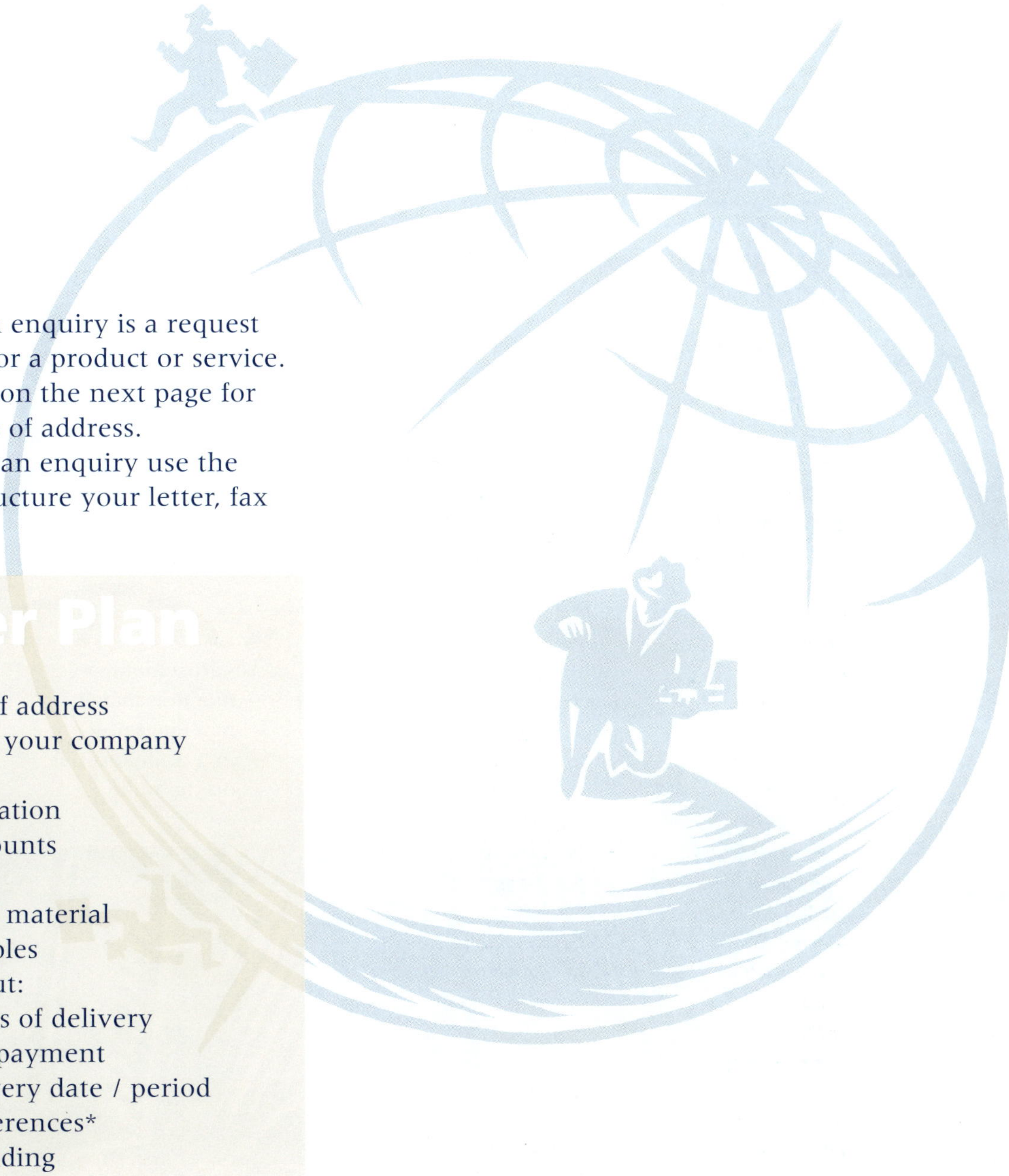

Introduction

In most cases, an enquiry is a request for a quotation for a product or service. See the diagram on the next page for common sources of address.

When writing an enquiry use the letter plan to structure your letter, fax or e-mail.

Letter Plan

Enquiries

1. Source of address
2. Describe your company
3. Ask for:
   - quotation
   - discounts
4. Ask for:
   - sales material
   - samples
5. Ask about:
   - terms of delivery and payment
   - delivery date / period
6. Give references*
7. Polite ending

*As appropriate

Fig. 7

Sources of Address

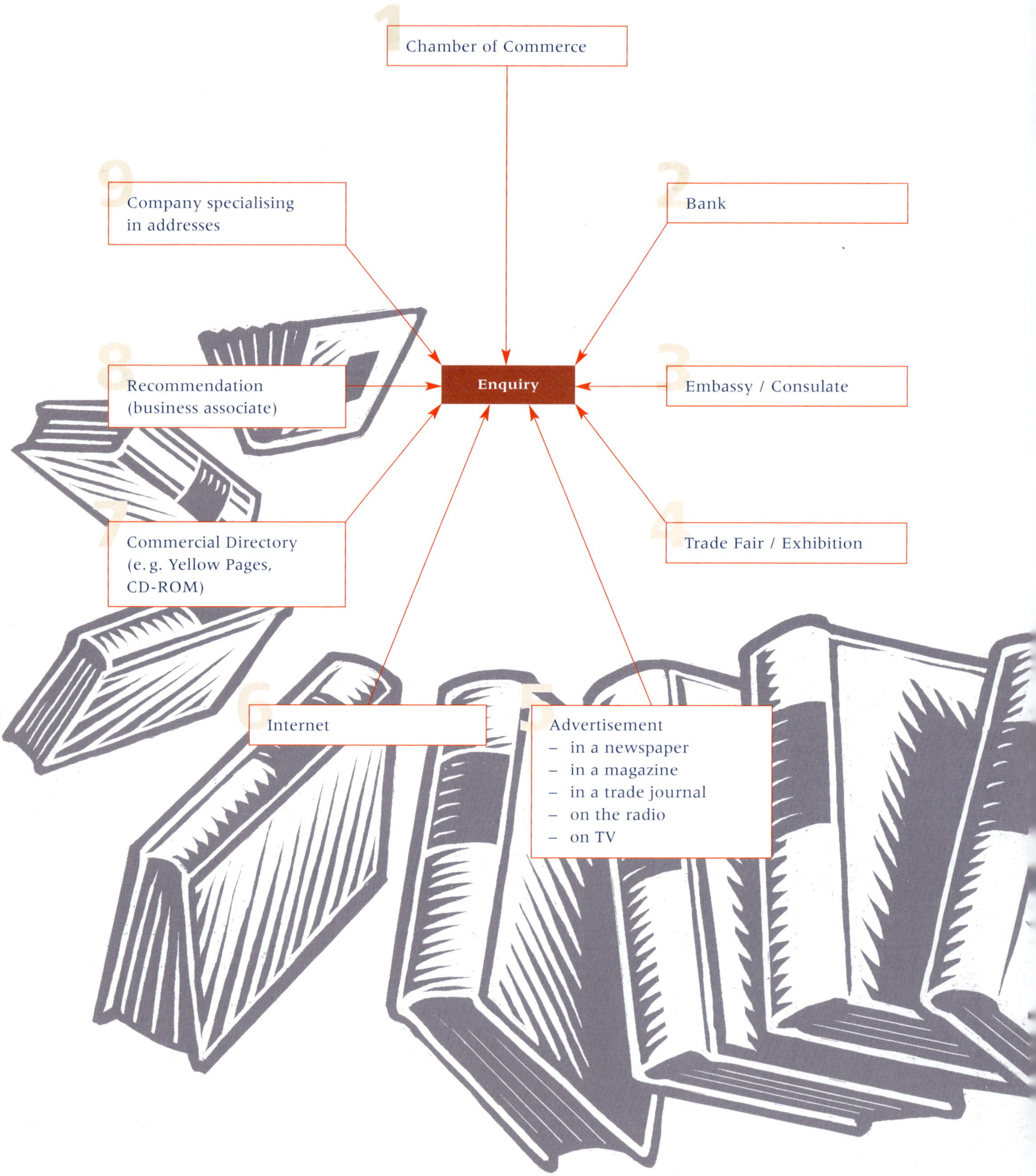

Specimen Letter

Neutech GmbH
Bahnhofstr. 98
45277 Essen
Germany

DS/RB
21 October ..

Electronic Equipment Ltd
13 London Road
OXFORD
OX2 7XY
England

Dear Sirs

Your ICUC Videophone

We recently visited your stand at the Hanover Trade Fair and were most impressed by your new videophone.

As a leading importer of electronic equipment with excellent business contacts throughout Germany, we feel that your product will sell well here.

Please send us an illustrated colour brochure, your current export price list and details of your discounts for quantity, cash, early payment and initial orders.
We would also like some information on your terms of delivery and payment and delivery periods.

Should you require a reference, please contact Deutsche Bank in Essen.

We look forward to hearing from you soon.

Yours faithfully
Neutech GmbH

Dagobert Schneider

Dagobert Schneider
Managing Director

Specimen Fax

sheet

FAO:	Mr Chiou Fang Yeh Export Sales Manager Ziang Kong Garments Co. Ltd Taipei Taiwan
Fax No:	+8 86 (2) 3 92 90 44
From:	Ursula Klein Head Buyer Neumoden GmbH Düsseldorf Germany Tel.: +49 (2 11) 89 75 43 Fax: +49 (2 11) 89 75 44 E-mail: neu.moden@firmlink.de
Date:	2 February ..
Subject:	Request for Quotation for "Summer Vogue Fashions"
Total Pages:	1

Dear Mr Chiou Fang Yeh

We have seen your advertisement in the latest edition of "The Rag Trade" for "Summer Vogue Fashions".

Our company is a major distributor of ladies' fashion clothes in Düsseldorf, Germany and has customers all over the European Union.

Please send us a quotation for your "Summer Vogue Fashions" including sales literature and an export price list. We also require details of your terms of payment and delivery and all discounts.

References on our company can be obtained from Ruhrbank or Kaufhof AG in Düsseldorf.

If your offer meets our requirements, we will be pleased to place a trial order with you.

We hope to hear from you shortly.

Yours sincerely

Ursula Klein

Case Study

You are Andrea Link, the Import Manager at Möbelimport Schulz GmbH in Essen. Your company imports furniture of all types and at the moment it is looking for office furniture for the German market.

Last month you saw some of the furniture made by "Office Style Manufacturing UK" at the "Modern Office" Exhibition in Birmingham, England. You also talked to Eileen Conway, Office Style's Export Sales Manager. Having now also looked at the company's web site on the Internet, you decide to contact them and ask for further information.

Activity

Write Andrea's letter / fax / e-mail to Office Style Manufacturing UK. Add further details as appropriate.

From:	Andrea Link, Import Manager, Möbelimport Schulz GmbH, Kupferdreher Str. 99, 45257 Essen, fax +49 (2 01) 44 45 00, e-mail: moebel.schulz.essen@aol.com
To:	Ms Eileen Conway, Export Sales Manager, Office Style Manufacturing UK, Toxteth Business Park, Liverpool LO3 8LJ, England, fax +44 (151) 89 77 44, e-mail: office.style@firmnet.uk

Standard Expressions

1 Source of address	We have been given your address by We have obtained your company's address from		the Chamber of Commerce in … (location) the London Chamber of Commerce the … (nationality, e.g. Japanese) embassy/consulate		who tell us you	specialise in … supply manufacture distribute	(product/service)
	We have seen your (company's)		web site on the Internet				
			advertisement in the latest edition of … (publication, e.g. "Business Weekly")				
	Having seen your stand We saw your (company's) stand We were most impressed by the products your company demonstrated				at the recent	… Fair (e.g. Young Style Clothes Fair)	in … (location)
	… we would now like to know more about your company's products						
2 Description of your company	As a Our company is a We are a	well-established leading successful fast-growing	wholesaler of importer of distributor of	high-quality	… (product, e.g. wines and spirits)		from suppliers all over the world with excellent business contacts throughout Germany with many long-standing customers
	… we have … we also have		extensive business contacts a well-established sales network		all over Germany throughout the EU and beyond		
3 Ask for quotation	We are particularly interested in importing		… (product/service)		at the moment		
	As goods of this nature are in demand at present		please (therefore) send us we would be grateful if you would let us have		a quotation		(for) … (goods/services)
– discounts	Please include … including details of … with information on … stating … indicating		all discounts granted				
	Do you grant a(n)		introductory offer discount/initial order discount/quantity discount/trade discount/cash discount/early payment discount?				

4	Ask for sales material	We would be grateful if you would provide us with Please also let us have	your latest illustrated colour your latest comprehensive your latest comprehensive colour	catalogue	on your entire range of products
			detailed comprehensive	sales literature sales material	
		... and ... together with ... as well as	your current export price list	including all discounts	
	– samples	Are you willing to provide us with (a) sample(s)?			
5	Ask about terms (of delivery and payment)	Please also let us have details of your terms of delivery and payment Please also state your terms of delivery and payment ... including full details of your terms of delivery and payment			
		Are you willing to deliver		... (term of delivery, e.g. CIF Hamburg)? franco to our premises?	
	– delivery date/period	Details of Information on	your delivery periods/dates/times	would also be appreciated	
		... as well as your delivery periods/dates			
		Delivery would need to be made We would require delivery	within 3 weeks after receipt of our order	at the latest	
6	References	References are available First-class trade and bank references can be supplied		on request	
		Should you require a reference,		... (name of bank/company) in ... will be happy to provide you with any information you may require please contact ... (name of bank/company)	
7	Polite ending	If your company's ... (product/goods) correspond(s) to our customers' wishes,		we will we will be willing to	place a trial order place a sizeable order with you
		As the market for such products is growing rapidly, we will be in a position to place a substantial order if your goods meet our requirements			
		We look forward to hearing from you soon We look forward to your (early) reply with interest			

Phraseology

1	**Source of address**	***Quelle der Anschrift***
	We have seen your advertisement in the latest edition of … (publication)	*Wir haben Ihre Anzeige in der letzten Ausgabe der … (Veröffentlichung) gesehen*
	We have been given your company's address by the Chamber of Commerce in Düsseldorf	*Wir erhielten die Anschrift Ihrer Firma von der Handelskammer in Düsseldorf*
	We have seen your (company's) web site / home page / advertisement on the Internet	*Wir haben Ihre (die) Website / Homepage / Anzeige (Ihrer Gesellschaft) im Internet gesehen*
	Having seen your stand at the recent Young Style Clothes Fair …	*Wir haben Ihren Stand auf der letzten Young Style Bekleidungsmesse gesehen …*
	We were most impressed by the products your company demonstrated at the recent Car Show	*Wir waren von den Produkten Ihrer Firma, die auf der letzten Automesse vorgeführt wurden, höchst beeindruckt*
2	**Describe your company**	***Beschreiben Sie Ihre Gesellschaft***
	As a well-established wholesaler of high-quality wines and spirits …	*Als gut eingeführter Großhändler von hochwertigen Weinen und Spirituosen …*
	Our company is a leading importer of photographic equipment from suppliers all over the world	*Unsere Gesellschaft ist ein führender Importeur von Fotoausrüstungen von Herstellern aus der ganzen Welt*
	… with many long-standing customers	*… mit vielen langjährigen Kunden*
	… we have extensive business contacts all over Germany	*… wir verfügen über umfangreiche Geschäftskontakte in ganz Deutschland*
	… we also have a well-established sales network throughout the EU and beyond	*… wir besitzen ebenfalls ein gut eingeführtes Verkaufsnetz in der ganzen EU und darüber hinaus*
3	**Ask for quotation**	***Bitten Sie um ein (Preis-)Angebot***
	We are particularly interested in importing … (goods) at present	*Wir sind zur Zeit besonders daran interessiert, … (Waren) zu importieren*
	As goods of this nature are in demand at present, we would like you to send us a quotation	*Da Waren dieser Art zur Zeit nachgefragt werden, möchten wir Sie bitten, uns ein Angebot zu schicken*
	– discounts	***– Nachlässe***
	We would be grateful if you would let us have information on all discounts granted	*Wir wären Ihnen dankbar, wenn Sie uns über alle gewährten Nachlässe informieren würden*
	Do you grant a(n) quantity discount / initial order discount / trade discount / cash discount?	*Gewähren Sie einen Mengenrabatt / Erstauftragsrabatt / Handelsnachlass / Barzahlungsrabatt?*

4	**Ask for sales material**	***Bitten Sie um Verkaufsmaterial***
	Please also let us have your latest comprehensive colour catalogue on your entire range of products	*Bitte lassen Sie uns auch Ihren neuesten umfassenden Farbkatalog über Ihre gesamte Produktpalette zukommen*
	– samples	***– Muster / Proben***
	Are you willing to provide us with (a) sample(s)?	*Sind Sie bereit, uns (ein) Muster / (eine) Probe(n) zukommen zu lassen?*
5	**Ask about terms of delivery and payment**	***Bitten Sie um Angabe der Liefer- und Zahlungsbedingungen***
	Please also state your terms of delivery and payment	*Bitte geben Sie auch Ihre Liefer- und Zahlungsbedingungen an*
	We would require delivery franco to our premises	*Wir benötigen die Lieferung frei unseren Geschäftsräumen*
	– delivery date / period	***– Lieferdatum / Lieferzeit***
	Delivery would need to be made within 3 weeks after receipt of order	*Die Lieferung sollte innerhalb von 3 Wochen nach Erhalt unserer Bestellung erfolgen*
	Details of your delivery periods would also be appreciated	*Einzelheiten Ihrer Lieferzeiten würden wir ebenfalls begrüßen*
6	**References**	***Referenzen***
	References are available on request	*Referenzen sind auf Wunsch erhältlich*
	Should you require a reference, please contact … (name of bank / company	*Sollten Sie eine Referenz benötigen, setzen Sie sich bitte mit … (Name der Bank / Gesellschaft) in Verbindung*
7	**Polite ending**	***Höfliche Schlussformel***
	If your company's … (product / goods) correspond(s) to our customers' wishes, we will be willing to place a sizeable order with you	*Wenn das (die) Produkt(e) / Waren Ihrer Gesellschaft den Wünschen unserer Kunden entspricht (entsprechen), sind wir bereit, Ihnen einen größeren Auftrag zu erteilen*
	As the market for such products is growing rapidly, we will be in a position to place a substantial order if your goods meet our requirements	*Auf Grund steigender Nachfrage wird ein größerer Auftrag möglich sein, wenn Ihre Ware unseren Anforderungen entspricht*
	We look forward to hearing from you soon	*Wir freuen uns, bald von Ihnen zu hören*
	We look forward to your (early) reply with interest	*Wir sehen Ihrer (baldigen) Antwort mit Interesse entgegen*

Exercises

Exercise 1: Jumbled Letter

The sentences in the letter below are in the wrong order. Use the letter plan on page 17 to put them in the correct order.

a. References are available on request.

b. Our company is a leading importer of high-quality furniture from suppliers all over the world and has extensive business contacts in Germany.

c. We would also be grateful if you would provide us with your latest illustrated colour catalogue on your entire range of products.

d. We have been given your address by the Chamber of Commerce in Düsseldorf, who tell us that you specialise in office furniture.

e. If your company's goods correspond to our customers' wishes, we will place a trial order.

We look forward to hearing from you soon.

f. As goods of this nature are in demand at present, please send us a quotation for your "Millennium Comfort" computer table including details of all discounts granted.

g. Are you willing to deliver CIP Düsseldorf Airport? Delivery would need to be made 4 weeks after receipt of our order at the latest.

Exercise 2: Anagrams

1. First read through the specimen letter on page 19 from Neutech GmbH to Electronic Equipment Ltd.
2. The letters of ten of the words have been mixed up. Re-arrange them to make words from the specimen letter.

1. tryelenc
2. deeprmiss
3. gindeal
4. xtelnlece
5. ttgruuoohh
6. dluestratil
7. trucern
8. sinutocd
9. tiiilan
10. smert

Exercise 3: Matching

1. First read through the specimen fax on page 20 from Neumoden GmbH to Ziang Kong Garments Co. Ltd in Taipei.
2. Next use the text of the fax to match the verbs in Column A with the nouns in Column B.

Column A

Verbs

1. to see
2. to send
3. to include
4. to require
5. to obtain
6. to meet
7. to place

Column B

Nouns

a. our requirements
b. references
c. an order
d. an advertisement
e. details
f. sales literature
g. a quotation

Exercise 4: Crossword

Look at the phraseology and vocabulary list for this unit on pages 24 / 25 and 31 / 32 to help you find some of the answers to this crossword. Write your answers on the worksheet provided.

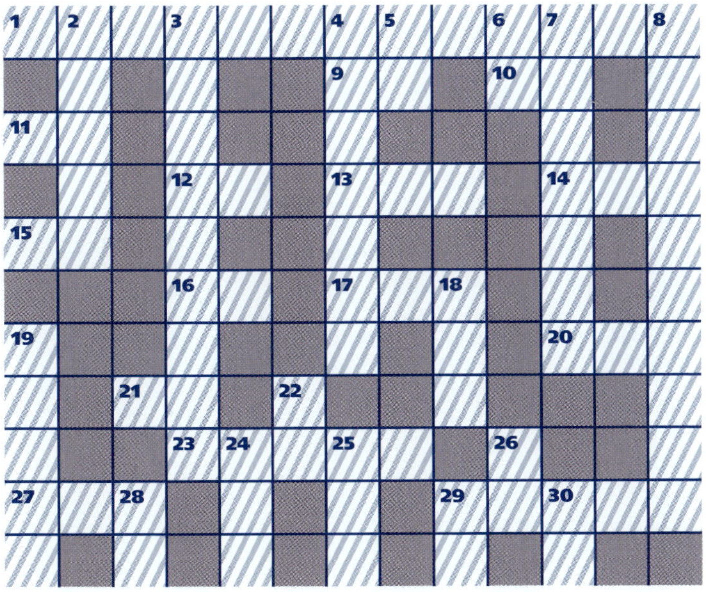

Clues

Across

1. "We have seen your ____ in the latest edition of 'Business Weekly'..."
9. opposite of "yes"
10. short form of the answer to clue no. 1
11. I am, you are, he ____.
12. "Look at that car. How much does ____ cost?"

13. another word for a "can"
14. In England most people drink ______.
15. "______ goods of this nature are in demand at present …"
16. "I can see you and you can see ______."
17. *Teacher:* Is anybody away today?
    Class: No, we're ______ here.
20. Neither Sally ______ Martin can speak French.
21. "We're interested ______ importing your products."
23. conditions
27. If you're hungry it's best to ______ something.
29. "If your products correspond to our customers' wishes, we'll place a substantial ______."

Down

2. In offices people sit at ______.
3. Computers, fax machines, photocopiers and telephone answering machines are all examples of office ______.
4. a *first* order – an ______ order
5. The goods were ______ expensive that we didn't buy them.
6. another word for "mum"
7. "We have seen your advertisement in the latest ______ of 'PhotoPro' …"
8. If you want to test a product, you place a ______. (*2 words*)
18. "We would be grateful if you would ______ us have a quotation."
19. "If your ______ meets our requirements, …"
22. "Would you like large, medium ______ small T-shirts?"
24. the part of the body you see with
25. "Pat isn't a woman. He's a ______."
26. "You can either take the goods now ______ come back tomorrow."
    (*same as no. 22*)
28. "We look forward ______ hearing from you soon."
29. "We've seen your company's web site ______ the Internet."
30. "Do you speak English?" – "Yes, I ______."

Aufgaben

1.

Name	Eigener Name	–
Position	Einkaufsleiter/in	–
Firma	Hoffmann AG	Jeremy Boulster Ltd
Anschrift	Münsterwalder Straße 11–15, 12651 Berlin, Germany	P.O. Box 110593, London W1M 7DA, England
Fax	+49 (30) 5 49 61 03	+44 (1 71) 23 90
E-Mail	hoffmann.ag@aol.com	boulster.ltd@firmnet.co.uk

Geschäftsfall:
Die Firma Hoffmann AG ist Großhändler für Weine und Spirituosen (*wholesaler of wines and spirits*). Sie hat von der IHK London den Namen der britischen Firma Jeremy Boulster Ltd erhalten, die sich auf die Lieferung von Sherry spezialisiert hat.

Aufgabe:
Schicken Sie als Einkaufsleiter/in von Hoffmann der Boulster Ltd eine Anfrage und berücksichtigen Sie dabei folgende Punkte:

- Sie haben die Adresse von der IHK London erhalten
- Vorstellung Ihres Unternehmens:
  - Großhändler für Weine und Spirituosen
  - langjährig bei deutschen Kunden eingeführt
- Interesse besonders an dem Sherry „Old England"
- Bitte um Preisangebot mit Angabe von Liefer- und Zahlungsbedingungen und allen Nachlässen
- Lieferzeit?
- Lieferung auch frei Haus?
- Erstklassige Bank- und Handelsreferenzen können auf Wunsch gestellt werden
- Aussicht auf größeren Auftrag, falls Sherry Ihren Kunden zusagt

2.

	Von	An
Name	Eigener Name	–
Position	Importleiter/in	The Export Director
Firma	Textilimport GmbH	Woolware Inc.
Anschrift	Postfach 395860, 90776 Fürth, Germany	1480 Granville St., Vancouver, BC, Canada V6C 1T2
Fax	+49 (9 11) 20 78 19	+1 (6 04) 2 30-38 04
E-Mail	textilimport.gmbh@t-online.de	woolware.inc@linkall.com

Geschäftsfall:
Sie haben vor 14 Tagen auf der „Natural Style" Bekleidungsmesse in Vancouver den Stand der kanadischen Firma Woolware Inc. gesehen und möchten jetzt Näheres über deren Produkte erfahren.

Aufgabe:
Schreiben Sie eine Anfrage an den Exportleiter der Woolware Inc. unter Berücksichtigung folgender Punkte:

- Bezug auf Messe
- Beschreibung Ihrer Firma:
  - führender Importeur von Damen-, Herren- und Kinderstrickwaren (*knitwear*) aus aller Welt
  - großer Kundenstamm in der EU
- Bitte um Übersendung eines aktuellen, umfassenden Katalogs mit Exportpreisliste
- Liefer- und Zahlungsbedingungen?
- Lieferzeiten?
- Referenz von der Handelsbank in Fürth erhältlich
- Auf Grund wachsender Nachfrage ist größerer Auftrag möglich, wenn Ware Ihren Anforderungen entspricht

Vocabulary List

ad (advertisement)	*Anzeige; Reklame*
add	*hinzufügen*
advertisement	*Anzeige*
after receipt of our order	*nach Erhalt unseres Auftrags*
appreciate	*schätzen; dankbar sein für*
appropriate, as ~	*wie geeignet, wie passend*
as	*da*
available	*erhältlich*
beyond	*darüber hinaus*
chamber of commerce	*Handelskammer*
commercial directory	*Handelsadressbuch*
common	*häufig; üblich*
comprehensive	*umfassend*
consulate	*Konsulat*
correspond to	*entsprechen*
current	*aktuell*
decide	*entscheiden*
delivery date / period	*Liefertermin, -zeit*
demonstrate	*vorführen*
describe	*beschreiben*
discount (see p. 24, Phraseology)	*Rabatt, Nachlass*
distribute	*vertreiben*
distributor	*Vertriebsfirma*
edition	*Ausgabe*
embassy	*Botschaft*
equipment	*Ausstattung; Geräte*
EU	*Europäische Union*
exhibition	*Ausstellung*
extensive	*ausgedehnt*
fashions	*Mode*
fast-growing	*schnell wachsend*
franco to our premises	*frei Haus, frei zu unseren Geschäftsräumen*
furniture	*Möbel*
further	*weitere(r, s)*
grant, to ~	*gewähren*
grateful	*dankbar*
growing	*wachsend*
head buyer	*Chefeinkäufer/in*
illustrated	*bebildert*
impress	*beeindrucken*
in demand	*begehrt; gefragt*
include	*einschließen*
indicate	*angeben*
initial order	*Erstauftrag*
jumbled	*durcheinander gewürfelt, in der falschen Reihenfolge*
latest	*neueste(r, s)*
latest, at the ~	*spätestens*
leading	*führend*
location	*Ort*
long-standing	*hier: längjährig*
look, to ~ forward to	*sich freuen auf*
major	*größere(r, s)*
managing director	*Geschäftsführer/in*
manufacture, to ~	*herstellen, fertigen, erzeugen*
meet our requirements	*unseren Anforderungen entsprechen*
neither … nor	*weder … noch*
obtain	*erhalten; hier: erhältlich sein*
of this nature	*dieser Art*
particularly	*insbesondere*
place an order	*einen Auftrag erteilen*
polite	*höflich*
premises	*Geschäftsräume*
provide with	*hier: zukommen lassen*
quotation	*Preisangebot*
rapidly	*schnell, rasch*
recent	*letzte(r, s)*
recommendation	*Empfehlung*
reply, a ~	*Antwort*
request, a ~	*Bitte*
require	*benötigen*
sales literature / material	*Verkaufsliteratur*
sales network	*Verkaufsnetz*
sample, a ~	*Muster; Probe*
sell well	*hier: sich gut verkaufen lassen*
shortly	*bald, in Kürze*
should you …	*sollten Sie …*
sizeable	*größere(r, s)*
source	*Quelle*
specialise in	*sich spezialisieren auf*
specimen	*Muster*
spirits	*Spirituosen*
state, to ~	*angeben*
substantial	*beträchtlich*
successful	*erfolgreich*
supplier	*Lieferant*
supply, to ~	*(be)liefern mit*
terms of delivery	*Lieferbedingungen*

terms of payment	*Zahlungsbedingungen*
throughout ...	*in ganz ...*
trade fair	*Handelsmesse*
trade journal	*Fachzeitschrift*
trial order	*Probeauftrag*
well-established	*gut eingeführt*
wholesaler	*Großhändler*
willing, to be ~	*bereit sein*

Unit 3

Offers

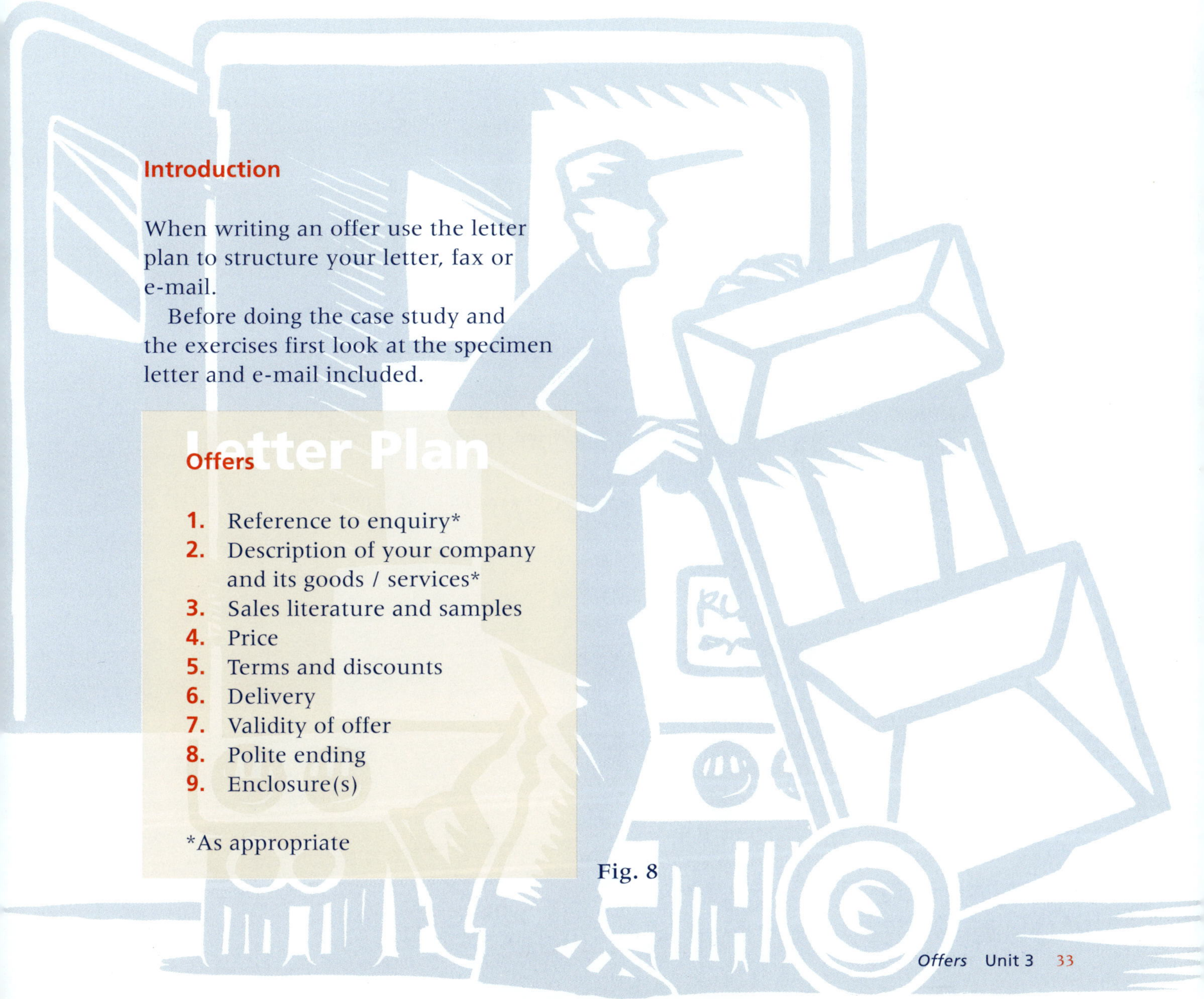

Introduction

When writing an offer use the letter plan to structure your letter, fax or e-mail.

Before doing the case study and the exercises first look at the specimen letter and e-mail included.

Letter Plan

Offers

1. Reference to enquiry*
2. Description of your company and its goods / services*
3. Sales literature and samples
4. Price
5. Terms and discounts
6. Delivery
7. Validity of offer
8. Polite ending
9. Enclosure(s)

*As appropriate

Fig. 8

Specimen Letter

1. Offer for wine

Talstr. 2
54293 Trier
Germany

Reichsgraf
Weinkellerei GmbH

IK/TT
10 June ..

Mr John Massecar
Purchasing Director
Famous Wines and Spirits Ltd
95 London Road
MANCHESTER
MA3 7HL
England

Dear Mr Massecar

Your Enquiry about Wine

Many thanks for your enquiry of 2 June .. about Mariahof Spätlese. As a major German wine-grower with excellent business contacts throughout the European Union and beyond, we have been producing top-grade wines for the past 75 years.

We enclose a leaflet on Mariahof Spätlese together with our catalogue on the rest of our range of products. We will be pleased to supply you with samples if requested.

Our prices are quoted FOB German port. Special quotations are available on request. Deliveries can be made within 7 days after receipt of order while stocks last.

Our terms are cash with order or 10 days 2%, 30 days net on receipt of our invoice, subject to favourable references.

This offer is valid for 30 days.

We look forward to receiving your order.

Yours sincerely

Ingo Kornharpen

Ingo Kornharpen
Sales Manager

Encs

Specimen E-mail

2. Offer for confectionery

e-mail

Mail to:	sweetmate.ltd@linkall.co.uk	**Cc:**	
Subject:	Offer for Confectionery	**Attachment:**	prices.doc

Dear Ms Sweeney

Thank you for your enquiry about our products.

I'm sending you our export price list with this e-mail as a file attachment.
All prices are quoted CIF UK port, and include packing. Our terms of payment are 10 days 2%, 30 days net and we can deliver from stock. This offer is valid for 30 days.

Please let me know if you need any more information.

I look forward to receiving your order in the next few days.

Yours sincerely

Henrietta von Jauch

Export Sales

Case Study

Martina Hensch is the European Sales Director at Designer Mode GmbH, Bahnhofstr. 110, 45128 Essen, fax +49 (0) 201 99 87 69. Her company is a leading wholesaler of fashionwear for young people, which it sells in boutiques all over Germany and the rest of Europe. It has been doing this for the last ten years.

The company also has a home page with an e-mail address on the Internet and when Martina checks the company's latest e-mails, she finds a lot of enquiries, including the one shown from TopFit Ltd. Martina now puts together an offer to be sent to all the firms interested in Designer Mode's clothes.

She tells them that her company's terms of delivery are CIF UK port or CIP UK airport and delivery takes about three weeks. With trade and / or bank references, the terms of payment are 10 days 2%, 30 days net, otherwise CWO (cash with order). The offer is valid for a month. She also sends each firm some information by separate post. Finally, she points out that there is a lot of demand for these goods, so she recommends ordering soon before stocks run out.

e-mail

Mail from:	TopFit@webserve.uk (TopFit Ltd)	**Cc:**	
Subject:	"Young Style" Fashionwear	**Attachment:**	

Dear Designer Mode

We have seen your home page on the Internet and are most interested in your young people's fashions.

As a major wholesaler of fashionwear in the UK we have excellent business contacts.

Please send us an offer for your new "Young Style" range. Our address is as follows:

TopFit Ltd
Unit 4
White Cross
LANCASTER
LA1 3DF
England
Tel: +44 (15 24) 3 44 87
Fax: +44 (15 24) 3 44 80

We would require the goods in time for the coming season.

References can be obtained from the NatWest Bank plc in Lancaster or C & A UK in London.

Many thanks in advance.

Yours sincerely

Diana Dors

Director

Activity

Write Martina's letter / fax / e-mail to TopFit Ltd. Add further details as appropriate.

Incoterms

Incoterms (international commercial terms) are used in international trade to define the rights and obligations of the buyer and the seller as regards transport and insurance. They are regularly revised by the Chamber of Commerce in Paris.

The Incoterms are in four groups – the "E", "F", "C" and "D" groups. Seen from the seller's point of view the "E" term is the most favourable and the "D" terms are most expensive.

The seller's obligations:

	Pay for Main Carriage?	Bear Risk ?
E-term	No	No
F-terms	No	Only until the goods are in the custody of the carrier
C-terms	Yes	Only until the goods are in the custody of the carrier
D-terms	Yes	All the way

Incoterms 2000

EXW	ex works	*ab Werk*
FCA	free carrier	*frei Frachtführer*
FAS	free alongside ship	*frei Längsseite Schiff*
FOB	free on board	*frei an Bord*
CFR	cost and freight	*Kosten und Fracht*
CPT	carriage paid to …	*frachtfrei*
CIF	cost, insurance, freight	*Kosten, Versicherung, Fracht*
CIP	carriage and insurance paid to …	*frachtfrei versichert*
DAF	delivered at frontier	*geliefert Grenze*
DES	delivered ex ship	*Lieferung ab Schiff*
DEQ	delivered ex quay	*Lieferung ab Kai*
DDU	delivered duty unpaid	*geliefert unverzollt*
DDP	delivered duty paid	*geliefert verzollt*

Other Useful Expressions

1	franco domicile	*frei Haus*
2	franco to (y)our premises	*frei bis zu unseren (Ihren) Geschäftsräumen, frei Haus*
3	carriage paid	*frachtfrei, Fracht bezahlt*
4	carriage forward	*unfrei, Fracht zahlt der Empfänger*

Standard Expressions

1 Reference to enquiry*	Thank you for Many thanks for			your the above-mentioned	letter fax e-mail enquiry phone call	of/dated … of today	about our … enquiring about … asking us to send you details of …	… (goods/services)
	We were	delighted pleasantly surprised	to receive			this morning		
2 Description of your company and its goods/services*	We are a	leading major	wholesaler of manufacturer of	high-quality first-rate	… (goods)	with excellent business contacts with an excellent reputation		throughout Europe both at home and abroad
			family business					
	… and have been supplying a wide selection of high-quality			(product, e.g. furniture, fashionwear) products of this type			for the last 10 years since … (date, e.g. 1990)	
	… with more than 100 years' experience of		producing growing	wines				
3 Sales literature and samples	As requested, For your information,	we are sending you	our current our latest	illustrated illustrated colour	catalogue brochure	and (a/an) and a current	price list export price list	by separate post
		we enclose						–
	… and … as well as … together with	a sample samples the samples requested		of … (product, material etc, e.g. our perfume)			in the next few days by … (date, e.g. 30 June/the end of the month)	
4 Price	Please refer to our (export) price list/catalogue for details							
5 Terms and discounts: – terms of delivery	Our terms of delivery are All (our) prices are quoted			… (Incoterm, e.g. CIF UK port or CIP UK airport)				
– terms of payment	Our terms of payment		for an initial order	are would be	10 days 2%, 30 days net		subject to favourable references	
					CWO (cash with order)			
	Open account terms may be granted if regular orders are placed with our company							
	Without references		they are	CWO the opening of an irrevocable and confirmed letter of credit				

	– discounts	… (we) would point out that	wholesalers	are granted	a discount of …	on the prices listed
		Please refer to our sales literature for details of our terms of delivery and discounts				
6	Delivery	Delivery Deliveries	can be made	immediately immediately from stock in approx. … (time, e.g. three weeks)		
7	Validity of offer	This offer is valid We can offer you firm	for one month while stocks last			
		Since there has been heavy demand for these items, As this … (product, e.g. wine) is selling particularly well at the moment,		I/we (urgently) recommend	you order now while stocks last	
8	Polite ending	I/We look forward to hearing from you soon I/We hope our offer is to your liking and look forward to doing business with you in the near future I/We feel sure that a trial order will convince you of the quality of our goods and look forward to doing business with you in the near future				
9	Enclosure(s)	Catalogue(s), brochure(s), leaflet(s), (export) price list, sample(s)				

Phraseology

1	**Reference to enquiry***	***Bezugnahme auf Anfrage****
	Many thanks for your enquiry of 15 June .. about our fashionwear	*Vielen Dank für Ihre Anfrage vom 15. Juni .. bezüglich unserer Modebekleidung*
	We were delighted to receive the above-mentioned letter this morning enquiring about our equipment	*Wir waren erfreut, heute Morgen den oben erwähnten Brief mit Ihrer Anfrage über unsere Ausrüstung / Geräte zu erhalten*
2	**Description of your company and its goods / services***	***Beschreibung Ihrer Firma und ihrer Waren / Dienstleistungen****
	We are a leading / major grower of first-rate wines with an excellent reputation both at home and abroad / throughout Germany	*Wir sind ein führender / größerer Anbauer von erstklassigen Weinen mit einem ausgezeichneten Ruf im In- und Ausland / in ganz Deutschland*
	... and have been exporting a wide selection of high-quality products of this type since 1990	*... und exportieren seit 1990 eine große Auswahl von hochwertigen Produkten dieser Art*
	We have more than 100 years' experience of growing wines	*Wir verfügen über eine mehr als 100-jährige Erfahrung im Anbau von Weinen*
3	**Sales literature and samples**	***Verkaufsmaterial und Muster***
	For your information / As requested, we are sending you our current illustrated colour catalogue and an export price list by separate post	*Zu Ihrer Information / Wie gewünscht senden wir Ihnen mit separater Post unseren aktuellen bebilderten Farbkatalog und eine Exportpreisliste*
4	**Price**	***Preis***
	Please refer to the enclosed (export) price list for details	*Bitte schauen Sie wegen der Einzelheiten in der beigefügten (Export-) Preisliste nach*
5	**Terms and discounts:** **– terms of delivery**	***Bedingungen und Nachlässe:*** ***– Lieferbedingungen***
	Our terms of delivery are CIF UK port or CIP UK airport	*Unsere Lieferbedingungen verstehen sich CIF britischem Hafen oder CIP britischem Flughafen*
	– terms of payment	***– Zahlungsbedingungen***
	Our terms of payment for an initial order are 10 days 2%, 30 days net, subject to favourable references	*Unsere Zahlungsbedingungen für einen Erstauftrag sind, günstige Referenzen vorausgesetzt, 10 Tage mit 2%, 30 Tage netto*
	Our terms of payment for a new customer would be CWO (cash with order)	*Unsere Zahlungsbedingungen für einen neuen Kunden wären Barzahlung bei Auftragserteilung*

	– discounts	*– Nachlässe*
	We would point out that wholesalers are granted a discount of …% on the prices listed	*Wir möchten darauf hinweisen, dass Großhändler einen Nachlass von …% auf die aufgeführten Preise erhalten*
	Open account terms may be granted if regular orders are placed with our company	*Ein offenes Zahlungsziel kann gewährt werden, wenn Sie unserer Firma regelmäßige Aufträge erteilen*
	Please refer to our sales literature for details of our terms and discounts	*Bitte ziehen Sie bezüglich der Einzelheiten unserer Bedingungen und Nachlässe unser Verkaufsmaterial zu Rate*
6	**Delivery**	***Lieferung***
	Deliveries can be made (by air freight) immediately from stock	*Lieferungen können (per Luftfracht) sofort ab Lager erfolgen*
	Delivery can be made in three months' time	*Die Lieferung kann in drei Monaten erfolgen*
7	**Validity of offer**	***Gültigkeit des Angebots***
	This offer is valid for one month	*Dieses Angebot ist einen Monat lang gültig*
	Since there has been heavy demand for these items, we (urgently) recommend you place your order as soon as possible	*Da für diese Positionen große Nachfrage besteht, empfehlen wir Ihnen (dringend), Ihre Bestellung so bald wie möglich aufzugeben*
	As this product is selling particularly well at the moment …	*Da dieses Produkt sich zur Zeit besonders gut verkauft …*
8	**Polite ending**	***Höfliche Schlussformel***
	I / We look forward to hearing from you soon	*Ich / Wir freuen uns, bald von Ihnen zu hören*
	I / We hope our offer is to your liking and look forward to doing business with you in the near future	*Ich / Wir hoffen, dass unser Angebot Ihnen zusagt und freuen uns darauf, in naher Zukunft mit Ihnen Geschäfte zu machen*
	We feel sure that a trial order will convince you of the quality of our goods and look forward to doing business with you in the near future	*Wir sind sicher, dass ein Probeauftrag Sie von der Qualität unserer Waren überzeugen wird, und freuen uns darauf, bald mit Ihnen in Geschäftsverbindung zu treten*
9	**Enclosure(s)**	***Anlage(n)***
	Catalogue(s), brochure(s), leaflet(s), (export) price list, sample(s)	*Katalog(e), Prospekt(e), Faltblatt(blätter), (Export)Preisliste, Muster*

Exercises

Exercise 1: Jumbled Letter

The sentences in the letter below are in the wrong order. Use the letter plan on page 33 to put them in the correct order.

a. Deliveries can be made from stock.

b. We hope our offer is to your liking and look forward to doing business with you in the near future.

c. This offer is valid while stocks last.

d. We are a leading wholesaler of first-class computer products with an excellent reputation both at home and abroad.

e. 1 Catalogue
1 Export Price List

f. For your information we enclose our current illustrated colour catalogue and price list.

g. Many thanks for the above-mentioned e-mail, which we received this morning.

h. All our prices are quoted CIF UK port. Our terms of payment for an initial order are CWO.

i. Please refer to our price list for details.

Exercise 2: Instructions I

1. First read through the specimen letter on page 34 from Reichsgraf Weinkellerei GmbH to Mr John Massecar at Famous Wines and Spirits Ltd.
2. Next write the words missing in the letter below on a piece of your own paper. Do this *without* looking at the specimen letter at the same time.

Ms Mary Stokes
1. ______ Director
TopSound Car Stereo Equipment Ltd
54 Terence Road
GUILDFORD
GU1 9JG
England

2. ______ Ms Stokes

Your 3. ______ about our VVG Car Radio/Cassette

Many 4. ______ for your enquiry of 2 June ... about our product. As a 5. ______ German manufacturer with 6. ______ business contacts throughout the European Union and 7. ______, we have been 8. ______ top-grade car stereos for the 9. ______ 20 years.

We 10. ______ a brochure on the VVG car radio/cassette together with our 11. ______ on the rest of our 12. ______ of products.

Our prices are 13. ______ FOB German 14. ______. Special 15. ______ are available on request. 16. ______ can be made within 7 days after 17. ______ of order while stocks last.

Our 18. ______ are cash with order or 10 days 2%, 30 days net on receipt of our invoice, subject to favourable 19. ______.

We look forward to 20. ______ your order.

Yours sincerely
etc.

Encs

Exercise 3: Instructions II

First read through the specimen e-mail on page 35. Next write the words missing in the e-mail below on a piece of your own paper. Do this *without* looking at the specimen e-mail at the same time.

Offer 1. ____ software

e-mail

Mail to:	software.ltd@linkall.co.uk	**Cc:**	
Subject:	Your Enquiry 2. ____ Software	**Attachment:**	prices.doc

Dear Mr Johnson

Many thanks 3. ____ your enquiry 4. ____ our goods.

For your information I have included our export price list 5. ____ this e-mail as a file attachment. All prices are quoted CIF UK port. Our terms 6. ____ payment are 10 days 2%, 30 days net and we are able to deliver 7. ____ stock. We can offer you firm 8. ____ 30 days.

Please contact me if you need any more information.

I look forward 9. ____ hearing from you 10. ____ the next few days.

Yours sincerely

Germaine Starnberg

Export Sales

Exercise 4: Crossword

Look at the phraseology and vocabulary list for this unit on pages 40 / 41 and 49 / 50 to help you find some of the answers to this crossword. Write your answers on the worksheet provided.

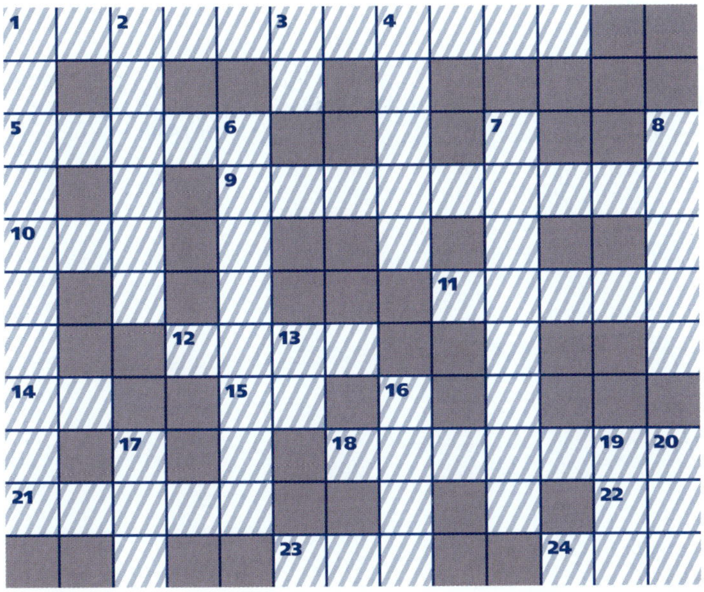

Clues

Across

1. a word for the clothes you can buy in a boutique
5. "We can offer you firm for one month." – "This offer is ___ for one month."
9. If you send something with a letter, this (e. g. a catalogue or a brochure) is called an ___
10. "I normally ___ a pen to write a letter."
11. "Please *look at* our catalogue for details." – "Please ___ to our catalogue for details."
12. "We have boutiques *in every part of* Germany." – "We have boutiques all ___ Germany."; another meaning: opposite of "under"
14. "*The latest date* for delivery is 30 June." – "You must deliver ___ 30 June."
15. two letters meaning "for example"
18. In order to thank someone now for something they are going to do later you say "Many thanks in ___."
21. "We work 7 days a week." – "We work ___ day."
22. "It isn't a fax. It's ___ e-mail."
23. opposite of "no"
24. "We send letters ___ faxes."

Down

1. "We'll give you credit *if your references are good.*" – "We'll give you credit subject to ___ references."
2. opposite of "buyer"
3. "Thank you for your letter *dated* 30 June." – "Thank you for your letter ___ 30 June."
4. "This offer is valid ___ stocks last."
6. "You will receive the goods immediately." – "___ will be made immediately."
7. "We enclose our catalogue ___ (*3 words*) our current price list."
8. past form of the the verb "to hear"
13. two letters meaning "for example"
16. If someone ___ 3 and 3 the answer is 6.
17. "We *receive* a lot of letters." – "We ___ a lot of letters."
19. another word for a "tin"
20. opposite of "beginning"

Aufgaben

1.

	Von	An
Name	Helmut Tannerbauer	Messrs Johnson & Remington
Position	Firmeninhaber	–
Firma	Weinbau Tannerbauer OHG	
Anschrift	Weinbergallee 90–92, 67435 Neustadt a. d. Weinstraße	30 Blackhill Road, Manchester MA4 1HQ, England
Fax	+49 (63 21) 4 48 79	+44 (1 61) 3 32-89 45
E-Mail	tannerbauer.ohg@aol.com	j.r@firmnet.co.uk

Geschäftsfall:
Die Helmut Tannerbauer OHG exportiert seit vielen Jahren ihre Pfälzer Weine (*wines from the Palatinate*) erfolgreich ins Ausland. Heute erhält die deutsche Firma eine Anfrage von der Firma Johnson & Remington in Manchester, England.

Aufgabe:
Verfassen Sie ein Angebot an die englische Firma unter Berücksichtigung folgender Punkte:

- Dank für Anfrage
- Beschreiben Sie kurz Ihr Unternehmen:
  - Winzerfamilie mit mehr als 100 Jahren Erfahrung
- Beschreiben Sie Ihr Produkt:
  - erstklassige Weine mit hervorragendem Ruf im In- und Ausland
- Fügen Sie den aktuellen Prospekt und die Preisliste bei
- Nachlass für Großhändler: 25 %
- Sofortige Lieferung (ab Lager) möglich
- Zahlung: bei Auftragserteilung; günstige Referenzen vorausgesetzt innerhalb von 30 Tagen
- Gültigkeit des Angebots: 3 Monate
- Dringende Bestellung erwünscht, da Angebot nur gültig, solange der Vorrat reicht (Weine lassen sich momentan besonders gut verkaufen)
- Höfliche Schlussformel

2.

	Von	An
Name	Annemarie (Thorsten) Strauch	Ms. Jennifer Bartholomew
Position	Exportabteilung	Vice President
Firma	Gebr. Lothar Hansen KG	Gifts & Presents Inc.
Anschrift	Zeppelinstr. 9, 51373 Limburg an der Lahn	205 Chesapeake Park Plaza, Baltimore, MD 21220, USA
Fax	+49 (64 31) 7 76 52	+1 (4 10) 6 82-04 95
E-Mail	lothar.hansen.kg@allfirm.de	gifts.presents@gnn.net

Geschäftsfall:
Sie sind Annemarie (Thorsten) Strauch, Sachbearbeiter(in) in der Exportabteilung bei Gebr. Lothar Hansen KG in Limburg an der Lahn. Sie stellen Geschenkartikel für den Export her und hatten kürzlich in der internationalen Zeitschrift „The Herald“ eine Annonce aufgegeben. Auf diese Annonce meldet sich telefonisch die amerikanische Fa. Gifts & Presents Inc. in Maryland, USA, mit der Bitte um ein kurzgefasstes Angebot.

Aufgabe:
Verfassen Sie dieses Angebot mit folgenden Einzelheiten:
- Dank für erhaltene telefonische Anfrage
- Sie werden mehrere Muster, Prospekte und eine aktuelle Exportpreisliste mit getrennter Post zusenden
- Lieferbedingungen und Nachlässe sind aus Unterlagen ersichtlich
- Zahlungsbedingungen: bei Erstauftrag Zahlung bei Auftragserteilung; bei regelmäßigen Aufträgen offenes Zahlungsziel möglich
- Lieferung ab Lager
- Hoffnung auf baldigen Probeauftrag

Vocabulary List

30 days net	*30 Tage netto*
abroad, at home and ~	*im In- und Ausland*
account, open ~ terms	*offenes Zahlungsziel*
add	*hinzufügen*
advance, in ~	*im Voraus*
appropriate, as ~	*wie geeignet, wie passend*
approx.	*ca.*
as well as	*sowie*
attachment, file ~	*Anlage (Datei)*
available	*erhältlich*
bank reference	*Bankauskunft*
bear (risks)	*tragen (Risiken)*
brochure	*Prospekt, Broschüre*
business, family ~	*Familienbetrieb*
business, to do ~	*Geschäfte tätigen / machen*
by 30 June	*bis 30. Juni*
by separate post	*mit getrennter Post*
carriage	*Transport-, Fracht- (kosten)*
carrier	*Frachtführer*
cash with order (CWO)	*Barzahlung bei Auftragserteilung*
catalogue (AE: catalog)	*Katalog*
chamber of commerce	*Handelskammer*
clothes	*Kleider, Kleidung*
confectionery	*Süßigkeiten*
confirmed	*bestätigt*
convince	*überzeugen*
current	*aktuell*
custody	*Obhut*
delighted	*sehr erfreut*
delivery	*Lieferung*
demand for	*Nachfrage nach*
description	*Beschreibung*
discount	*Rabatt, Nachlass*
enclosure	*Anlage*
expensive	*teuer*
experience	*Erfahrung*
famous	*berühmt*
fashionwear	*Modebekleidung*
favourable	*günstig*
few, in the next ~ days	*in den nächsten Tagen*
file, a ~	*Datei*
firm	*hier: fest*
first-rate	*erstklassig*
FOB	*frei an Bord*
for your information	*zu Ihrer Information*
from stock	*ab Lager*
furniture	*Möbel*
future, in the near ~	*bald, in Kürze*
grant, to ~	*gewähren*
heavy (demand)	*hier: erheblich(e Nachfrage)*
illustrated	*bebildert*
immediately	*sofort, umgehend*
including	*einschließlich*
initial order	*Erstauftrag*
insurance	*Versicherung*
irrevocable	*unwiderruflich*
irrevocable, the opening of an ~ and confirmed letter of credit	*Eröffnung eines unwiderruflichen und bestätigten Akkreditivs*
jumbled	*durcheinander gewürfelt, in der falschen Reihenfolge*
leading	*führend*
leaflet	*Faltblatt*
letter of credit	*Akkreditiv*
liking, to be to your ~	*(Ihnen) zusagen*
liquor	*Alkohol, Spirituosen*
look, to ~ forward to	*sich freuen auf*
major	*größere(r, s)*
manufacturer	*Hersteller*
net	*netto*
obligations	*hier: Pflichten*
obtain	*erhalten, bekommen, erwerben*
packing	*Verpackung*
particularly	*insbesondere*
place an order	*einen Auftrag erteilen*
pleasantly surprised	*angenehm überrascht*
point of view	*hier: Sicht*
point out	*darauf hinweisen*
port (e.g. Hamburg)	*Hafen*
purchasing director	*Einkaufsleiter/in*
put together	*zusammenstellen*
quotation	*Preisangebot*
quoted, our prices are ~	*unsere Preise verstehen sich*
range	*Palette, Sortiment*
receipt, after ~ of order	*nach Erhalt des (Ihres) Auftrags*
receipt, on ~ of our invoice	*bei Erhalt unserer Rechnung*
receive	*erhalten*
recommend	*empfehlen*

refer to	*sich beziehen auf; zu Rate ziehen, entnehmen*
reference to	*Bezug auf*
regards, as ~	*bezüglich*
regular(ly)	*regelmäßig*
reputation	*Ruf*
request, on ~	*auf Wunsch*
requested, if ~	*auf Wunsch*
requested, as ~	*wunschgemäß*
revise	*revidieren*
rights	*Rechte*
run out	*zu Ende gehen, erschöpft sein*
sales literature	*Verkaufsliteratur*
sample, a ~	*Muster; Probe*
season	*Saison, Jahreszeit*
selection	*Auswahl*
seller	*Verkäufer/in*
since	*hier: da*
stocks, before ~ run out	*hier: solange der Vorrat reicht*
subject to favourable references	*günstige Referenzen vorausgesetzt, sofern wir günstige Referenzen erhalten*
supply s. o. with	*jdn. mit etwas beliefern*
terms	*Bedingungen*
terms of delivery	*Lieferbedingungen*
throughout (Europe)	*in ganz (Europa)*
together with	*zusammen mit*
top-grade	*erstklassig*
trade reference	*Handelsreferenz*
trial order	*Probeauftrag*
until	*bis*
urgent(ly)	*dringend*
use, to ~	*verwenden, gebrauchen*
valid	*gültig*
validity	*Gültigkeit*
while stocks last	*solange der Vorrat reicht*
wholesaler	*Großhändler/in*
wine-grower	*Winzer/in, Weinbauer/in*
within	*hier: binnen*

Unit 4

Orders

Introduction

Orders are best in tabular form. For more than one item use a table with columns and rows. Add separate headings under the table for extra information such as shipping charges, insurance etc. (see page 52 "Specimen Letter"). For a single item just use headings (see page 53 "Specimen Fax").

Before doing the case study and the exercises, first look at the specimen letter and fax.

Letter Plan

Orders

1. Reference to offer*
2. Details of goods / services required
3. Prices and discount(s)
4. Terms of delivery
   – delivery
   – shipment
   – shipping charge
5. Payment
6. Instructions*
   – insurance
   – packing
   – acknowledgement / invoice
7. Polite ending
8. Enclosure(s)

*As appropriate

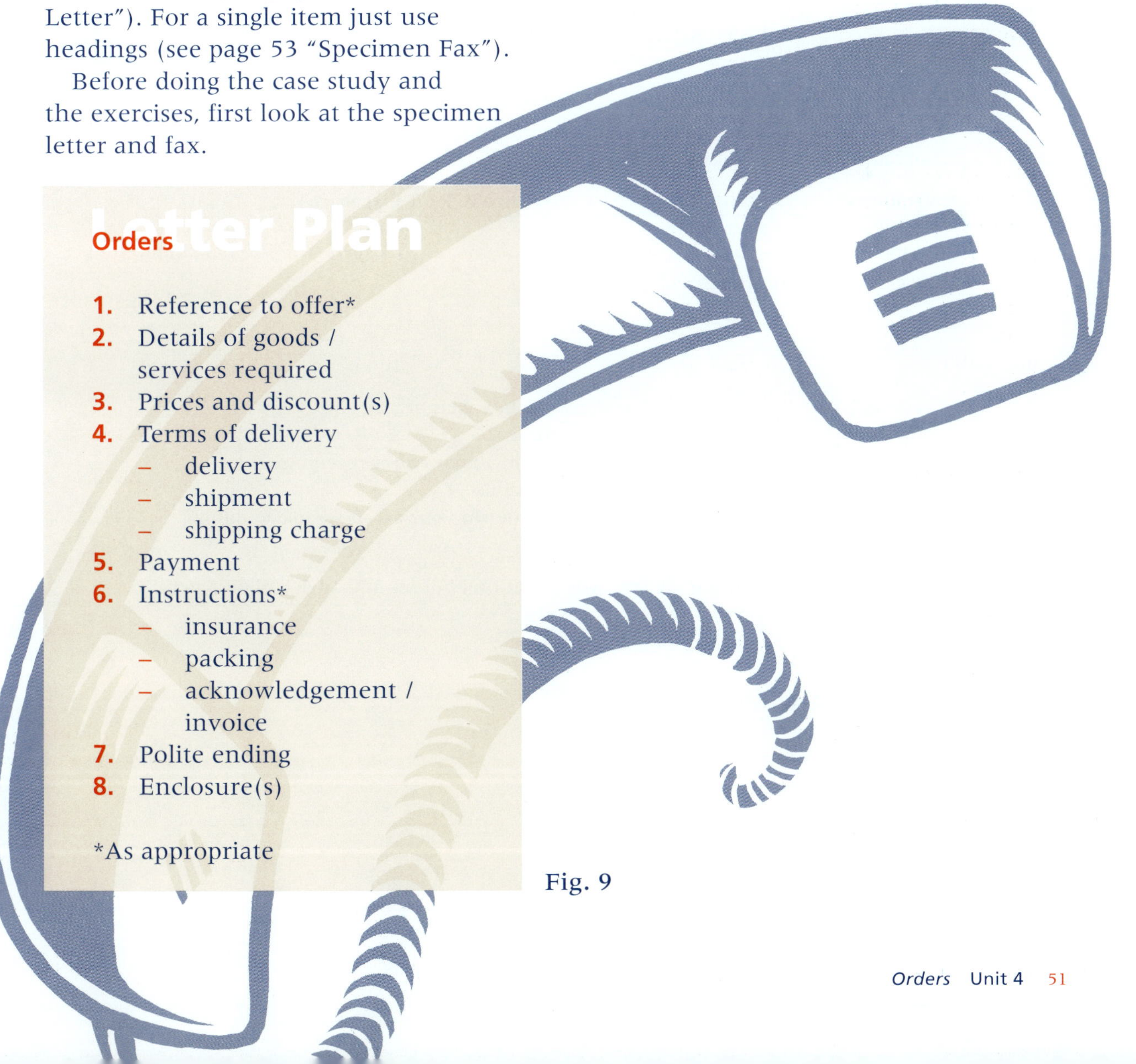

Fig. 9

Specimen Letter

1. An order in tabular form

Sweetmate Ltd
8 Coppergate
YORK
YO1 1NR
England

MS/HH
1 February ..

Ms Henrietta von Jauch
European Sales Director
Stecker Süßwaren Deutschland GmbH
Ringstr. 88
012607 Dresden
Germany

Dear Ms von Jauch

Order for Confectionery

We have studied the catalogue and export price list sent to us on 10 January .. and now wish to order as follows:

Quantity	Description	Article No.	List Price	Total
2,500	"Easter Bunnies"	EB25	€1.00	€2,500.00
100	Boxes of "Brown Sugar" chocolates	BS99	€5.00	€ 500.00
			Sub-total	€3,000.00
			–5% discount	–€ 150.00
			Total	**€2,850.00**

Insurance: Warehouse to warehouse, to be taken out by you
Shipment: InterTrans Freight Forwarding Co.
Delivery: Franco to our premises, within 10 days after receipt of order
Packing: See enclosed packing instructions
Payment: On receipt of invoice by transfer to your a/c at Deutsche Bank, Dresden

We look forward to receiving your confirmation of order and advice of despatch.

Yours sincerely
Sweetmate Ltd

Miranda Sweeney

Miranda Sweeney
Purchasing Director

Enc:
Packing Instructions

Specimen Fax

2. Order with headings for a single item

sheet

FAO:	Ms Anita Schenk, Export Sales Director Westerhagen EDV Vertriebs GmbH Erlenweg 20–26 97076 Würzburg Germany
Fax No:	00 49 (0) 9 31-97 76 59
From:	Joanna Johnson Purchasing Director EP Distributors Ltd 109 Stanwell Road ASHFORD MA2 6HH England Tel. +44 (17 84) 4 53-98 99 Fax +44 (17 84) 4 53-98 77 E-mail: ep.distributors@firmnet.co.uk
Date:	16 March ..
Subject:	Order for Computer Power Units
Total Pages:	1

Dear Ms Schenk

Thank you for your quotation dated 10 March .. .

On the basis of the terms stated we now wish to place an order as follows:

Article:	50A power unit
Quantity:	500
Unit price:	€ 50.00
Trade discount:	30%
Total price:	€ 17,500.00
Delivery:	CIP London Heathrow Airport, within 30 days after receipt of order
Terms of payment:	1/3 with order, 1/3 on delivery, 1/3 within 30 days after delivery, by transfer to your a/c
Packing:	Sturdy cartons
Insurance:	Warehouse to warehouse, to be taken out by you

Please send us your advice of despatch as soon as the consignment has been shipped.

We look forward to taking delivery of the goods in the near future.

Yours sincerely

Joanna Johnson

Case Study

Melanie Giese works in the purchasing department at Allwetter Sport AG in Düsseldorf. Her company is now buying backpacks for the summer season so she sends an e-mail enquiry to Wilderness Adventure Inc. in Nevada, USA. The American company sends her a quotation so Melanie now wants to order 5 "Trekker" backpacks, article number PK155, list price $ 89.95 each; 5 "Outback" backpacks, article number PK160, list price $ 124.95 each; 5 "Kelty" backpacks, article number PK157, list price $ 144.95 each.

Payment is to be made in advance by international money order (IMO) and the goods are to be shipped by WorldWide Parcels Service. She wants the backpacks to be delivered to her company's premises within three weeks after receipt of order and expects to be receiving the sales invoice soon.

She also receives a 5% quantity discount on the list prices, which she includes when placing her order.

There is also a shipping charge of approx. $ 195.00 and Melanie wants Wilderness Adventure Inc. to take out warehouse-to-warehouse insurance for the goods.

e-mail

An: wain@communique.net **Cc:**

Betreff: Backpacks for Europe + payment **Anlage:**

Dear Wilderness Adventure:

I have seen your advertisement for backpacks on the Internet and would like to know more about your service. Please let me have the following information:

a) What are your shipping charges to Europe for 15 backpacks?
b) How should I pay?
c) How soon can you deliver?

Many thanks in advance for your attention to this enquiry.

Sincerely,
Melanie Giese

Activity

Write Melanie's letter / fax / e-mail to Mr. John D. Thomas at Wilderness Adventure Inc. Make it friendly and informal by writing in the "I" form and using short forms (e.g. "I'd", "it's" etc.). Add further details as appropriate.

From: Melanie Giese, Purchasing Department, Allwetter Sport AG, Eichenkreuzstr. 40–44, 40589 Düsseldorf, tel. +49 (211) 2098-0, fax +49 (211) 2098-110, e-mail: allwetter.ag@t-online.de

To: Mr. John D. Thomas, Export Sales Director, Wilderness Adventure Inc., 330 California Ave., Reno, NV 89509, tel. +1 (916) 272-7097, fax +1 (916) 272-7002, e-mail: wain@communique.net

Standard Expressions

1 Reference to offer*	Many thanks for Thank you for We thank you for	your offer your quotation the above-mentioned offer	of/dated ...	for	... (goods/services, e.g. electronic equipment/ software installation) the above-mentioned ... (goods, e.g. air conditioning units)
	We have studied/examined your		offer quotation catalogue brochure sales literature		and ...
	I/We have seen your advertisement		in the latest/current edition of ... (name of publication, e.g. "Climber's Weekly")/on the Internet		
	On (on) the basis of		the terms stated	in the/your	offer/quotation
2 Details of goods/ services required	... and, on the basis of the terms stated	we now wish to place	an order an order as follows: the following order: the following trial order:		(→ table/heading)
	We (now) wish to place I'd like to place	an order a trial order an initial order	for ... (goods)	on the basis of the conditions stated in your offer dated/of ...	as follows: (→ table/heading)
	I'd like to order We now wish to order				
3 Prices and discount(s)	→ table/heading				
	We (are pleased to) note there is a(n)	trade initial order introductory offer quantity cash	discount of	...% (e.g. 10%)	
4 Terms of delivery	→ heading				
	Please deliver the goods/consignment ... delivery to be made		... (Incoterm, e.g. CIF Hamburg/CFR Bremen) CIP German airport franco to our premises FOB San Francisco		

– delivery	→ heading		
	Within 14 days after receipt of order To our premises within 3 weeks after receipt of order 8 weeks after receipt of order Within the next 4 weeks In (the next) 4 weeks As soon as possible		
– shipment	→ heading		
	Shipment is to be made by CargoTrans International International Parcel Service		
– shipping charge	→ heading		
	(Approx.) $200/€200 etc.		
5 Payment	→ heading		
	Payment will be made We will make payment	as agreed as requested in advance	by IMO by irrevocable letter of credit by transfer to your a/c (account) on receipt of the goods 90 days after receipt of invoice
6 Instructions *	→ heading		
– insurance	Warehouse to warehouse To be taken out by us/you		
– packing	→ heading		
	Please pack the goods	in (sturdy) cartons/cardboard boxes/crates on pallets	
– acknowledge-ment/invoice	Please confirm receipt of our order I/We expect to be receiving your sales invoice in the near future We look forward to receiving your acknowledgement/sales invoice in the next few days We would be grateful if you would send us your acknowledgement and state the date of delivery		
7 Polite ending	Thank you for your prompt attention to our order I/We look forward to taking delivery of the … (goods, e.g. backpacks, tents) in the near future We trust the goods will be delivered punctually and in good condition and look forward to placing further orders with your company if this article sells well		
8 Enclosure(s)	Order Form Packing Instructions		

Phraseology

1	**Reference to offer***	***Bezugnahme auf Angebot****
	Many thanks for your offer of 10 May .. for electronic equipment	*Vielen Dank für Ihr Angebot vom 10. Mai .. für elektronische Ausrüstung*
	We have seen your advertisement in the latest edition of "Climber's Weekly"	*Wir haben Ihre Anzeige in der letzten Ausgabe des „Climber's Weekly" gesehen*
	We have studied your sales literature ...	*Wir haben Ihre Verkaufsliteratur geprüft ...*
	We thank you for the above-mentioned offer	*Wir danken Ihnen für das oben erwähnte Angebot*
2	**Details of goods / services required**	***Einzelheiten der benötigten Waren / Dienstleistungen***
	On the basis of the terms stated in your quotation ...	*Auf der Grundlage der in Ihrem Angebot genannten Bedingungen ...*
	... we now wish to place the following (trial) order:	*... möchten wir jetzt den folgenden (Probe)Auftrag erteilen:*
	We now wish to place an (initial) order for air conditioning units on the basis of the conditions stated in your offer dated 25 October .. as follows:	*Wir möchten nunmehr auf der Basis der in Ihrem Angebot vom 25. Oktober .. enthaltenen Bedingungen einen (Erst)Auftrag über Klimaanlagen wie folgt erteilen:*
	I / We now wish to order ...	*Ich / Wir möchte(n) jetzt ... bestellen*
3	**Prices and discount(s)**	***Preise und Nachlass (Nachlässe)***
	We wish to order 10×T50 generators at €1,000 each	*Hiermit bestellen wir 10 Generatoren vom Typ T50 zu je 1.000 €*
	We are pleased to note there is a trade discount of 10%	*Wir nehmen erfreut zur Kenntnis, dass ein Handelsrabatt von 10% gewährt wird*
4	**Terms of delivery**	***Lieferbedingungen***
	Please deliver the goods franco to our premises	*Bitte liefern Sie die Waren frei Haus (frei bis zu unseren Geschäftsräumen)*
	... delivery to be made FOB San Francisco	*... die Lieferung soll FOB San Francisco erfolgen*
	– delivery	***– Lieferung***
	Please deliver the goods to our premises within 3 weeks after receipt of order	*Bitte liefern Sie die Waren innerhalb von 3 Wochen nach Erhalt des Auftrags in unsere Geschäftsräume*
	Within 14 days after receipt of order	*Innerhalb von 14 Tagen nach Erhalt des Auftrags*
	– shipment	***– Versand (Verschiffung)***
	– shipping charge: Approx. $200	***– Versand (Verschiffungs)gebühr: ca. 200 $***
5	**Payment**	***Zahlung***
	Payment will be made as agreed by irrevocable letter of credit	*Die Zahlung wird, wie vereinbart, durch unwiderrufliches Akkreditiv erfolgen*

	… as requested by transfer to your a/c (account)	*… wie gewünscht durch Überweisung auf Ihr Konto*
	… after receipt of invoice	*… nach Rechnungserhalt*
7	**Instructions***	***Anweisungen****
	– insurance	***– Versicherung***
	To be taken out by us / you	*Ist von uns / Ihnen abzuschließen*
	From warehouse to warehouse	*von Lager bis Lager*
	– packing	***– Verpackung***
	Please pack the goods in sturdy cartons / cardboard boxes	*Bitte verpacken Sie die Waren in stabile Pappkartons*
	– acknowledgement / invoice	***– Auftragsbestätigung / Rechnung***
	Please confirm receipt of our order	*Bitte bestätigen Sie den Erhalt unseres Auftrags*
	We expect to be receiving your sales invoice in the next few days	*Wir erwarten den Erhalt Ihrer Verkaufs-rechnung in den nächsten Tagen*
8	**Polite ending**	***Höfliche Schlussformel***
	I / We expect to be receiving your advice of despatch in the next few days	*Ich erwarte / Wir erwarten den Erhalt Ihrer Versandanzeige in den nächsten Tagen*
	We look forward to taking delivery of the goods in the near future	*Wir freuen uns, die Waren in Kürze entgegenzunehmen*
	We look forward to taking delivery of the tents in the near future	*Wir freuen uns, die Zelte in nächster Zeit zu erhalten*
	We trust the goods will be delivered punctually and in good condition and look forward to placing further orders with your company if this article sells well	*Wir vertrauen darauf, dass die Güter pünktlich und in gutem Zustand geliefert werden, und werden gern weitere Aufträge erteilen, wenn sich dieser Artikel gut verkauft*
9	**Enclosure(s)**	***Anlage(n)***
	Order Form	*Auftragsformular*
	Packing Instructions	*Verpackungsanweisungen*

Exercises

Exercise 1: Jumbled Letter

1. In this exercise the headings are missing and the information is in the wrong order. Use the letter plan on page 51, the specimen letter on page 52 and the specimen fax on page 53 (a) to find the correct headings (e.g. "Article:") and (b) to put them in the right order (i.e. 1, 2, 3 etc.). The first answer has been done for you.

Order	Heading	Text
10)	Insurance	Warehouse to warehouse
2)	quantity	100 units
5)	total price	€30,000.00
4)	Trade discount	40%
3)	Unit price	€500.00
9)	packing	Sturdy cartons
7)	terms of payment	As agreed by transfer to your a/c
8)	shipment	CargoTrans International
6)	delivery	CIF Hamburg, within 8 weeks after receipt of order
1	Article:	EZ PC "Netsurf 1"

2. Now put the whole letter in the correct order using the ten headings and the following sentences.

a. We trust the goods will be delivered punctually and in good condition and look forward to placing further orders with your company if this article sells well.

b. We thank you for the above-mentioned offer for electronic equipment.

c. On the basis of the terms stated we now wish to place the following trial order:

d. Please confirm receipt of our order.

e. Headings (answers to exercise no. 1.)

Exercise 2: Instructions I

First read through the specimen letter on page 52 from Sweetmate Ltd to Ms Henrietta von Jauch. Next write the words missing in the letter below on a piece of your own paper. Do this *without* looking at the specimen letter at the same time.

Ms Henrietta von Jauch
European 1. ____ Director
Stecker Süßwaren Deutschland GmbH
Ringstr. 88
012607 Dresden
Germany

Dear Ms von Jauch

Order 2. ____ Confectionery

We have 3. ____ the catalogue and export price list sent to us on 10 January .. and now 4. ____ to order as follows:

5. ____	6. ____	Article No.	List Price	7. ____
2,500	"Easter Bunnies"	EB25	€1.00	€2,500.00
100	Boxes of "Brown Sugar" chocolates	BS99	€5.00	€ 500.00
			8. ____	€3,000.00
			–5% 9. ____	–€ 150.00
			Total	**€2,850.00**

10. ____: Warehouse to warehouse, to be 11. ____ ____ (*2 words*) by you
Shipment: InterTrans Freight Forwarding Co.
12. ____: Franco to our 13. ____, within 10 days after 14. ____ of order
15. ____: On receipt of invoice by 16. ____ to your a/c at Deutsche Bank, Dresden

We look forward to 17. ____ your confirmation of order and 18. ____ of despatch.

Yours 19. ____
Sweetmate Ltd

Miranda Sweeney

Miranda Sweeney
20. ____ Director

Exercise 3: Instructions II

First read through the specimen fax on page 53 from Joanna Johnson to Ms Anita Schenk. Next write the words missing in the fax below on a piece of your own paper. Do this *without* looking at the specimen fax at the same time.

Fax 1._____ Sheet

2._____:	Ms Anita Schenk, Export Sales Director
Fax No:	+49 (9 31) 97 76 59
From:	Joanna Johnson Purchasing Director
3._____:	16 March ..
4._____:	Order for Computer Power Units
5._____ Pages:	1

Dear Ms Schenk

Thank you for your 6._____ dated 10 March .. .
On the basis of the 7._____ stated we now wish to 8._____ an order as follows:

Article:	50A power unit
Quantity:	500
Unit price:	€ 50.00
9._____ *(2 words):*	30 %
Total price:	€ 17,500.00
Delivery:	CIP London Heathrow Airport, within 30 days after receipt of order
Terms of payment:	$^1/_3$ with order, $^1/_3$ on delivery, $^1/_3$ within 30 days after delivery, by transfer to your 10._____
Packing:	11._____ cartons
Insurance:	12._____ to _____ (*same word again*), to be taken out by you

Please send us your advice of 13._____ as soon as the 14._____ has been shipped.
We look forward to taking 15._____ of the goods in the near future.

Yours sincerely

Joanna Johnson

Exercise 4: Crossword

Look at the vocabulary list on pages 65 / 66 and pick out all the words ending in "-tion" or "-tions". You should find eight in all.

Now complete the crossword using the eight words you have found and the clues below. Write your answers on the worksheet provided.

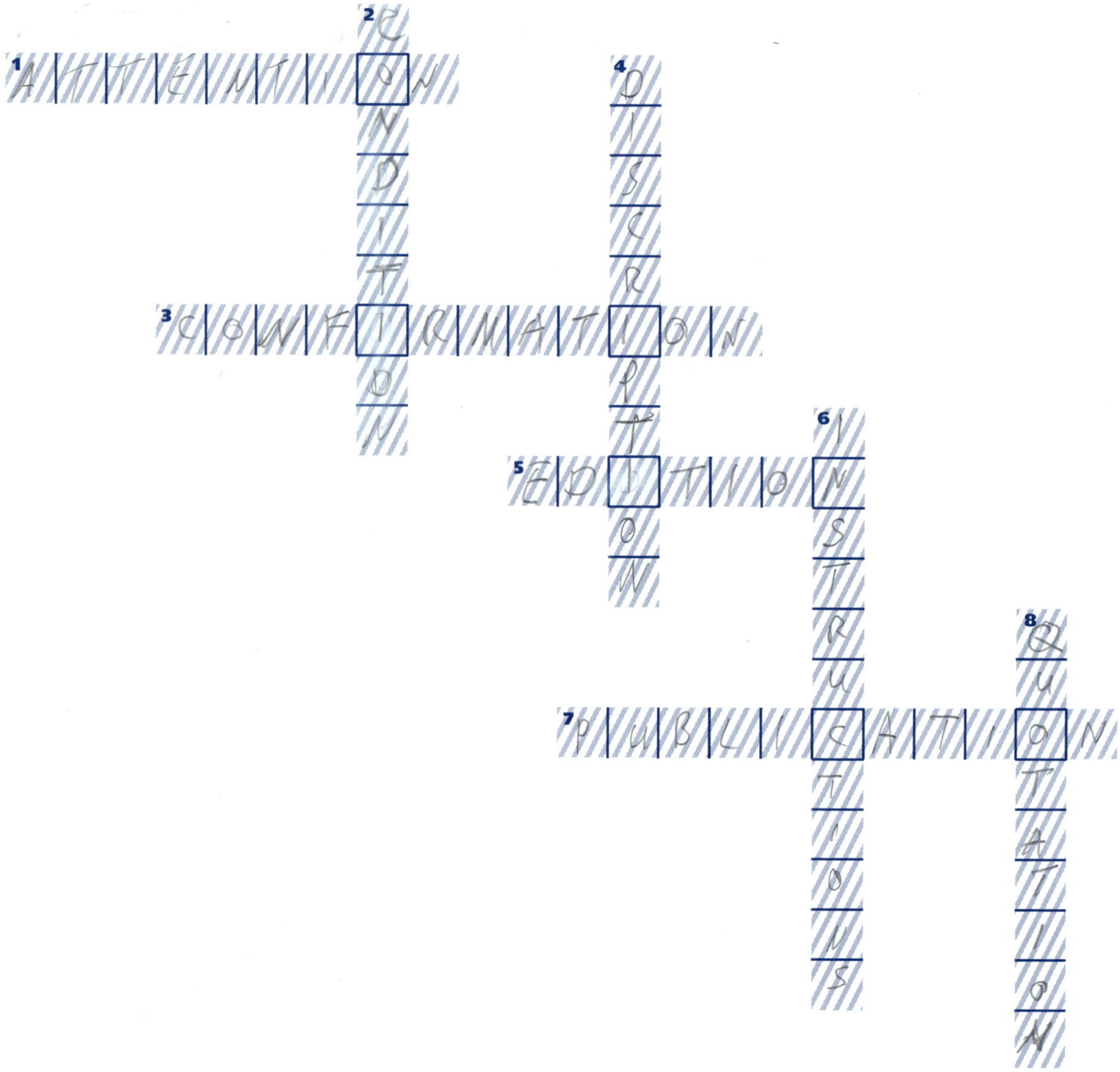

1. "Thank you for your ____ to our order."
2. "We trust the goods will be delivered punctually and in good ____."
3. "We look forward to receiving your ____ of order."
4. Policeman: "What do the missing goods look like? Can you give me a ____?"
5. "We have seen your advertisement in the latest ____ of 'North Face'."
6. "We enclose our packing ____."
7. "Climber's Weekly" is a ____ for climbers.
8. A ____ is an offer for goods or services which includes the price.

Aufgaben

1.

	Von	An
Name	Felicitas (Paul) Werner	–
Position	Einkauf	–
Firma	Adams & Partner	Enduro Tents Ltd
Anschrift	Reichenberger Allee 39–41 24146 Kiel, Germany	90 Staines High Street Staines, ML1 1DB England
Fax	+49 (4 31) 88 34 99	+44 (17 84) 89-32 51
E-Mail	adams.partner@webnet.com.de	enduro.tents@firmnet.co.uk

Geschäftsfall:
In der letzten Ausgabe der britischen Fachzeitschrift "North Face" haben Sie eine Anzeige für Zelte und Zubehör (*accessories*) der Fa. Enduro Tents Ltd in Staines, England gesehen.

Aufgabe:
Erteilen Sie der britischen Firma folgenden Probeauftrag:

- Zelt „Rocky Mountain“ (Katalog-Nr. RM50) zu 180,–€, 5 Stück;
  Zelt „Outback 49 (Katalog-Nr. OB45)“ zu 250,–€, 6 Stück;
  Schlafsack (*sleeping bag*) „Arctic 2000“ (Katalog-Nr. AT40) zu 150,–€, 10 Stück
- Bringen Sie auch einen Wiederverkäuferrabatt von 50 % in Abzug und errechnen Sie den Endpreis!
- Lieferung: CIP deutschem Flughafen
- Lieferzeit: innerhalb von 14 Tagen nach Erhalt des Auftrags
- Zahlungsbedingungen: Zahlung bei Erhalt der Waren
- Bitte um Auftragsbestätigung

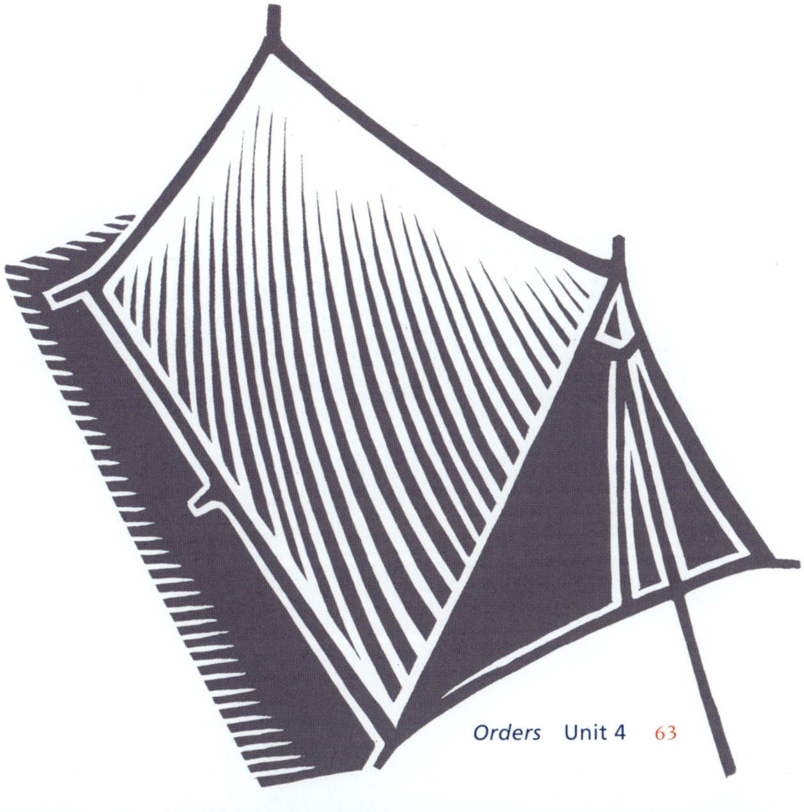

2.

	Von	An
Name	Eigener Name	Mr. Hank Perkins
Position	Einkaufsleiter/in	Sales Division
Firma	Siebel Elektronik AG	Roosevelt Inc.
Anschrift	Postfach 50 30 98, 77656 Offenburg	P.O. Box 1073, Big Bear Lahu, CA 92315, USA
Fax	+49 (7 81) 4 90 08	+1 (9 13) 35 86-90 45
E-Mail	siebelelektronik@t-online.de	roosevelt.inc@ aol.com

Geschäftsfall:
Der amerikanische Klimageräte-Hersteller Roosevelt Inc. in Kalifornien hatte der deutschen Firma Siebel Elektronik AG in Offenburg ein Angebot über sein neuestes Klimagerät AK 37 (*air conditioning unit*) zum Stückpreis von 1.500 US$ gemacht.

Aufgabe:
Erteilen Sie als Einkaufsleiter/in der deutschen Firma dem amerikanischen Unternehmen einen Auftrag unter Berücksichtigung folgender Punkte:

- Bezug auf Angebot
- 100 Stück zum Preis von je 1.500 US$
- Bringen Sie einen Mengenrabatt von 20 % in Abzug und errechnen Sie den Endpreis!
- Lieferzeit: 8 Wochen nach Auftragseingang
- Lieferbedingung: FOB San Francisco
- Zahlungsbedingung: per unwiderruflichem Akkreditiv
- Bitte um Auftragsbestätigung
- Aussicht auf weitere Aufträge, wenn die Ware sich gut verkaufen lässt

Vocabulary List

a/c (account)	*Konto*
acknowledgement of order	*Auftragsbestätigung*
add	*hinzufügen*
advertisement	*Anzeige*
advice of despatch	*Versandanzeige*
agreed, as ~	*wie vereinbart*
air conditioning unit	*Klimaanlage*
appropriate, as ~	*wie geeignet, wie passend*
approx. (approximately)	*ca. (circa)*
attention	*hier: Erledigung*
backpack	*Rucksack*
basis, on the ~ of	*auf der Grundlage von*
cash discount	*Skonto, Barzahlungsrabatt*
chocolates	*Pralinen*
column	*Spalte*
computer power unit	*Netzteil*
condition, in good ~	*in gutem Zustand, wohlbehalten*
confectionery	*Süßwaren*
confirm	*bestätigen*
confirmation of order	*Auftragsbestätigung*
consignment	*Lieferung*
crate, a ~	*(Latten)Kiste*
current	*aktuell*
date of delivery	*Liefertermin*
description	*Beschreibung*
discount	*Rabatt, Nachlass*
each	*je*
edition	*Ausgabe*
equipment	*Geräte, Ausstattung*
European sales director	*Verkaufsleiter/in für Europa*
examine	*hier: prüfen*
few, in the next ~ days	*in den nächsten Tagen*
follows, as ~	*wie folgt*
franco	*hier: frei*
franco to our premises	*frei zu unseren Geschäftsräumen, frei Haus*
further	*weitere (r, s)*
further details	*weitere Einzelheiten*
grateful	*dankbar*
heading	*Überschrift*
IMO (international money order)	*internationale Postanweisung*
in advance	*im Voraus*
include	*hier: mit angeben*
initial order	*Erstauftrag*
instructions	*Anweisungen*
insurance	*Versicherung*
introductory offer discount	*Angebots-Einführungsrabatt*
invoice	*Rechnung*
irrevocable letter of credit, by ~	*per unwiderruflichem Akkreditiv*
item	*Posten, Artikel*
jumbled	*durcheinander gewürfelt, in der falschen Reihenfolge*
latest	*neueste(r, s)*
missing	*fehlende(r, s)*
note, to ~	*feststellen, zur Kenntnis nehmen*
order form	*Auftragsformular*
pallet	*Palette*
place an order	*einen Auftrag erteilen*
premises	*Geschäftsräume*
prompt attention	*hier: umgehende Erledigung*
publication	*Veröffentlichung*
punctually	*pünktlich*
purchasing department	*Einkaufsabteilung*
purchasing director	*Einkaufsleiter/in*
quantity discount	*Mengenrabatt*
quotation	*Preisangebot*
receipt of the goods, on ~	*bei Erhalt der Ware*
reference	*hier: Bezug*
requested, as ~	*wunschgemäß*
required	*benötigt*
row, a ~	*Reihe*
sales invoice	*Verkaufsrechnung*
sales literature	*Verkaufsliteratur*
season	*Saison*
sells well, if this article ~	*wenn dieser Artikel sich gut verkaufen lässt*
ship, to ~	*versenden*
shipment	*hier: Versand*
shipping charge	*Versandgebühr*
state, to ~	*angeben*
study, to ~	*hier: prüfen*
sturdy	*stabil*
sub-total	*Zwischensumme*
table	*hier: Tabelle*
tabular form, in ~	*tabellarisch*
take out	*abschließen*
terms	*Bedingungen*
total	*gesamt (Betrag)*
trade discount	*Wiederverkäuferrabatt, Handelsrabatt*

transfer, a ~	*hier: Überweisung*
trial order	*Probeauftrag*
unit price	*Stückpreis*
use, to ~	*verwenden*
warehouse	*Lager*
within	*innerhalb*
wrong order, in the ~	*in der falschen Reihenfolge*

Unit 5
Acknowledgements

Introduction

An acknowledgement is often sent in foreign trade if
- an order is refused
- delivery will take some time
- substitutes are offered
- new terms are suggested

When writing an acknowledgement use the letter plan to structure your letter, fax or e-mail.

Letter Plan
Acknowledgements

1. Reference to order
2. Confirmation of order*
3. Offer of substitutes
4. Price(s) and discount(s)
5. Terms of delivery and payment
6. Date and mode of delivery
7. Technicalities
   - packing / shipping
   - advice of despatch
8. Request for confirmation
9. Polite ending
10. Enclosure(s)

*As a table, with headings or both. See Unit 4 Orders, pages 52 / 53.

Fig. 10

The following table shows when acknowledgements are sent in foreign trade:

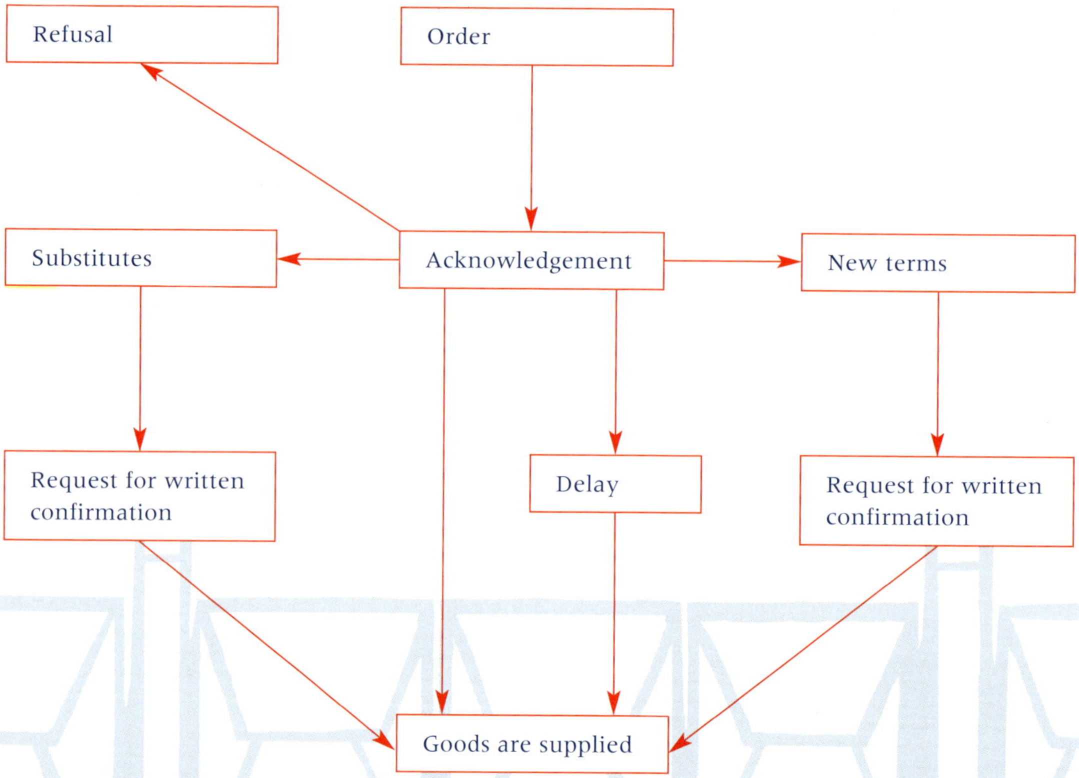

Specimen Letter

1. Letter from Schäfer u. Jost acknowledging an order

Schäfer u. Jost
Großhandel GmbH
Sanitär-Heizung-Sauna

Erlenweg 20–26
97076 Würzburg
Germany

ET / TT
25 February ..

Mrs Janet Watson
Purchasing Department
EP Distributors Ltd
109 Stanwell Road
ASHFORD
MA2 6HH
England

Dear Mrs Watson

Your Order No. 409/20A dated 20 February .. for a Jacuzzi, Article No. GF101

Many thanks for the above-mentioned order. We are pleased to confirm that, as stated in our offer, our company will grant a 10 % discount on the list price of € 10,000, making the total amount € 9,000.

Delivery will be made CIF Dover within 30 days. Please make payment by transfer to our account at Deutsche Bank in Würzburg within 30 days after receipt of invoice. For payment within 14 days a cash discount of 2 % is granted.

You will be receiving our advice of despatch shortly.

Thank you for choosing to place your order with our company.

Yours sincerely
Schäfer u. Jost Großhandel GmbH

Elke Tannenberg

Elke Tannenberg
Export Sales

Tel.: +49 (9 31) 88 79 05
Fax: +49 (9 31) 88 79 00
E-mail: schaefer.jost@firmenet.de

Specimen E-mail

2. Offer of substitutes

e-mail

Mail from:	hnowotny@online.de	**Cc:**	
Subject:	Your Order for Exercise Cycles	**Attachment:**	

Dear Mr Johnson

Thank you for your order dated 4 July .. .

We are unfortunately unable to supply the 5 "Keep Fit" exercise cycles ordered for the next two months. May we therefore recommend our "Top Fit" model instead? It has its own, on-board fitness computer and sells at almost the same price, i. e. €500 per unit, CIP UK airport.

Our new offer is therefore as follows:

Article:	"Top Fit" exercise cycle
Price:	€500 per unit
Quantity:	5
Total price:	€2,500
Terms of delivery:	CIP UK airport
Delivery period:	30 days

We will start processing your order as soon as you confirm the new terms.

Please do not hesitate to contact us if you require further information.

Yours sincerely

Harald Nowotny

Export Sales

Case Study

Neulicht GmbH in Bochum has just received an order from ShowStar International, an Australian company in Perth, to supply lasers for their new musical called "Goethe Get your Gun!" in Hamburg, opening in six months' time.

The Australian company wants 10 × LS15 lasers with delivery franco to the St. Pauli Theater in Hamburg within three months after receipt of order. The price quoted by Neulicht in its sales literature for this laser is € 1,500 per unit.

This model is now no longer manufactured so Gabriele Naumann, the sales manager at Neulicht in Bochum, contacts ShowStar International in Perth today to suggest substituting LS20 lasers for the LS15 models ordered and encloses a brochure on the new model. The new laser is better and more economical than the old one but the list price is € 1,750 per unit. In this case, however, Neulicht is prepared to grant a special discount of 10 %, (i. e. a reduction of € 175 per unit).

Activity

Write Gabriele's letter / fax / e-mail to ShowStar International in which she gives details of Neulicht's new offer and asks ShowStar to confirm it.

From: Gabriele Naumann, Sales Manager, Neulicht GmbH, Castroper Hellweg 40, 44805 Bochum, Germany, fax: +49 (2 34) 98 76 00, e-mail: neu.licht@aol.com

To: Ms Sheilagh Mackenzie, Project Director, ShowStar International Pty, 346 Coronation Street, Perth, Western Australia 6000, fax: +61 (9) 3 22-70 06, e-mail: show.star@aussienet.pw.com

Standard Expressions

1	Reference to order	Many thanks for Thank you for We were delighted to receive		the above-mentioned order your order dated 4 July .. your order		for … (goods, e.g. LS15 lasers, Workplace 3000 swivel chairs)	
2	Confirmation of order*	We are pleased to confirm that		as stated in our offer		our terms are as follows: → table/ headings (*See Unit 4: Orders*)	
		… which we are pleased to confirm … which we hereby confirm					
3	Offer of substitutes	We are unfortunately unable to supply		the … (article, e.g. "Keep Fit" exercise cycles ordered)		at present for the next two months	
		We unfortunately only have … (quantity, e.g. 300)	in stock	and will not be able to send you the other … (quantity, e.g. 200)		for … (time, e.g. another four weeks)	
		… (but we) regret to inform you that this article is now no longer manufactured					
		May we therefore recommend		our … (article, e.g. "Top Fit" model) instead?	The new model	sells at almost the same price is very similar but is more reliable and economical	
		Might we therefore suggest substituting		… (new article, e.g. LS20s)		for … (old article, e.g. LS15s)?	
		Our new offer is therefore as follows: → headings (*See Specimen E-mail on page 70*)					
4	Prices and discounts	→ heading (e.g. Price: € 500 per unit/Total price: € 15,750.00)					
		Our prices and discounts are as stated in our offer					
		We must unfortunately point out that	we are unable to supply	the new model this model this item	at at the price of	… (price, e.g. € 1,500)	per unit
		(… but) in this case	our company will we are prepared to we would be prepared to	grant give you	a …% (e.g. 10%) a special	discount reduction	of … (e.g. 10%, € 25 per unit)
		For payment within … (time, e.g. 14 days)		after receipt of invoice		a cash discount of …% is granted	
5	Terms of delivery	→ heading (e.g. Terms of delivery: CIP UK airport/franco to the St. Pauli Theater Hamburg)					
		Delivery will be made		… (Incoterm, e.g. CIF Dover, CPT London Airport)		in within	30 days

Terms of payment	→ heading (e. g. Terms of payment: 30 days net, 3% cash discount for payment within 10 days)							
	Our terms of payment are	CWO (cash with order) 30 days net						
	Please make payment	by transfer to our account at Deutsche Bank in Würzburg	within 30 days after receipt of invoice					
	Our invoice is enclosed and we would ask you to settle it within 30 days by transfer to our account at the Handelsbank in Munich							
6 Date and mode of delivery	→ heading (e. g. Delivery period: 30 days/within 3 months after receipt of order/from stock)							
	Delivery will be made by	cross-Channel ferry rail road air sea	… (Incoterm, e. g. CIF Harwich, CPT London Airport) franco to your premises	in approx. 8 days' time by … (date, e. g. 30 June ..)				
	The goods will be shipped to … (location)	by …	for delivery and delivered					
	This article can be	supplied sent shipped	immediately from stock					
7 Technicalities – packing/ shipping	The … (article) The goods	will be are	sent shipped transported	in cartons in (large) crates	to … (location, e. g. London, the Hook of Holland)	by	road rail air sea	as requested as stated as agreed
– advice of despatch	You will be receiving our advice of despatch shortly Or advice of despatch will be sent to you in the next few days							
8 Request for confirmation	We will start processing your order as soon as you confirm the new terms Please let us have your confirmation in writing if you accept our new offer and do not hesitate to contact us if you require further information We look forward to receiving your instructions on this matter							
9 Polite ending	Thank you for choosing to place your order with … (e. g. our company/Seidler GmbH etc.) Please do not hesitate to contact us if you require further information We enclose a brochure for your information We look forward to hearing from you soon							
10 Enclosure(s)	Brochure(s) Catalogue(s) Invoice							

Phraseology

1	**Reference to order**	*Bezugnahme auf Auftrag*
	Many thanks for the above-mentioned order for …	*Vielen Dank für den oben erwähnten Auftrag über …*
	We were delighted to receive your order dated 4 July .. for …	*Wir waren erfreut, Ihren Auftrag vom 4. Juli .. für … zu erhalten*
2	**Confirmation of order***	*Auftragsbestätigung**
	We are pleased to confirm that, as stated in our offer, our terms are as follows:	*Wir bestätigen gern, dass, wie in unserem Angebot erwähnt, unsere Bedingungen wie folgt lauten:*
	Thank you for your order dated …, which we are pleased to confirm	*Vielen Dank für Ihren Auftrag vom …, den wir gern bestätigen*
3	**Offer of substitutes**	*Angebot von Ersatzware*
	We are unfortunately unable to supply the "Keep Fit" exercise cycles ordered for the next two months	*Leider sind die „Keep Fit"-Heimtrainer, die Sie bestellt haben, erst in zwei Monaten wieder lieferbar*
	We unfortunately only have 100 in stock and will not be able to send you the other 100 for another four weeks	*Wir haben leider nur 100 auf Lager und können Ihnen die anderen 100 erst in vier Wochen liefern*
	We regret to inform you that this article is now no longer manufactured	*Wir bedauern Ihnen mitzuteilen, dass dieser Artikel jetzt nicht mehr hergestellt wird*
	May we therefore recommend our "Top Fit" model instead?	*Dürfen wir Ihnen daher stattdessen unser Modell „Top Fit" empfehlen?*
	The new model sells at almost the same price and is very similar but more reliable and economical	*Das neue Modell wird zu fast dem gleichen Preis verkauft und ist sehr ähnlich, jedoch verlässlicher und wirtschaftlicher*
	Might we therefore suggest substituting A20s for A15s?	*Dürfen wir deshalb vorschlagen, die A15er durch A20er zu ersetzen?*
	Our new offer is therefore as follows:	*Unser neues Angebot lautet daher wie folgt:*
4	**Prices and discounts**	*Preise und Nachlässe*
	We must unfortunately point out that we are unable to supply the new model at the price of €1,500 per unit	*Wir müssen leider darauf hinweisen, dass wir nicht in der Lage sind, das neue Modell zum Preis von 1.500,– € pro Stück zu verkaufen*
	In this case we would be prepared to grant a special discount of …	*In diesem Fall wären wir bereit, einen Sondernachlass von … zu gewähren*
	For payment within 14 days after receipt of invoice a cash discount of 5% is granted	*Für Zahlung innerhalb von 14 Tagen nach Rechnungserhalt wird ein Barzahlungsrabatt von 5% gewährt*

5	**Terms of delivery**	***Lieferbedingungen***
	Delivery will be made CIF Dover within 30 days	*Die Lieferung erfolgt CIF Dover innerhalb von 30 Tagen*
	Terms of payment	***Zahlungsbedingungen***
	Please make payment by transfer to our account at Deutsche Bank in Würzburg within 30 days after receipt of invoice	*Bitte leisten Sie die Zahlung durch Überweisung auf unser Konto bei der Deutschen Bank in Würzburg innerhalb von 30 Tagen nach Erhalt der Rechnung*
	Our invoice is enclosed and we would ask you to settle it within 30 days by transfer to our account at …	*Unsere Rechnung ist beigefügt und wir bitten Sie, diese innerhalb von 30 Tagen durch Überweisung auf unser Konto bei … zu begleichen*
6	**Date and mode of delivery**	***Datum und Art der Lieferung***
	Delivery will be made by cross-Channel ferry, franco to your premises, in approx. 8 days' time	*Die Lieferung erfolgt durch Kanalfähre frei Ihren Geschäftsräumen in ca. 8 Tagen*
	The goods will be delivered CPT Victoria Station by 30 June ..	*Die Waren werden bis zum 30. Juni .. CPT Victoria Station geliefert*
	This article can be supplied immediately from stock	*Dieser Artikel kann sofort ab Lager geliefert werden*
7	**Technicalities – packing / shipping**	***Technische Einzelheiten – Verpackung / Versand***
	The goods will be shipped in large crates to the Hook of Holland by rail as requested	*Die Waren werden wie gewünscht in großen Lattenkisten per Schiene nach Hook von Holland versandt*
	– advice of despatch	***– Versandavis***
8	You will be receiving our advice of despatch shortly	*Sie werden in Kürze unser Versandavis erhalten*
	Request for confirmation	***Bitte um Bestätigung***
	We will start processing your order as soon as you confirm the new terms	*Wir werden mit der Bearbeitung Ihres Auftrages beginnen, sobald Sie die neuen Bedingungen bestätigen*
	Please let us have your confirmation in writing if you accept our new offer	*Bitte lassen Sie uns Ihre schriftliche Bestätigung zukommen, wenn Sie unser neues Angebot annehmen*
9	We look forward to receiving your instructions on this matter	*Wir freuen uns darauf, Ihre Anweisungen in dieser Angelegenheit zu erhalten*
	Polite ending	***Höfliche Schlussformel***
	Thank you for choosing to place your order with our company	*Vielen Dank, dass Sie sich entschlossen haben, unserer Firma Ihren Auftrag zu erteilen*
	Please do not hesitate to contact us if you require further information	*Bitte zögern Sie nicht, mit uns in Verbindung zu treten, wenn Sie weitere Informationen benötigen*

	We enclose a brochure for your information	*Wir fügen zu Ihrer Information eine Broschüre bei*
	We look forward to hearing from you soon	*Wir freuen uns darauf, bald von Ihnen zu hören*
10	Enclosure(s)	*Anlage(n)*
	Brochure(s)	*Broschüre(n)*
	Invoice	*Rechnung*

Exercises

Exercise 1: Jumbled Letter

The sentences in the letter below are in the wrong order. Use the letter plan on page 67 to put them in the correct order.

a. In this case we would be prepared to grant a special discount of 15 %.

b. We enclose a brochure on the "E-Shock" for your information and look forward to hearing from you soon.

c. Please let us have your confirmation in writing if you accept our new offer.

d. Many thanks for the above-mentioned order for digital watches.

e. The new model sells at almost the same price.

f. We unfortunately only have 200 "D-Shock" watches in stock and will not be able to send you the other 300 for another four weeks.

g. Brochure

h. The watches are shipped in cartons by air.

i. The "E-Shock" can be supplied from stock.

j. Might we therefore recommend our "E-Shock" instead?

k. Delivery will be made CPT London Airport.

l. Our terms of payment are CWO.

Exercise 2: Instructions I

1. First read through the specimen letter on page 69 from Schäfer u. Jost Großhandel GmbH to Mrs Janet Watson.
2. Next write the words missing in the letter below on a piece of your own paper. Do this *without* looking at the specimen letter at the same time.

> Dear Mrs Marlowe
>
> Order No. 508/AB of 1 July .. 1. ___ 5x C-Safe Security Cameras
>
> We thank you 2. ___ the above-mentioned order and are able to confirm that, as mentioned 3. ___ our quotation, we can grant you a discount of 15% 4. ___ the catalogue price of €5,000, making the total amount €4,250.
>
> The cameras will be shipped CIP Gatwick Airport 5. ___ 30 days. We would ask you to make payment 6. ___ transfer 7. ___ our account 8. ___ the Hypobank in Erfurt within 30 days 9. ___ receipt of invoice. For payment within 10 days a cash discount of 3% is granted.
>
> We will be sending you our advice of despatch in the next few days.
>
> Thank you for choosing to place your order 10. ___ our company.
>
> Yours sincerely
> etc.

Exercise 3: Instructions II

1. First read through the specimen e-mail on page 70 from Harald Nowotny to Mr Johnson.
2. Next write the words missing in the e-mail below on a piece of your own paper. Do this *without* looking at the specimen e-mail at the same time.

e-mail

Mail from: sfaulstroh@aol.com **Cc:**

Subject: Your Order for Chest Expanders **Attachment:**

Dear Ms Roberts

Many thanks for your fax of 1 April .. .

We will unfortunately not be able to 1. ____ the 25 "Ripple" chest expanders 2. ____ for the next six weeks. 3. ____ we therefore 4. ____ our "Swell" model instead, which 5. ____ at the same price and is very similar?

We therefore wish to make you a new offer as 6. ____

Article:	"Swell" chest expander
Price:	€ 100 per unit
Quantity:	25
Total price:	€ 2,500
Terms of delivery:	CPT UK airport
Delivery period:	30 days

As soon as you 7. ____ the new terms we will begin 8. ____ your order.

Should you 9. ____ any more details, please do not 10. ____ to contact us.

Yours sincerely

Silke Faulstroh

Export Section

Exercise 4: Word Groups

Look at the vocabulary list on page 82 to find the following groups of words and expressions.

A. Verbs beginning with "re-"

Find the right verbs for the following meanings:

	Meaning
1	to need
2	to be sorry
3	to say "no"
4	to get
5	to say something is good

B. Transport

How many expressions can you find beginning with "by" to mean a form of transport? Make a list.

C. Money

Use the vocabulary list on page 82 to find the words, expressions or abbreviations defined in the table below. All the answers have something to do with money.

	Meaning
1	how much money must be paid for the goods (*2 words*)
2	e. g. 30 days net (*3 words*)
3	sending money from one bank to another
4	You put your money in this at a bank. It has a number.
5	a bill
6	If you buy a lot, we'll give you a 10% ____.
7	You have to pay for the goods when ordering them. (*abbreviation*)

Aufgaben

1.

	Von	An
Name	Eigener Name	–
Position	Verkauf	–
Firma	Gebrüder Johnen KG	Griffith & Co.
Anschrift	Rosenheimerstr. 90–100, 81667 München	21–27 Church St., Oxford OX9 5HH, England
Fax	+49 (89) 9 98 55 70	+44 (18 65) 3 42 67
E-Mail	gebrueder.johnen@t-online.de	griffith.co@firmlink.co.uk

Geschäftsfall:

Die Firma Griffith & Co. hat bei Ihnen 200 Diktiergeräte (*dictaphones*) vom Typ DP49 zum Preis von 25,–€ pro Stück bestellt.

Aufgabe:

Schreiben Sie die entsprechende Auftragsbestätigung und berücksichtigen Sie dabei folgende Punkte:

- Dank für Auftrag über 200 Diktiergeräte (Datum von vor ca. 4 Tagen)
- Geräte werden wunschgemäß per Bahn nach Hook van Holland (*the Hook of Holland*) abgeschickt (4 große Kisten)
- Weitertransport und Lieferung CIF Harwich (GB) erfolgt per Kanalfähre in ca. 8 Tagen
- Rechnung ist beigefügt

- Um Begleichung innerhalb 30 Tagen per Überweisung auf Ihr Konto bei der Handelsbank München wird gebeten
- 3% Skonto für Zahlung innerhalb 10 Tagen nach Rechnungserhalt
- Höfliche Schlussformel

2.

	Von	An
Name	Maria (Max) Pircher	–
Position	Exportabteilung	–
Firma	Jakob Schleyer Computer-Möbel	Norman & Partners Ltd
Anschrift	Reiterstr. 66, 79100 Freiburg	9 Albert Court, Prince Consort Road, London SW7 2BT, England
Fax	+49 (7 61) 8 65 59	+44 (1 81) 2 56-34 27
E-Mail	jakob.schleyer@infoserve.de	norman.partners@bt.com

Geschäftsfall:
Sie sind Maria (Max) Pircher und arbeiten in der Exportabteilung bei der Firma Jakob Schleyer Computer-Möbel in Freiburg. Norman & Partners Ltd in London hat bei Ihnen 500 Drehstühle (*swivel chairs*) Marke „Workplace 3000“, Listenpreis 250,–€ pro Stück, bestellt.

Aufgabe:
Schreiben Sie eine Auftragsbestätigung und berücksichtigen Sie dabei folgende Punkte:
- Dank für den Auftrag (Schreiben vom ... (vor ca. 4 Tagen))
- Von den bestellten Stühlen haben Sie leider nur noch 300 auf Lager
- Die restlichen 200 können in ca. 4 Wochen nachgeschickt werden
- Alternativvorschlag: Sie schicken stattdessen das verbesserte Modell „Workplace 3001“ (Listenpreis 300,–€), das sofort ab Lager lieferbar ist, und gewähren darauf einen Sonderrabatt von 25,–€ pro Stück
- Sie fügen einen Prospekt über den Drehstuhl „Workplace 3001“ bei
- Ihre übrigen Bedingungen: Lieferung CIF Dover, Zahlungsbedingungen 30 Tage netto, 3% Skonto für Zahlung innerhalb 10 Tagen
- Bitte um Benachrichtigung bezüglich der gewünschten Alternative

Vocabulary List

abbreviation	*Abkürzung*
account, an ~	*Konto*
acknowledgement	*Auftragsbestätigung*
advice of despatch	*Versandanzeige*
agreed, as ~	*wie vereinbart*
air, by ~	*auf dem Luftweg*
approx.	*ca.*
CIF (cost, insurance, freight)	*Kosten, Versicherung, Fracht*
confirmation	*Bestätigung*
crate, a ~	*(Latten)Kiste*
cross-Channel ferry	*Kanalfähre*
CWO (cash with order)	*Barzahlung bei Auftragserteilung*
date of delivery	*Liefertermin*
delay, the ~	*Verzögerung*
delighted, we were ~	*wir haben uns gefreut*
delivery	*Lieferung*
discount	*Rabatt*
economical	*sparsam*
enclose	*beifügen*
exercise cycle	*Heimtrainer*
ferry	*Fähre*
foreign trade	*Außenhandel*
franco to your premises	*frei zu Ihren Geschäfts-räumen*
further	*weitere(r, s)*
grant, to ~	*gewähren*
heading	*Überschrift*
hereby	*hiermit*
hesitate	*zögern*
i. e.	*d. h.*
immediately	*sofort*
instead	*hier: dafür; statt*
instructions	*Anweisungen*
invoice	*Rechnung*
item	*Posten*
jacuzzi	*Whirlpool*
jumbled	*durcheinander ge-würfelt, in der falschen Reihenfolge*
location	*Ort*
look, to ~ forward to	*sich freuen auf*
manufacture, to ~	*herstellen*
matter, on this ~	*in dieser Angelegenheit*
mode of delivery	*Versandart*
net, 30 days ~	*30 Tage netto*
packing	*Verpackung*
place an order	*einen Auftrag erteilen*
point out	*darauf hinweisen*
premises	*Geschäftsräume*
process, to ~	*bearbeiten*

purchasing department	*Einkaufsabteilung*
quoted	*hier: angeboten*
rail, by ~	*per Bahn*
receipt, after ~ of invoice	*nach Rechnungserhalt*
receive	*erhalten*
recommend	*empfehlen*
reference to	*Bezug auf*
refusal	*Ablehnung*
refuse, to ~	*ablehnen*
regret, to ~	*bedauern*
reliable	*zuverlässig*
request, a ~ for	*Bitte um*
requested, as ~	*wunschgemäß*
require	*benötigen, brauchen*
road, by ~	*per Straße*
sales literature	*Verkaufsliteratur*
sea, by ~	*per Schiff*
settle, to ~	*begleichen*
ship, to ~	*versenden*
shipping	*Versand*
shortly	*in Kürze*
similar	*ähnlich*
specimen	*Muster*
state, to ~	*angeben*
stated, as ~	*wie angegeben*
stock, from ~	*ab Lager*
stock, in ~	*auf Lager*
substitute, to ~	*ersetzen*
substitute(s)	*Ersatz(waren)*
suggest	*vorschlagen*
supply, to ~	*liefern*
swivel chair	*Drehstuhl*
table	*hier: Tabelle*
technicalities	*technische Einzelheiten*
terms of delivery	*Lieferbedingungen*
terms of payment	*Zahlungsbedingungen*
therefore	*deshalb, daher*
total amount	*Gesamtbetrag*
trade	*hier: Handel*
transfer, a ~	*Überweisung*
unfortunately	*leider*
within	*innerhalb*

Unit 6

Delivery

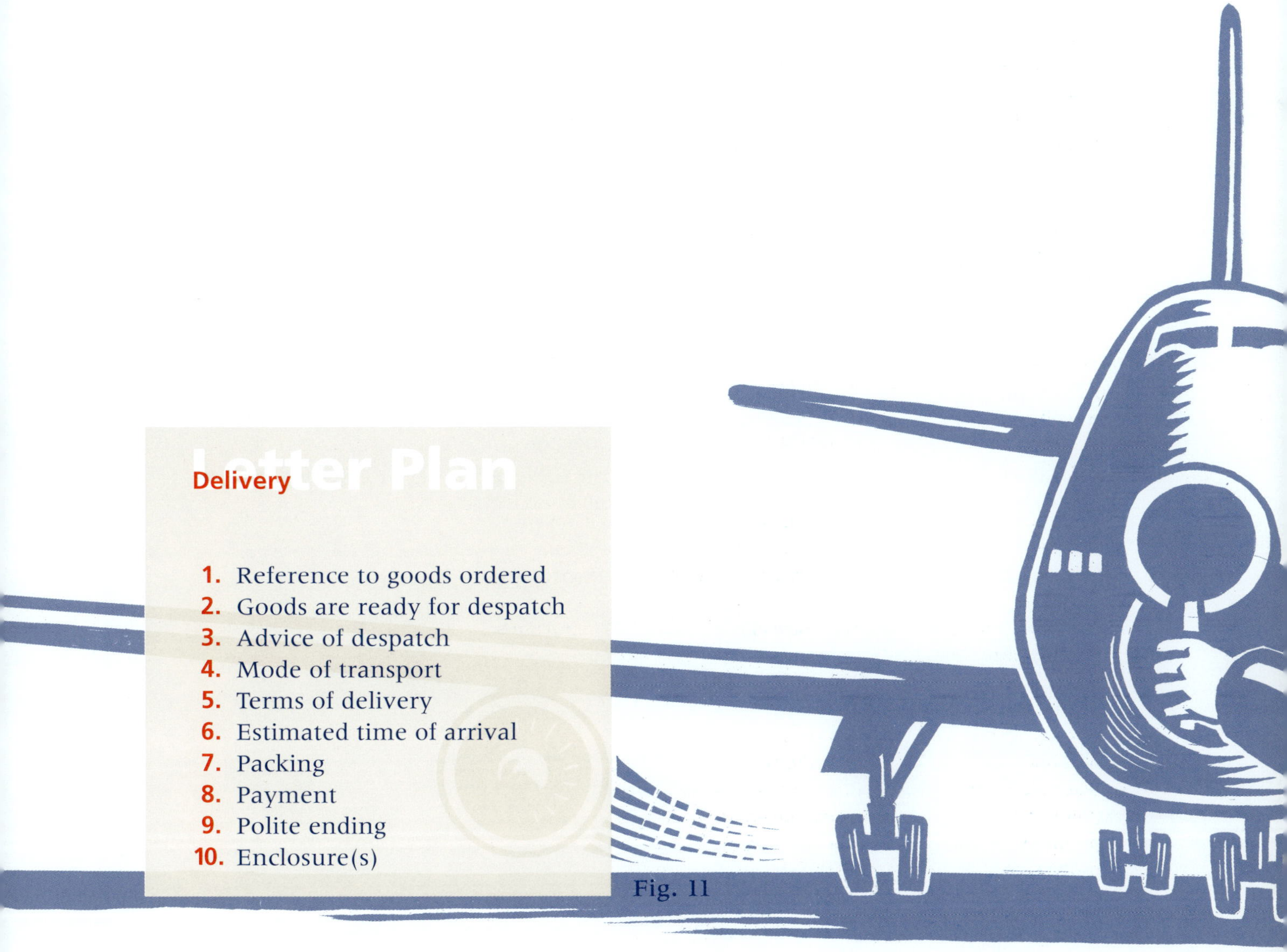

Letter Plan

Delivery

1. Reference to goods ordered
2. Goods are ready for despatch
3. Advice of despatch
4. Mode of transport
5. Terms of delivery
6. Estimated time of arrival
7. Packing
8. Payment
9. Polite ending
10. Enclosure(s)

Fig. 11

Introduction

When goods are shipped abroad, the supplier usually sends the buyer an advice of despatch, which tells the buyer when to expect the goods and how they will be transported.

In addition, documents are needed to ship, export, deliver and pay for goods. The most important shipping documents in foreign trade are as follows:

Documents

	Name of document	Important features
1	Bill of lading *Konnossement*	1. document of title (can be sold) 2. contract of carriage 3. receipt for the goods
2	Consignment note (road or rail transport) *Frachtbrief*	1. not a document of title (cannot be sold) 2. contract of carriage 3. receipt for the goods
3	Air waybill *Luftfrachtbrief*	1. not a document of title (cannot be sold) 2. contract of carriage 3. receipt for the goods
4	Commercial invoice *Handelsrechnung*	1. request for payment 2. the price of the goods
5	Pro-forma invoice *Proforma-Rechnung*	1. not a request for payment 2. the price of the goods
6	Insurance policy / certificate *Versicherungspolice / Versicherungsschein*	Shows the goods are insured
7	Certificate of origin *Ursprungszeugnis*	Shows where the goods are from
8	Bill of exchange (draft) *Wechsel (Tratte)*	The customer can pay by accepting or paying a bill of exchange

Use the letter plan to structure your letter, fax or e-mail.

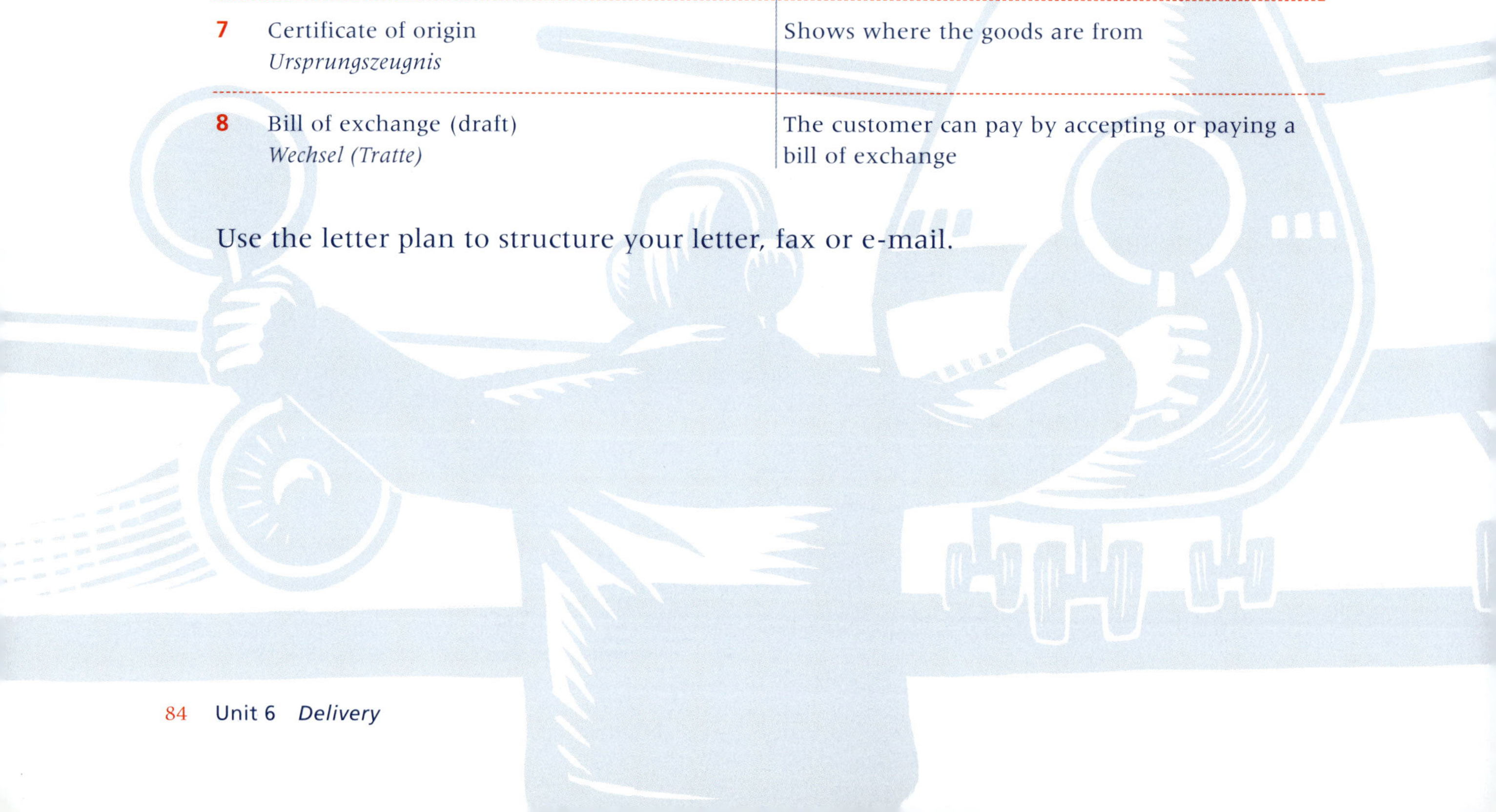

Specimen Letter

1. Home Draught Beer Units

Heymanns Kühl-Geräte-Bau confirms delivery of home draught beer units

Heymanns Kühl-Geräte-Bau	Am Neggenborn 98	44892 Bochum, Germany
Tel. +49 (2 34) 99 67-0	Fax. +49 (2 34) 99 67-35	E-mail: heymanns@firmnet.com

Our ref. hey.92-B
Your ref. –
15 June ..

Hyde Bros Catering Ltd
49 Tippletree Road
IPSWICH
SU5 9KK
England

For the attention of Mr Martin Wallis, Imports

Dear Mr Wallis

Shipment of 100 Home Draught Beer Units as per your Order dated 27 May ..

We are pleased to confirm that the above-mentioned units have now been sent to you by container. They will be shipped by cross-Channel ferry from the Hook of Holland to Felixstowe and then taken by road to your premises.

Delivery will be made by Eurotrans GmbH and the goods are expected to reach your warehouse by the end of the month. The Home Draught Beer Units have been packed in sturdy cartons with the usual marks.

We have instructed our correspondent bank, the Midland Bank in Ipswich, to release the documents to you on payment of our draft for € 15,500.

We trust that the goods will arrive punctually and in good condition and look forward to doing further business with you.

Yours sincerely
Heymanns Kühl-Geräte-Bau

Johannes Heymann

Johannes Heymann
Managing Director

Specimen Fax

2. Advice of despatch

sheet

Woosey and Hawkes Ltd,
Manufacturers of the Finest Brass Instruments
99 Tetherington Road, London EC2 9AH, England
Tel. +44 (0) 1 71 / 8 97-44 35, Fax +44 (0) 1 71 / 8 97-44 80
E-mail: woosey.hawkes@firmlink.co.uk

FAO:	Mr Harald Rottkamp Purchasing Department Musikhaus Berger Hauptstr. 99 73730 Euskirchen Germany
Fax No:	+49 (22 51) 88 97 65
From:	Rita King Export Sales Department
Date:	30 September ..
Subject:	Advice of Despatch: Order No. 998C for 25 Trombones dated 15 August ..
Total Pages:	1

Dear Mr Rottkamp

We are now able to confirm that the instruments ordered have been collected by our forwarding agents, CargoShip Ltd, and will be despatched to you CIP Cologne–Bonn Airport on Lufthansa Flight No. LH 8095 on 7 October. They have been packed in sturdy cases.

The shipping documents for the documentary credit (air waybill, commercial invoice, packing list, insurance certificate) have now been handed over to our bankers and payment has been received.

We trust the consignment will arrive safely and on schedule and look forward to receiving further orders.

Yours sincerely

Rita King

Case Study

Michael Schreiner is the export sales manager at Entech Umwelttechnik GmbH in Düsseldorf. His company has received an order from Mr Richard Tang, the plant manager at the Taiwan Metal Company Ltd, for six "SA1" Decontamination Units. The details of the transaction are as follows:

Mode of transport:	ship
Port of shipment:	Hamburg
Port of destination:	Kaohsiung in Taiwan
Name of ship:	MS "Angela"
Departure date:	end of the month (*give exact date*)
ETA (estimated time of arrival):	2 weeks after departure (*give approximate date*)
Terms of delivery:	CIF Kaohsiung
Total price:	€6,000
Payment:	D / A (through the Ruhrbank in Düsseldorf and the Bank of Taiwan in Taichung). The shipping documents will be released against acceptance of a 90-day sight draft

Activity

Using the letter plan on page 83 and the layouts in Unit 1 write Michael Schreiner's advice of despatch as a letter, fax or e-mail to the Taiwanese company.

From: Entech Umwelttechnik GmbH, Potsdamer Str. 44, 40599 Düsseldorf,
fax +49 (2 11) 56 48 99, e-mail: entech.recycling@compuserve.com

To: Taiwan Metal Company Ltd, P.O. Box 21–83, Taichung, Taiwan,
fax +8 86 (4) 2 81 24 23, e-mail: taiwan.metal@tainet.com

Standard Expressions

1	Reference to goods ordered	Many thanks Thank you	for your order	dated … (e.g. 2 February ..)	for	… (goods)	
						the above-mentioned	article(s) goods equipment

2	Goods are ready for despatch	We are pleased to We are now able to	confirm that	the article(s) the goods the above-mentioned goods the above-mentioned units	ordered …	… as per your	letter fax e-mail phone call	dated …	is are	now ready for despatch

3	Advice of despatch	We are pleased to	confirm that advise you that	your order for … (goods, e.g. crystal glass items) the above-mentioned units/goods the … (goods, e.g. instruments) ordered	has have	(now) been	sent to you by container collected by our forwarding agents, CargoShip Ltd

4	Mode of transport	The consignment The goods The units They	will be sent will be shipped	by sea by cross-Channel ferry as sea freight on board MS "Angela"			from … (sea port, e.g. the Hook of Holland) to … (sea port, e.g. Felixstowe)
		… and then	taken to transported to shipped to delivered to	your premises your warehouse your company	by	road lorry rail train	by … (name of forwarder, e.g. Eurotrans GmbH)
		The consignment has It has The goods have They have		now been loaded on board … (name of ship, e.g. MS "Seagull")	which is due to leave the port of … (name of port, e.g. Hamburg)		on … (date) at the end of the month
		… and is expected to dock … and is due to arrive		in … (location, e.g. Taiwan)			on … (date, e.g. 5 March ..) in two weeks' time on … (date) on or around … (date)
		The goods will be despatched to you on British Airways Flight No. BA 7062 Delivery will be made by Eurotrans GmbH					on … (date)

5	Terms of delivery	Delivery will be made The goods will be delivered The goods will be despatched to you	... (Incoterm, e.g. CIF Kaohsiung, CIP Cologne–Bonn Airport)		on board ... (name of ship, e.g. MS "Angela") on Lufthansa Flight No. LH 8095		as instructed as requested as agreed
		The goods have now been loaded on board ... (name of ship, e.g. MS "Seagull")			for delivery ... (Incoterm, e.g. CIF Hong Kong)		
6	Estimated time of arrival	Your order is The consignment is The goods are	expected	to arrive at to reach	your warehouse your premises	on ... (date) in 3 days' time by ... (date, e.g. 15 June ..) by the end of the month	
7	Packing	As requested, As instructed,	the ... (article, e.g. crystal) your order the consignment the ... (goods)	has have	been packed in	boxes crates sturdy cartons sturdy cases	marked ... (shipping marks) marked with your address with the usual marks
8	Payment	We have instructed	... (name of bank in foreign buyer's country , e.g. the Bank of India) our correspondent bank, the Midland Bank in Ipswich,	to release the documents to you		on payment of	the invoice amount the sum of ... our draft for ... (e.g. €5,500)
		The documents The shipping documents	have now been		given to handed over to	... (seller's bank in Germany, e.g. Deutsche Bank in Düsseldorf)	
		Our correspondent bank, ... (name of bank in foreign buyer's country, e.g. the Bank of Taiwan in Taichung)	will release them to you		as soon as	payment has been made our 90-day sight draft has been accepted	
		The shipping documents for the documentary credit	(air waybill, commercial invoice, packing list, insurance certificate)	have now been handed over to		... (name of bank) our bankers	and payment has been received
		We have handed over the shipping documents	(complete set of 3 clean, on-board bills of lading, 3 copies of the commercial invoice, certificate of origin, insurance certificate)				to ... (name of seller's bank, e.g. Deutsche Bank in Mettmann)

	… (name of seller's bank, e.g. Deutsche Bank in Mettmann) They	will forward	the documents them	to our correspondent bank, … (name of bank in foreign buyer's country, e.g. the Bank of Hong Kong, China)	who will release them to you who have been instructed to release them to you	as soon as after	payment has been made our draft has been accepted
	The invoice Our invoice	is enclosed will be sent to you by separate post					
9 Polite ending	We trust that the goods will arrive punctually and in good condition and look forward to doing further business with you We trust the consignment will arrive safely and on schedule and look forward to receiving further orders We trust your order has been executed to your satisfaction and that the consignment will arrive safely and on schedule Should you have any queries, please do not hesitate to contact us						
10 Enclosure(s)	Invoice Copy/Copies of shipping document(s) Shipping documents						

Phraseology

1	**Reference to goods ordered**	***Bezugnahme auf bestellte Waren***
	Many thanks for your order dated … for the above-mentioned equipment	*Vielen Dank für Ihren Auftrag vom … für die oben erwähnte Ausrüstung*
2	**Goods are ready for despatch**	***Die Waren sind versandbereit***
	We are pleased to confirm that the above-mentioned goods, ordered as per your letter dated …, are now ready for despatch	*Wir freuen uns zu bestätigen, dass die oben erwähnten Güter, die gemäß Ihrem Schreiben vom … bestellt wurden, jetzt versandbereit sind*
3	**Advice of despatch**	***Versandavis (-anzeige)***
	We are pleased to advise you that your order for crystal glass items has now been sent to you by container	*Wir freuen uns Ihnen mitzuteilen, dass Ihre Bestellung für Kristallglasteile Ihnen jetzt per Container zugesandt worden ist*
4	**Mode of transport**	***Transportart***
	The goods will be sent by cross-Channel ferry from the Hook of Holland to Felixstowe	*Die Waren werden mit der Kanalfähre von Hook van Holland nach Felixstowe geschickt*
	They will be shipped as sea freight on board MS "Angela", and then taken to your premises by road	*Sie werden als Seefracht an Bord der MS „Angela" verschifft und dann per Straße zu Ihren Geschäftsräumen gebracht*
	The consignment has now been loaded on board MS "Seagull", which is due to leave the port of Hamburg at the end of the month	*Die Sendung ist nun an Bord der MS „Seagull" verladen worden, die Ende des Monats aus dem Hamburger Hafen auslaufen soll*
	… and is expected to dock in Taiwan on or around 15 June	*… und am oder um den 15. Juni in Taiwan andocken soll*
	The goods will be despatched to you on British Airways Flight No. BA 7062 on …	*Die Waren werden Ihnen mit dem Flug der British Airways Nr. BA 7062 am … zugeschickt*
	The goods have now been loaded on board MS "Anastasia" for delivery CIF Hong Kong	*Die Waren sind jetzt für Lieferung CIF Hongkong an Bord der MS "Anastasia" verladen worden*
	Delivery will be made by Eurotrans GmbH	*Die Lieferung erfolgt durch die Eurotrans GmbH*
5	**Terms of delivery**	***Lieferbedingungen***
	Delivery will be made CIP Cologne–Bonn Airport on Lufthansa Flight No. LH 8095, as instructed	*Die Lieferung erfolgt nach Anweisung CIP Köln-Bonner Flughafen mit dem Lufthansa Flug Nr. LH 8095*
	The goods will be delivered CIF Kaohsiung on board MS "Juliana", as requested	*Die Waren werden wie gewünscht CIF Kaohsiung an Bord der MS „Juliana" geliefert*

6	**Estimated time of arrival**	***Geschätzte Ankunftszeit***
	The goods are expected to arrive at your premises in 3 days' time	*Die Waren sollen in 3 Tagen in Ihren Geschäftsräumen ankommen*
7	**Packing**	***Verpackung***
	As requested, the crystal has been packed in sturdy cartons marked with your address	*Wie gewünscht, ist das Kristall in festen Kartons, die mit Ihrer Adresse markiert sind, verpackt worden*
	The goods have been packed in crates with the usual marks	*Die Waren wurden mit den üblichen Markierungen in Verschläge gepackt*
8	**Payment**	***Zahlung***
	We have instructed our correspondent bank, the Midland Bank in Ipswich, to release the documents to you on payment / acceptance of our draft for €5,500	*Wir haben unsere Korrespondenzbank, die Midland Bank in Ipswich, angewiesen, die Dokumente bei Zahlung / Akzept unseres Wechsels über 5.500,– € an Sie herauszugeben*
	The shipping documents have now been handed over to the Handelsbank in Düsseldorf	*Die Versand-(Verschiffungs-)dokumente sind jetzt der Handelsbank in Düsseldorf übergeben worden*
	Our correspondent bank, the Bank of Taiwan in Taichung, will release them to you as soon as our 90-day sight draft has been accepted	*Unsere Korrespondenzbank, die Bank von Taiwan in Taichung, wird sie Ihnen übergeben, sobald unser 90-Tage-Sichtwechsel akzeptiert worden ist*
	We have handed over the shipping documents (*list of documents*) to Deutsche Bank in Mettmann	*Wir haben der Deutschen Bank in Mettmann die Versand-(Verschiffungs-)dokumente (Liste der Dokumente) übergeben*
	The bank will forward the documents to our correspondent bank, the Bank of Hong Kong, China	*Die Bank wird die Dokumente unserer Korrespondenzbank, der Bank of Hong Kong, China, zusenden*
	The shipping documents for the documentary credit (*list of documents*) have now been handed over to our bankers and payment has been received	*Die Versand-(Verschiffungs-)dokumente für das Dokumentenakkreditiv (Liste der Dokumente) sind nun unserer Bank übergeben worden und die Zahlung ist erfolgt*
	Our invoice will be sent to you by separate post	*Unsere Rechnung wird Ihnen mit separater Post zugehen*
9	**Polite ending**	***Höfliche Schlussformel***
	We trust that the goods will arrive punctually and in good condition	*Wir sind zuversichtlich, dass die Waren pünktlich und in gutem Zustand ankommen werden*
	We trust the consignment will arrive safely and on schedule and look forward to receiving further orders	*Wir vertrauen darauf, dass die Sendung sicher und gemäß Zeitplan ankommen wird, und freuen uns darauf, weitere Aufträge zu erhalten*

	We trust your order has been executed to your satisfaction	*Wir hoffen, dass Ihr Auftrag zu Ihrer Zufriedenheit ausgeführt wurde*
	Should you have any queries, please do not hesitate to contact us	*Sollten Sie irgendwelche Fragen haben, zögern Sie bitte nicht, mit uns Verbindung aufzunehmen*
10	Enclosure(s)	*Anlage(n)*
	Invoice	*Rechnung*
	Shipping documents	*Versand-(Verschiffungs-)dokumente*

Shipping Documents

1	complete set of 3 clean, on-board bills of lading	*kompletter Satz von 3 reinen, an-Bord-Konnossementen*
2	air waybill	*Luftfrachtbrief*
3	(3 copies of the) commercial invoice	*(3 Ausfertigungen der) Handelsrechnung*
4	certificate of origin	*Ursprungszeugnis*
5	insurance certificate	*Versicherungszertifikat*
6	packing list	*Packliste*

Exercises

Exercise 1: Jumbled Letter

The sentences below are in the wrong order. Use the letter plan on page 83 to put them in the correct order.

a. The consignment is expected to arrive at your warehouse by the end of the month.

b. Many thanks for your order dated 10 July .. for mobile phones.

c. We have instructed the Midland Bank in Colchester to release the documents to you on payment of the sum of €2,000.

d. We are pleased to advise you that the goods have now been collected by our forwarding agents, QuickShip GmbH.

e. Delivery will be made CIP Colchester, as instructed.

f. They will be shipped by cross-Channel ferry from Rotterdam to Harwich and then taken to your premises by road.

g. We trust that the goods will arrive punctually and in good condition and look forward to doing further business with you.

h. As requested, the mobile phones have been packed in sturdy cartons marked with your address.

Exercise 2: Instructions

1. First read through the specimen letter on page 85 from Heymanns Kühl-Geräte-Bau to Hyde Bros Catering Ltd.
2. Next use the words in the list and write the words missing in the letter below on a piece of your own paper. One of the words is used five times.

List
by ◆ correspondent bank ◆ draft ◆ draught ◆ marks ◆ premises ◆ punctually ◆ release ◆ sturdy ◆ trust ◆ warehouse

Dear Ms Wells

Your Order for 2,000 Home 1. ___ Beer Units dated 10 July ..

We are now able to confirm that the above-mentioned goods have now been shipped to you 2. ___ container. They will be sent 3. ___ cross-Channel ferry from Rotterdam to Harwich and then taken 4. ___ road to your 5. ___.

Delivery will be made 6. ___ QuickShip GmbH and we expect the load to reach your 7. ___ 8. ___ the end of the month. They have been packed in 9. ___ cartons with the usual 10. ___.

We have told our 11. ___, Lloyds TSB in Colchester, to 12. ___ the documents to you on payment of our 13. ___ for € 10,000.

We 14. ___ that the goods will arrive 15. ___ and in good condition and look forward to doing further business with you.

Yours sincerely
etc.

Exercise 3: Anagrams

1. First read through the specimen fax on page 86 from Woosey and Hawkes Ltd to Musikhaus Berger.
2. The letters of ten of the words have been mixed up. Re-arrange them to make words from the specimen fax.

1. vadcie
2. gnrupchisa
3. mnttrpdeea
4. fromnic
5. dirrogfawn
6. yudrst
7. eaiucnnrs
8. typneam
9. tnnmgsnceio
10. rreutfh

Exercise 4: Word Groups

Look at the vocabulary list on page 99 / 100 to find the following groups of words and expressions. Write your answers on a piece of your own paper.

A.

Verbs which go with "goods". The first letter is of the word is given.

1	c		goods
2	d		
3	e		
4	i		
5	l		
6	r		
7	s		

B.

Write down the six different persons named in the vocabulary list.

C.

Write down the four methods of payment given in the vocabulary list.

D.

Write down the names of three more documents in the vocabulary list (excluding the ones named under **C.**)

Aufgaben

1.

Name	eigener Name	Ms Fiona MacNamara
Position	Versandabteilung	Purchasing Director
Firma	Schulenburg KG	Jonston & Farmer Ltd
Anschrift	Gutenbergstr. 99, 75206 Keltern, Germany	P.O. Box 200, Romford, RM3 8UX, UK
Fax	+49 (72 36) 88 12 40	+44 (3 70) 8 62-19 88
E-Mail	schulenberg.kg@netlink.de	jonston.farmer@firmnet.co.uk

Geschäftsfall:
Sie haben von der Jonston & Farmer Ltd am ... (vor einer Woche) einen Auftrag über verschiedene Kristallwaren (*crystal glass*) erhalten.

Aufgabe:
Verfassen Sie mit Datum von heute die Versandanzeige per Brief / Fax / E-Mail unter Berücksichtigung der folgenden Einzelheiten:

- Ware wurde dem Spediteur, der Firma Expressgut Schmidt KG, heute übergeben
- voraussichtliches Ankunftsdatum beim Kunden: in 3 Tagen
- Ware wurde in stabilen Kartons verpackt
- Markierung der Kisten mit Kundenanschrift, wie gewünscht
- Rechnung wird mit separater Post geschickt
- Höfliche Schlussformel

2.

	Von	An
Name	Patricia (Patrick) Angerer	–
Position	Verkaufssachbearbeiter/in	–
Firma	Braukunst-Gaststätten-Brauerei GmbH	Hong Kong Gastronomy Ltd
Anschrift	Gold-Zack-Str. 11, 40822 Mettmann, Germany	Suite 9–11, 18 / F Kinwick Centre, 48 Hollywood Road, Central, Hong Kong, China
Fax	+49 (21 04) 87 86 54	+8 53 (9 80) 3 42 55
E-Mail	angerer.bgb.gmbh@aol.com	hk.gastronomy@chinaweb.com

Geschäftsfall:
Sie haben vor einer Woche einen Auftrag über eine Brauereiausrüstung (*brewing equipment*) erhalten.

Aufgabe:
Teilen Sie der Hong Kong Gastronomy Ltd mit, dass die Ausrüstung heute Morgen an Bord der MS „Seagull" verschifft worden ist. Weitere Einzelheiten:

Auslaufhafen:	Rotterdam
Bestimmungshafen:	Hong Kong
Ankunftsdatum:	2 Wochen (ab heute!)
Lieferbedingung:	CIF Hong Kong
Dokumente:	Reines Bordkonnossement 3-fach, Handelsrechnung 3-fach, Ursprungszeugnis, Versicherungsschein. Diese wurden der Deutschen Bank in Mettmann übergeben zur Weiterleitung an die Bank of Hong Kong, China.
Zahlung:	Die Bank of Hong Kong, China wird die Dokumente gegen Akzept der Hong Kong Gastronomy Ltd aushändigen

– Höfliche Schlussformel

Vocabulary List

90-day sight draft	*90-Tage-Sichttratte*
able, to be ~ to	*können*
above-mentioned	*oben erwähnt*
accept	*akzeptieren*
advice of despatch	*Versandanzeige*
agreed, as ~	*wie vereinbart*
airport	*Flughafen*
amount	*Betrag*
approximate	*ungefähr*
as per	*gemäß*
bill of exchange	*Wechsel*
brass instruments	*Blechblasinstrumente*
business, to do ~	*Geschäfte tätigen*
buyer	*Käufer/in*
by, ~ the end of the month	*bis Ende des Monats*
case, a ~	*(Latten)Kiste*
catering	*Gastronomie, Restauration*
CIF (cost, insurance, freight)	*Kosten, Versicherung, Fracht*
CIP (carriage and insurance paid)	*frachtfrei versichert*
clean	*rein (siehe Phraseology)*
collect	*abholen*
condition, in good ~	*wohlbehalten*
consignment	*Lieferung*
contract of carriage	*Beweisurkunde für den Frachtvertrag*
correspondent bank	*Korrespondenzbank*
crate, a ~	*Kiste, Verschlag*
cross-Channel ferry	*Kanalfähre*
crystal glass items	*Kristallwaren*
decontamination unit	*Dekontaminierungs-, Entgiftungsanlage*
delivery, for ~ ...	*zur Lieferung ...*
departure date	*Abfahrtszeit*
despatch, the ~	*Versand*
despatch, ready for	*versandbereit*
despatch, to ~	*versenden*
destination, port of ~	*Bestimmungshafen*
dock, to ~	*anlegen*
document of title	*Warenwertpapier, Eigentumsurkunde*
documentary credit	*Dokumentenakkreditiv*
draft, a ~	*Tratte*
due to leave (ship)	*auslaufen sollen (Schiff)*
enclosed	*beigefügt*
equipment	*Ausrüstung*
estimate, to ~	*schätzen*
estimated time of arrival (ETA)	*geschätzte Ankunftszeit*
execute	*ausführen*
expect	*rechnen mit (Waren); davon ausgehen*
flight	*Flug*
foreign trade	*Außenhandel*
forward, to ~	*weiterleiten*
forwarding agent(s)	*Spediteur(e)*
freight, sea ~	*Seefracht*
further	*weitere(r, s)*
hand over	*übergeben*
hesitate	*zögern*
home draught beer unit	*Bierzapfanlage für zu Hause*
in addition	*darüber hinaus*
instruct	*anweisen*
instructed, as ~	*gemäß Ihren Anweisungen*
insure	*versichern*
invoice	*Rechnung*
invoice amount	*Rechnungsbetrag*
jumbled	*durcheinander gewürfelt, in der falschen Reihenfolge*
load, to ~	*verladen*
location	*Ort*
managing director	*Geschäftsführer/in*
marks	*hier: Versandmarkierungen*
mixed up	*durcheinander gewürfelt, in der falschen Reihenfolge*
mobile phone	*Handy*
mode of transport	*Versandart*
on board	*an Bord*
on schedule	*pünktlich, planmäßig, termingerecht*
on-board bill of lading	*Bordkonnossement (siehe Phraseology)*
payment	*Zahlung*
per, as ~	*gemäß*
phone call	*Telefonanruf*
plant manager	*Werksleiter/in*
port, sea ~	*Seehafen*
premises	*Geschäftsräume*
punctually	*pünktlich*
purchasing department	*Einkaufsabteilung*
query, a ~	*(Rück)Frage*
ready for despatch	*versandbereit*
re-arrange	*hier: in die richtige Reihenfolge bringen*
receipt for the goods	*Empfangsbescheinigung für die Waren*

receive	*erhalten*
reference to	*Bezug auf*
release, to ~	*aushändigen*
request for payment	*Zahlungsaufforderung*
requested, as ~	*wunschgemäß*
safely	*wohlbehalten*
satisfaction, to your ~	*zu Ihrer Zufriedenheit*
schedule, on ~	*gemäß Zeitplan*
seller	*Verkäufer/in*
separate post, by ~	*mit getrennter Post*
ship, to ~	*versenden*
shipment	*Lieferung*
shipment, port of ~	*Verschiffungshafen*
sturdy	*stabil*
sum	*Summe*
supplier	*Lieferant/in*
trombone	*Posaune*
trust, to ~	*hoffen; zuversichtlich sein; davon ausgehen*
usual	*üblich*
warehouse	*Lager*

Unit 7

Payment

Letter Plan 1

Payment

A. Buyer

1. Reference to goods
2. Reference to invoice / statement*
3. Mode of payment
4. Polite ending
5. Enclosure(s)

*As appropriate

Fig. 12

Letter Plan 2

Payment

B. Seller

1. Reference to invoice / statement*
2. Payment
3. Reference to other goods / services
4. Polite ending
5. Enclosure(s)

*As appropriate

Fig. 13

Introduction

Letters about payment are normally brief. In most cases the seller advises the buyer how to make payment (see table *Methods of payment in foreign trade* below) or the buyer confirms or promises payment.

Methods of payment in foreign trade

1	Documentary letter of credit	*Dokumentenakkreditiv*
2	Bank transfer (by SWIFT – Society for Worldwide Interbank Financial Telecommunication)	*Banküberweisung*
3	Bill of exchange (draft)	*Wechsel (Tratte)*
4	International money order	*Internationale Zahlungsanweisung*
5	International banker's draft	*Bankscheck*

Terms of payment in international trade

In the following table the best terms of payment for the buyer are at the beginning and the least favourable are at the end.

Best for the buyer (least favourable for the seller)

1	Open account terms	*Offenes Zahlungsziel*
2	D/A (documents against acceptance)	*Dokumente gegen Akzept*
3	2% 14 days	*Zahlung innerhalb 14 Tagen abzüglich 2% Skonto*
4	30 days net	*Zahlung innerhalb 30 Tagen netto*
5	One third with order, one third on delivery, one third within 30 days after delivery	*1/3 bei Auftragserteilung, 1/3 bei Lieferung, 1/3 innerhalb von 30 Tagen nach Lieferung*
6	D/P (documents against payment)	*Kasse gegen Dokumente*
7	Payment by irrevocable (and confirmed) documentary letter of credit	*Zahlung durch unwiderrufliches (und bestätigtes) Dokumentenakkreditiv*
8	CWO (cash with order)	*Barzahlung bei Auftragserteilung*

Best for the seller (least favourable for the buyer)

Specimen Letter

1. Buyer pays for goods received

Massenbergstr. 8–10
4787 Bochum
Germany

Tonwaren
Hilpert GmbH

Our ref. Wosz/88.tw
Your ref. DJ/bk
2 March ..

Severn Potteries Ltd
95 Clifton Road
BRISTOL
BP4 8JK
England

For the attention of Ms Daphne Jones, Export Sales

Dear Ms Jones

Your Invoice No. EW7/HJG for €5,425.50 of 15 February ..

We have now taken delivery of the consignment of 200 earthenware bowls as per our order no. 88.tw/200 dated 30 January .. . The goods have been checked and we are pleased to confirm that they are as ordered.

We have therefore instructed our bank to remit the invoice amount by SWIFT to your account no. 2 672 876 at the Royal Bank of Commerce in Bristol as agreed. Please contact us should you not receive our remittance within the next few days.

Yours sincerely
Tonwaren Hilpert GmbH

Davina Wosz

Davina Wosz
Purchasing Department

Specimen E-mail

2. Seller requests payment for goods supplied

e-mail

Mail to:	AHG@firmenetz.de	**Cc:**	
Subject:	Your Order for Water Filters	**Attachment:**	

Dear Mr Konrad

The above-mentioned goods are now ready for despatch. Please remit the sum of €2,500 to our account no. 7 339 928 at Lloyds TSB in Eastbourne, sort code 30-92-86, quoting reference WP1/2000. The goods will then be shipped to you.

Thank you for choosing to place your order with Aqua Pure.

Yours sincerely

Piers Mountjoy

Export Sales Director

Case Study

A. Seller

Stafford Tableware Ltd in Stoke on Trent, England despatched several consignments of crockery to Megaware Handelsgesellschaft in Berlin last quarter.

Mr Humphrey Pritchard in the European Sales Section at Stafford Tableware now writes to Ms Marita Schneider in the Import Section at Megaware enclosing his company's quarterly statement no. 98DS-TS for the period … (i.e. 1 January–31 March .. or 1 April–30 June .. or 1 July–30 September .. or 1 October–31 December ..) and requests payment of €2,250 by SWIFT to his company's account no. 3 269 981 at Barclays Bank in Stoke on Trent. He adds that a 3% discount is granted for payment within 10 days.

For Megaware's information he also sends a brochure / data file and export price list about his company's latest "Prince William" series, which is on offer for the next 30 days.

B. Buyer

Marita Schneider works in the Import Section at Megaware in Berlin. Her company received several consignments of crockery from Stafford Tableware Ltd in Stoke on Trent, England last quarter ending … (date, i.e. 31 March .. or 30 June .. or 30 September .. or 31 December ..). Today, a week after the end of last quarter, she receives the English company's quarterly statement no. 98DS-TS.

The goods have been checked and found to correspond to the statement, so Marita now writes to Stafford Tableware Ltd to advise them that she has instructed her bank to remit €2,250 to their account no. 3 269 981 at Barclays Bank in Stoke on Trent by SWIFT. She asks them to let her know if they do not receive the money within the next few days.

Activities

A. Seller

Using the letter plan on page 101 and the layouts in Unit 1 write Humphrey Pritchard's letter / fax / e-mail to Marita Schneider at Megaware.

B. Buyer

Using the letter plan on page 101 and the layouts in Unit 1 write Marita Schneider's letter / fax / e-mail to Humphrey Pritchard at Stafford Tableware Ltd.

Addresses:

- Megaware Handelsgesellschaft mbH, Moltkestr. 10–12, 12203 Berlin, fax +49 (30) 5 33-87 97, e-mail: megaware.mbh@telnet.de
- Stafford Tableware Ltd, Long Man Business Park, Stoke on Trent, ST3 7AA, England, fax +44 (17 82) 58 97 53, e-mail: stafford.tableware@firmweb.co.uk

Standard Expressions

Buyer

1 Reference to goods	We have now taken delivery of	... (goods) the consignment of ... (goods, e.g. 200 earthenware bowls)	as ordered as per our order no. ... of/dated 30 January ..						
	The goods have been checked and Having (now) checked the goods	we are pleased to we are able to	confirm that they are						
2 Reference to invoice/statement	Thank you for Many thanks for We have received	your the above-mentioned	statement	dated ... for ... (period of time, e.g. the quarter ending 30 September ..)	showing a balance in your favour of ... (sum, e.g. €5,000)				
		your	invoice	of ... dated ...	for ... (sum of money, e.g. €5,000)	for ... (goods/services)			
		the above-mentioned invoice	and your draft for ... (sum, e.g. €5,000) together with your 30-day bill of exchange						
	Your invoice Your statement It	has now been	checked checked against our own records	and found	to be correct to correspond to the goods received				
	Having checked the invoice we We have now checked it and	can confirm that are pleased to confirm that	it is correct it corresponds to our records						
3 Mode of payment	We have (therefore)	instructed our bank	to remit to transfer	the sum in question the invoice amount	to your account no. ...	at ... (bank)	by SWIFT	as requested as agreed	
		accepted	your bill of exchange your draft	for ... (sum)	and are returning it to you which you will find enclosed	with this letter			
	It will be	honoured on the due date paid at maturity							
4 Polite ending	Please do not hesitate to contact us should you not receive our remittance within the next few days Please contact us should you not receive our remittance within the next few days Should you not receive our remittance in the next few days, please do not hesitate to contact us Please confirm that you have received the bill of exchange with our acceptance								

5 Enclosure(s)	Bill of exchange Draft					

Seller

1 Reference to invoice/statement*	Our Our company's The above-mentioned	invoice for statement for	… (goods) goods supplied to your company	on … (date) for the period … (date) – … (date) last quarter	is enclosed is included is attached	for settlement for payment
			… (services) services provided to your company			
	We enclose the above-mentioned					
2 Payment	The goods The above-mentioned goods		as per your order no. … dated …	are now	ready for despatch ready for collection	
	Please … and would ask you to	remit transfer	the sum in question the invoice amount	to account no. … to our company's account no. …	at … (bank) in … (location), sort code (branch code) …	by SWIFT by telegraphic transfer
	Please note that We would also point out that	you qualify for a(n) you are entitled to a(n)	early payment discount cash discount	of … %	on the invoice amount on the sum in question	if payment is made within … days
		you may deduct a(n)			from the invoice amount from the sum in question	
	The goods will be shipped to you as soon as payment has been received					

3	Reference to other goods/services	For your information		we are also enclosing we also enclose	our company's latest catalogue
				a brochure and an export price list some sales literature	on … (goods, e.g. our company's latest "Prince William" series) on our company's latest product … (details, e.g. the "Repro 3000" Fast Copying Machine)
		… which is	on offer on special offer	for the next … (period of time, e.g. 30 days) until … (date, e.g. the end of the month)	
4	Polite ending	Should you require further information please do not hesitate to contact us We look forward to receiving further orders from your company Thank you for choosing to place your order with … (name of company)			
5	Enclosure(s)	Invoice Statement Bill of exchange Brochure Catalogue Price list			

Phraseology

Buyer

1	**Reference to goods**	***Bezugnahme auf Waren***
	We have now taken delivery of the consignment of 200 earthenware bowls as per our order no. 415-A dated 30 January ..	*Wir haben nunmehr die Lieferung der Sendung von 200 Steingutschüsseln gemäß unserem Auftrag Nr. 415-A vom 30. Januar .. entgegengenommen*
	The goods have been checked and we are pleased to confirm that they are as ordered	*Die Waren sind geprüft worden, und wir freuen uns zu bestätigen, dass sie dem Auftrag entsprechen*
2	**Reference to invoice / statement**	***Bezugnahme auf Rechnung / Kontoauszug***
	Thank you for the above-mentioned statement for the quarter ending 30 September .. showing a balance in your favour of €5,000	*Vielen Dank für den oben erwähnten Kontoauszug für das am 30. September .. zu Ende gegangene Quartal, der einen Saldo zu Ihren Gunsten von 5.000,– € aufweist*
	Many thanks for the above-mentioned invoice together with your 30-day bill of exchange	*Vielen Dank für die obengenannte Rechnung zusammen mit Ihrem 30-Tage Wechsel*
	It has now been checked against our own records and found to correspond to the goods received	*Sie / Er ist jetzt mit unseren eigenen Aufzeichnungen verglichen worden, und es wurde festgestellt, dass sie / er den erhaltenen Waren entspricht*
3	**Mode of payment**	***Zahlungsweise***
	We have therefore instructed our bank to remit the sum in question to your account no. 456 123 at Lloyds TSB Bank in Leeds by SWIFT, as requested	*Wir haben daher unsere Bank angewiesen, die infrage stehende Summe wie gewünscht per SWIFT auf Ihr Konto Nr. 456 123 bei der Lloyds TSB Bank in Leeds zu überweisen*
	We have (therefore) accepted your bill of exchange for €5,000 and are returning it to you with this letter	*Wir haben (daher) Ihren Wechsel für 5.000,– € akzeptiert und schicken ihn zusammen mit diesem Brief an Sie zurück*
	It will be honoured on the due date	*Er wird am Fälligkeitstag eingelöst*
4	**Polite ending**	***Höfliche Schlussformel***
	Should you not receive our remittance in the next few days, please do not hesitate to contact us	*Sollten Sie unsere Überweisung nicht in den nächsten Tagen erhalten, zögern Sie bitte nicht, mit uns Verbindung aufzunehmen*
	Please confirm that you have received the bill of exchange with our acceptance	*Bitte bestätigen Sie, dass Sie den Wechsel mit unserem Akzept erhalten haben*
5	**Enclosure(s)**	***Anlage(n)***
	Bill of exchange	*Wechsel*
	Draft	*Tratte (Wechsel)*

Seller

1	**Reference to invoice / statement**	***Bezugnahme auf Rechnung / Kontoauszug***
	The above-mentioned statement for goods supplied to your company last quarter is enclosed for settlement	*Der obengenannte Kontoauszug für Waren, die im letzten Quartal an Ihre Firma geliefert wurden, ist zwecks Begleichung beigefügt*
	We enclose our invoice for services provided to your company on 1 January .. for payment	*Wir fügen unsere Rechnung für Dienstleistungen, die Ihrer Firma am 1. Januar .. geleistet wurden, zur Begleichung bei*
2	**Payment**	***Zahlung***
	The goods as per your order no. 415-A dated 28 December .. are now ready for despatch	*Die gemäß Ihrem Auftrag Nr. 415-A vom 28. Dezember .. gelieferten Waren sind jetzt versandbereit*
	Please remit the invoice amount to our company's account no. 107 149 993 at Commerzbank in Witten, sort code 452 400 56 by SWIFT	*Bitte überweisen Sie den Rechnungsbetrag per SWIFT auf das Konto unserer Firma Nr. 107 149 993 bei der Commerzbank in Witten, Bankleitzahl 452 400 56*
	Please note that you qualify for an early payment discount of 3% on the sum in question if payment is made within 10 days	*Bitte nehmen Sie zur Kenntnis, dass Sie wegen pünktlicher Zahlung zu einem 3%igen Rabatt auf die infrage stehende Summe berechtigt sind, wenn die Zahlung innerhalb von 10 Tagen erfolgt*
	If payment is made within 10 days, you may deduct a cash discount from the invoice amount	*Wenn die Zahlung innerhalb von 10 Tagen erfolgt, können Sie einen Barzahlungsrabatt vom Rechnungsbetrag abziehen*
	The goods will be shipped to you as soon as payment has been received	*Die Waren werden Ihnen geschickt, sobald die Zahlung eingegangen ist*
3	**Reference to other goods / services**	***Bezugnahme auf andere Waren / Dienstleistungen***
	For your information, we are also enclosing a brochure and an export price list on our company's latest "Prince William" series	*Zu Ihrer Information fügen wir ebenfalls eine Broschüre und eine Exportpreisliste über die neuste Serie „Prince William" unserer Firma bei*
	We also enclose a brochure on our company's latest product, the "Repro 3000" Fast Copying Machine	*Wir fügen auch einen Prospekt des neuesten Produkts unserer Gesellschaft bei, des „Repro 3000" Schnellkopiergeräts*
	... which is on special offer for the next 30 days	*... das für die nächsten 30 Tage als Sonderangebot zu haben ist*

4	**Polite ending**	***Höfliche Schlussformel***
	Should you require further information please do not hesitate to contact us	*Sollten Sie weitere Informationen benötigen, zögern Sie bitte nicht, mit uns in Verbindung zu treten*
	We look forward to receiving further orders from your company	*Wir freuen uns, weitere Aufträge von Ihrer Firma zu erhalten*
	Thank you for choosing to place your order with Aqua Pure	*Vielen Dank, dass sie sich entschlossen haben, Ihren Auftrag Aqua Pure zu erteilen*
5	**Enclosure(s)**	***Anlage(n)***
	Invoice	*Rechnung*
	Statement	*Kontoauszug*
	Bill of exchange	*Wechsel*
	Brochure	*Broschüre*
	Catalogue	*Katalog*
	Price list	*Preisliste*

Exercises

Exercise 1: Jumbled Letters

The sentences below are in the wrong order. Use the letter plans on page 101 to put them in the correct order.

Buyer

a. We have therefore instructed our bank to remit the invoice amount to your account no. 490 445 at Lloyds TSB by SWIFT as requested.

b. Your invoice has been checked against our own records and found to correspond to the goods received.

c. Should you not receive our remittance in the next few days please do not hesitate to contact us.

d. We have now taken delivery of the consignment of 100 mountain bikes as per our order no. 342-A dated 4 July ...

Seller

a. For your information, we are also enclosing some sales literature on our company's latest product, the "Xtra 3000" laptop computer.

b. Brochure

c. We enclose the above-mentioned statement for goods supplied to your company last quarter for settlement

d. The next consignment will be shipped to you as soon as payment has been received.

e. ... and would ask you to remit the sum in question to our company's account no. 800 499 377 at Deutsche Bank AG Bochum, sort code 430 800 83.

f. Thank you for choosing to place your order with CyberTech Ltd.

Exercise 2: Instructions

1. First read through the specimen letter on page 103 from Tonwaren Hilpert GmbH to Severn Potteries Ltd.
2. Next write the words missing in the letter below on a piece of your own paper. Do this *without* looking at the specimen letter at the same time.

Paxton Electronics Ltd
45 Paxton High Street
PAXTON
PA4 8GG
England

For the 1. ____ of Mr Miles Foreman, Sales Department

Dear Mr Foreman

2. ____ No. IT/44 for €7,000 of 1 April ..

This is to inform you that we have 3. ____ (*2 words*) of the 4. ____ of 10,000 soup plates 5. ____ (*2 words*) our order no. SP400 dated 15 March ... We have 6. ____ them and are pleased to 7. ____ that they are as 8. ____.

Our bank will now 9. ____ the 10. ____ (*2 words*) to your account at the International Bank of Commerce in Leeds as 11. ____. If our 12. ____ does not arrive 13. ____ the next 14. ____ days please 15. ____ us.

Yours sincerely
etc.

Exercise 3: Anagrams

1. First read through the specimen e-mail on page 104 to Mr Konrad from Astra Haustechnik GmbH.
2. The letters of ten of the words have been mixed up. Re-arrange them to make words from the specimen e-mail.
   Some answers are two words or a hyphenated word.

1. aoeeioedntnmvb	6. iougntq
2. aehctpsd	7. pdhseip
3. tmrie	8. oignshco
4. ctnuoac	9. eaclp
5. eoodctrs	10. cnrfreeee

Exercise 4: Crossword

Look at the phraseology and vocabulary list for this unit on pages 109–111 and 118 to help you find some of the answers to this crossword. Write your answers on the worksheet provided.

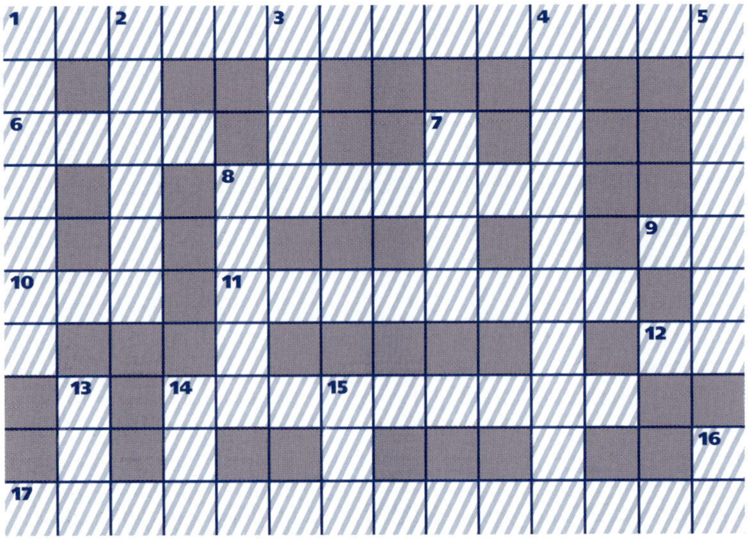

Clues

Across

1. We have accepted your ____ (*3 words*) for €5,000 and are returning it to you with this letter.
6. opposite of "early"
8. Should you ____ further information please do not hesitate to contact us.
9. opposite of "yes"
10. I don't go to work by bus. I go by ____.
11. Your bill of exchange will be paid at ____.
12. "There's Mr White. ____'s my boss."
14. We have received your ____ for the quarter ending 31 March ... It will be paid by SWIFT.
17. Payment will be made by documentary ____ (*3 words*).

Down

1. Thank you for your statement showing a ____ in your favour of €10,000.
2. "I didn't send him a fax or an e-mail. I sent him a ____."
3. When you send an e-mail you can't send a catalogue with it but you can send a ____.
4. Please confirm that you have received the bill of exchange with our ____.
5. For your information we ____ a brochure on our company's latest product with this letter.
7. Someone who doesn't tell the truth is a ____.
8. We have therefore instructed our bank to ____ the sum in question to your account at the National Westminster Bank in Eastbourne.
13. Question: "What's your ____?" Answer: "I'm 21."
14. the past form of "sit"
15. "I went to the conference and the Head of Sales came, ____."
16. We have an account ____ The Royal Bank of Commerce.

Aufgaben

1.

	Von	An
Name	eigener Name	Ms Lucy Clayton
Position	Buchhaltung	Imports Department
Firma	Ormanns Büromaschinen GmbH	ProntoPrint Ltd
Anschrift	Neusserstr. 13, 80807 München, Germany	48 Clarence Dock Road, Leeds LE1 8WW, England
Fax	+49 (89) 7 25 45 77	+44 (1 13) 2 33-65 48
E-Mail	ormanns.bm@germanyweb.de	prontoprint.ltd@webnet.co.uk

Geschäftsfall:
Sie haben im vergangenen Quartal mehrere Sendungen Büromaschinen an die englische Firma ProntoPrint Ltd in Leeds geliefert. Heute schicken Sie dieser Firma Ihre Quartalsabrechnung.

Aufgabe:
Verfassen Sie ein Schreiben an ProntoPrint Ltd unter Berücksichtigung folgender Einzelheiten:

- Bezugnahme auf beigefügte Quartalsabrechnung Nr. 554-TW über 34.950,–€ vom ... (Datum ca. 8 Tage nach Quartalsende)
- Bitte um Begleichung per Überweisung auf Ihr Konto Nr. 995 673 bei der Bayrischen Kreditbank, München
- Bei Zahlung innerhalb 10 Tagen 3% Skonto
- Sie legen auch Werbematerial über Ihr neuestes Produkt, den Schnellkopierer (*fast copying machine*) „Repro 3000", bei
- Sie sind jederzeit bereit, bei Rückfragen bezüglich dieses Geräts Auskunft zu erteilen
- Höfliche Schlussformel

2.

Name	eigener Name	Mr Colin Jones
Position	Buchhaltung	Accounts Department
Firma	Bauer & Döppner KG	Uppercut Fabrics Ltd
Anschrift	Fraasstr. 17, 70184 Stuttgart, Germany	62 Durham Street, London SE11 5JW, England
Fax	+49 (7 11) 90 66 54	+44 (1 71) 8 75-60 40
E-Mail	bauer.doeppner.kg@aol.com	uppercut@capitalweb.co.uk

Geschäftsfall:
Von Ihrem Londoner Lieferanten, der Uppercut Fabrics Ltd, haben Sie mit Schreiben vom ... (vor 5 Tagen) eine Rechnung über 3.500,–€ für eine Lieferung Stoff erhalten. Diesem Schreiben liegt ein 30-Tage-Wechsel zum Akzept bei.

Aufgabe:
Verfassen Sie ein Schreiben folgenden Inhalts an Uppercut Fabrics Ltd:
- Bezug auf Rechnung-Nr.GF-24 vom ... und den beigefügten Wechsel
- Die Rechnung ist geprüft worden und stimmt mit Ihren Aufzeichnungen überein
- Sie haben deshalb den Wechsel mit Ihrem Akzept versehen und diesem Schreiben beigelegt (bei Fax bzw. E-Mail mit getrennter Post an Uppercut Fabrics Ltd geschickt)
- Der Wechsel wird bei Fälligkeit eingelöst
- Sie bitten, den Erhalt des akzeptierten Wechsels zu bestätigen

Vocabulary List

able, to be ~ to	*können*
acceptance	*hier: Akzept*
add	*hinzufügen*
advise	*hier: informieren*
agreed, as ~	*wie vereinbart*
appropriate, as ~	*wie geeignet, wie passend*
attached	*beigefügt*
balance in your favour	*hier: Schuldsaldo*
bill of exchange	*Wechsel*
bowl	*Schüssel*
brief	*kurz*
brochure	*Broschüre, Prospekt*
business park	*Gewerbegebiet*
buyer	*Käufer/in*
check against	*hier: vergleichen mit*
check, to ~	*kontrollieren*
collection, ready for ~	*abholbereit*
confirm	*bestätigen*
consignment	*Lieferung*
correspond to	*entsprechen*
crockery	*Geschirr*
deduct	*abziehen*
despatch, ready for ~	*versandbereit*
despatch, to ~	*schicken, (ver)senden*
discount, cash ~	*Nachlass für Barzahlung*
discount, early payment ~	*Nachlass für sofortige Bezahlung*
draft, a ~	*Tratte*
due date, on the ~	*bei Fälligkeit*
earthenware bowls	*Steingutschüsseln*
enclosure(s)	*Anlage(n)*
entitled, to be ~ to	*Anspruch haben auf*
favour, in your ~	*zu Ihren Gunsten*
favourable	*günstig*
file, data ~	*Datei*
for your information	*zu Ihrer Information*
foreign trade	*Außenhandel*
further	*weitere(r, s)*
grant, to ~	*gewähren*
hesitate	*zögern*
honour, to ~	*hier: einlösen*
instruct	*anweisen*
invoice	*Rechnung*
least favourable	*ungünstigste(r, s)*
letter of credit	*Akkreditiv*
liar	*Lügner*
maturity, at ~	*bei Fälligkeit*
mode of payment	*Zahlungsweise*
note, please ~ that …	*etwa: Wir möchten Sie darauf hinweisen, dass …*
on offer	*im Angebot*
per, as ~	*gemäß*
period	*Zeitraum*
point out	*darauf hinweisen*
polite ending	*höfliche Schlussformel*
potteries (pottery)	*Töpfereien*
provide	*hier: erbringen*
qualify, to ~ for	*Anspruch haben auf*
quarter	*hier: Quartal*
quarterly statement	*Quartalsabrechnung*
ready for collection	*abholbereit*
ready for despatch	*versandbereit*
records	*hier: Aufzeichnungen*
reference to	*Bezug auf*
remit, to ~	*zahlen, z. B. überweisen*
remittance	*Zahlung, z. B. Überweisung*
requested, as ~	*wunschgemäß*
require	*benötigen*
return	*hier: zurückschicken*
seller	*Verkäufer/in*
series	*hier: Reihe*
several	*mehrere*
Severn	*englischer Fluss (the River Severn)*
ship, to ~	*versenden*
sort code	*Bankleitzahl*
statement	*Abrechnung*
tableware	*Tischgeschirr*
take delivery of, to ~	*in Empfang nehmen*
telegraphic transfer	*telegraphische Überweisung*
therefore	*deshalb, aus diesem Grund*
transfer, a ~	*Überweisung*
transfer, to ~	*überweisen*
within	*innerhalb*

Unit 8

Complaints

Introduction

The most common reasons for a complaint are shown in the diagram on page 120.

Whatever the case may be, the seller should be informed immediately. He / She should express regret that the customer finds it necessary to complain, investigate the problem, give an explanation and offer a solution.

Both the buyer and seller should be polite and factual at all times.

Letter Plan 1

A. Delay in Delivery

Buyer

1. Reference to delayed order
2. Request for an explanation for the delay*
3. Request for delivery by a certain date*
4. Consequences of (further) delay*
5. Polite ending

*As appropriate

Fig. 14

Letter Plan 2

B. Making a Complaint

Buyer

1. Refer to goods
2. Say what is wrong
3. Ask for an explanation*
4. Consequences for the buyer and seller*
5. Ask for appropriate action
6. Polite ending
7. Enclosure(s)*

*As appropriate

Fig. 15

Letter Plan 3

C. Dealing with a Complaint

Seller

1. Acknowledge receipt of the buyer's complaint immediately
2. Express regret
3. Give details of action taken*
4. Suggest a solution*
5. Apologise again
6. Polite ending

*As appropriate

Fig. 16

Why Complaints are Made

Fig. 17

Activity

What can the seller do if …?

Match the questions in the diagram with the solutions in the list below to make six more sentences. Remember the seller can sometimes do more than one thing.

Example

1. If the goods are delayed, the seller can make a part-delivery or reduce the price.

List

make a part-delivery
contact the freight forwarder
contact the insurance company
send replacements
take back the goods
take back the extra goods
reduce the price
send more goods
send the right goods

Specimen Fax

1. Delay in delivery

sheet

Wirichs Fruchtsäfte KG,
Dieselstr. 99, 46049 Oberhausen, Germany
Tel.-Nr. +49 (0)2 08-33 96 74
Fax-Nr. +49 (0)2 08-33 96 70

FAO:	Ms Sharon Waterstone Export Sales Dept. Heavytree Natural Fruit Juice Co. Willow Farm TAUNTON TA4 7HH England
Fax No:	00 44 (18 23) 7 92 10
From:	Brigitte Stein Import Section
Date:	18 February ..
Subject:	Delay in Delivery of our Order No. 997-OS for 5,000 Litres of Fruit Juice dated 3 January ..
Total Pages:	1

Dear Ms Waterstone

The above-mentioned goods are now 5 days overdue and we have received no explanation for the delay.

As some of our customers are now threatening to cancel their orders, we must be certain that the consignment will reach our premises by the end of this week at the latest.

If this deadline is not met, we will have to cancel the order.

Please let us know by return when the goods will arrive and why they have been delayed.

Prompt delivery is all that is needed to settle this matter.

Yours sincerely

Brigitte Stein

Specimen Letter

2. Complaint from an English company about touring cycles

Tel. +44 (171) 2 22 98 45
Fax +44 (171) 2 22 98 00
E-mail: ferris.wheel@ferriswheel.co.uk
Website: www.ferriswheel.co.uk

Ferris Wheel Cycle Stores Ltd
400 Commercial Road
London EC2 9JK
England

Ferris Wheel Cycle Stores Ltd

HB/MT
10 May ..

Ms Marita Henkel
Managing Director
Henkel Fahrradbau GmbH
Industriestr. 52
44577 Castrop-Rauxel
Germany

Dear Ms Henkel

Our Order No. RB-007-D dated 3 March .. for 500 Touring Cycles

The above-mentioned goods were delivered to us today and on checking them we found that 25 cycles were badly scratched. We enclose photographs of the damage for your information.

We therefore cannot sell these goods at the normal price and can only keep them if a reduction in price of 25% is granted on the damaged cycles.

We look forward to receiving your comments on this matter in the very near future.

Yours sincerely
Ferris Wheel Cycle Stores Ltd

Henry Butcher

Henry Butcher
Purchasing Director

Encs

Specimen E-mail

3. Reply to complaint about touring cycles

e-mail

Mail to:	ferris.wheel@ferriswheel.co.uk	**Cc:**	
Subject:	Your Order for Cycles	**Attachment:**	

Dear Mr Butcher

We have just received your letter regarding the above-mentioned order and are dismayed to hear that some of the cycles arrived scratched.

As the cycles left our premises in perfect condition, we have contacted our freight forwarders and are waiting for their report.

In the meantime, please accept our apologies for the inconvenience. We are sure that the matter will be settled to the satisfaction of all parties concerned and will be contacting you again in the very near future.

Yours sincerely

Marita Henkel

Managing Director

Case Study

A. Buyer

Nadine Lindemann works in the Purchasing Department at Möbel Muckemann GmbH in Hattingen. Her company has just taken delivery of a consignment of office furniture from Office Interiors Ltd in Leeds, England (order no. WM/2000 dated ...) and Nadine is dissatisfied with the goods because they arrived 5 days late and some of them are sub-standard. One of the desks is scratched and three of the swivel chairs are dirty. She thinks this is the result of rough handling in transit. She therefore writes to Terry Cotton in the Sales Department at Office Interiors to ask for an explanation and replacements or a considerable reduction in price. She encloses photographs of the sub-standard items.

B. Seller

Terry Cotton in the Sales Department at Office Interiors Ltd in Leeds, England receives Nadine's complaint and investigates. He contacts the freight forwarders, FreightLine Ltd, and discovers that the lorry was involved in an accident in the Netherlands two weeks ago. This explains the delay of 5 days and the damage.

Terry writes to Nadine, explains what went wrong and offers to replace the unsatisfactory items or reduce the price by 25%. He apologises for the inconvenience and asks Nadine to let him know which of his two offers her company is willing to accept.

Activities

A. Buyer

Using the letter plan (**Fig. 15**) on page 119 and the layouts in Unit 1 write Nadine Lindemann's letter / fax / e-mail to Terry Cotton at Office Interiors Ltd in Leeds, England.

B. Seller

Using the letter plan (**Fig. 16**) on page 119 and the layouts in Unit 1 write Terry Cotton's letter / fax / e-mail to Nadine Lindemann at Möbel Muckemann in Hattingen.

Addresses:

- Möbel Muckemann GmbH, Nierenhoferstr. 38, 45525 Hattingen / Ruhr, fax: +49 (23 24) 88 80 07, e-mail: moebel.muckemann@ruhrlink.de
- Office Interiors Ltd, 99 Witherstone Way, Leeds LG7 4JJ, England, fax: +44 (1 13) 2 33-50 92

A disastrous desk

This desk has ten things wrong with it. Match the words in the list with the numbers to describe what's wrong with it. Write on a piece of your own paper.

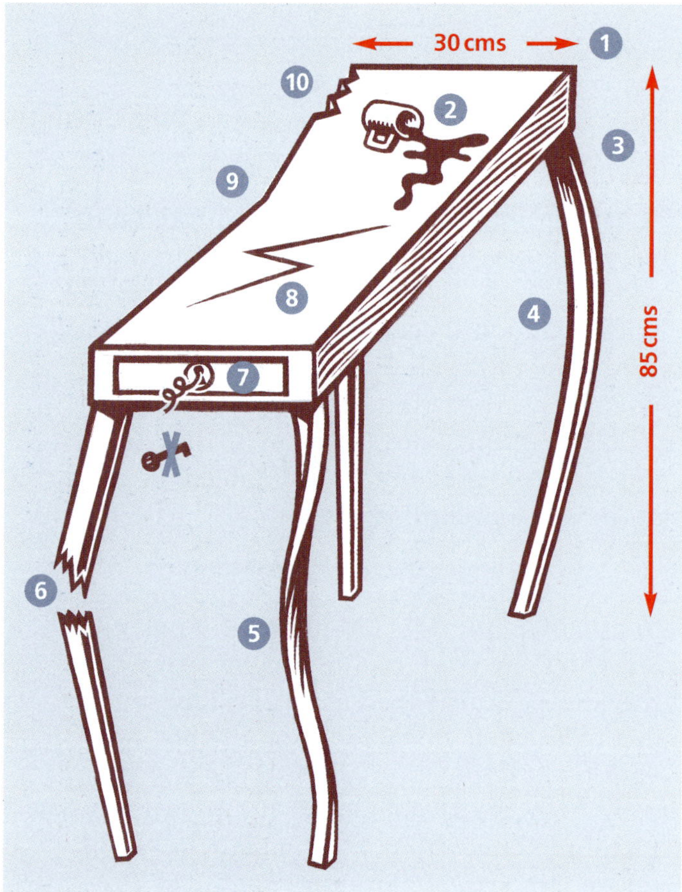

List

a. stained
b. scratched
c. too narrow
d. rough
e. crooked
f. too high
g. broken
h. bent
i. faulty
j. twisted

Standard Expressions

Delay in Delivery

Buyer

1 Reference to delayed order	On 1 November .. Four weeks ago	we placed an order	with you for with your company for	... (goods) the above-mentioned items	for delivery to be delivered	within 3 weeks by ... (date, e.g. 31 May ..) on ... (date)
		we ordered				
	... and it was agreed that delivery was to be made					
	Our order The goods The above-mentioned goods		is/are now	5 days one week more than a week	overdue late	
2 Request for explanation for the delay*	Please give us your reasons for We would welcome an explanation for So far we have not been given a reason for ... and we have received no explanation for			the delay		
	Please let us know why they (the goods) have been delayed					
3 Request for delivery by a certain date*	Please let us know We must know	by return immediately without delay		when	the goods will arrive we can expect the goods we will be able to take delivery of the goods	
	We must be certain that	the consignment the goods our order	will reach our premises	by the end of this week by 6 December .. within ... (number, e.g. 7) days		at the latest without fail
	... and make sure that we receive					
4 Consequences of (further) delay*	If this deadline is not		met, kept,	we will have to cancel the order we will be obliged to cancel this and all future orders		
	We must point out that the goods are needed urgently for our own customers, who might well look elsewhere for their supplies					
	... as ... since	several customers some of our customers		are now threatening to cancel their orders ... have now cancelled their orders ...		
5 Polite ending	Prompt delivery is all that is needed to settle this matter We trust that we will be hearing from you in the very near future					

Making a Complaint

Buyer

1 Refer to goods	The above-mentioned goods The consignment of … (goods) The above-mentioned consignment of … (goods, e.g. office supplies) The … (goods, e.g. 2,000 mobile phones) ordered on … (date) as per our order no. …			was/were delivered to us today arrived here yesterday		as promised 36 hours late
	We have just taken delivery of the above-mentioned		goods articles consignment	which arrived … (time, e.g. 5 days) later than		promised expected agreed
2 Say what is wrong	On Upon When	examining it/them checking it/them	we found that we discovered that	one of the … (article(s), e.g. desks) two/three/several of the … (articles) 25 … (articles, e.g. cycles) some of the … (articles) some of them	was were	dirty missing scratched badly scratched damaged damaged and therefore unusable sub-standard
	We	think believe are of the opinion that	this is the result of this was caused by	rough handling rough handling in transit poor packing	… and enclose photographs of the these items for your information We enclose photographs of the damage for your information (see photograph(s) enclosed)	
3 Ask for an explanation*	We would welcome your explanation of the damage Please explain how such a thing could happen					
4 Consequences for the buyer and seller*	We therefore You will understand that we You will appreciate that we		cannot sell will not be able to sell	these such sub-standard damaged	goods articles items	at the normal price at the usual price
	… and can only keep them … and will only be able to keep them			if a reduction in price of … % is granted on the damaged … (goods, e.g. cycles) if the price is reduced by … %		

	... if you reduce the price of the	dirty damaged scratched sub-standard	... (goods) goods articles items	by ... % considerably
	If they do not arrive here	by ... (date, e.g. 15 February) by then within ... (period of time, e.g. the next five days)	we will have to obtain them	from another supplier elsewhere
5 Ask for appropriate action	Whatever the case may be	we need the ... (goods, e.g. 250 mobile phones)	urgently as soon as possible by the end of the week at the latest	
	We / ... and — must therefore ask you to	send replacements send us these goods	or reduce the price (considerably) or grant us a considerable reduction in price	
	We trust you will	deal with this matter without delay attend to this matter immediately		
6 Polite ending	We look forward to receiving your comments on this matter We expect to hear from you ... and expect to hear from you		in the very near future	
7 Enclosure(s)	Photograph(s)			

Dealing with a Complaint

Seller

1 Acknowledge receipt of the buyer's complaint immediately	We thank you for We have just received	your letter/fax/e-mail the above-mentioned letter/fax/e-mail	about regarding	your the above-mentioned	order consignment of ... (goods, e.g. office furniture)	Your complaint is now being investigated
2 Express regret	We are sorry to hear (that) ... and are dismayed to hear (that)	it the consignment the goods		was/were delayed and that	one box of ... (goods, e.g. expanders) is some of the goods are	missing sub-standard unsatisfactory damaged
					some of the cycles arrived scratched	

3	Give details of action taken*	As the … (goods, e.g. cycles) left our premises in perfect condition Since hearing from you		we have contacted we have got in touch with	our freight forwarders the shipping company the railway company the airline		and are waiting for their report
							and found out that … and discovered that …
		their lorry the train the ship the plane	crashed broke down was involved in an accident	in … (location, e.g. the Netherlands) on the way to … (location)	on … (date) last week / month two weeks ago	This explains This is the reason for	the delay (of … time, e.g. of 5 days) (and) the damage
4	Suggest a solution*	Under the circumstances In the meantime		we are sending you	a replacement consignment replacements		at no extra charge by return
				we are willing to offer you			or a reduction in price of 25% on the unsatisfactory items
5	Apologise again	In the meantime,	we wish to apologise for please accept our apologies for please once again accept our apologies for		the inconvenience the inconvenience caused	which was due to circumstances beyond our control	
6	Polite ending	We look forward to hearing from you soon … and look forward to doing further business with you in the future We hope this suggestion will find your approval We are sure that the matter will be settled to the satisfaction of all parties concerned and will be contacting you again in the very near future					

Phraseology

A. Delay in Delivery

Buyer

1	**Reference to delayed order**	***Bezugnahme auf verzögerte Bestellung***
	On 1 November we placed an order with you for the above-mentioned items to be delivered within 3 weeks	*Am 1. November erteilten wir Ihnen einen Auftrag für die oben erwähnten Positionen, die innerhalb von 3 Wochen geliefert werden sollten*
	Four weeks ago we ordered a consignment of office furniture for delivery by 31 May ..	*Vor vier Wochen bestellten wir eine Sendung Büromöbel zur Lieferung bis 31. Mai ..*
	It was agreed that delivery was to be made within 3 weeks	*Es wurde vereinbart, dass die Lieferung innerhalb von 3 Wochen erfolgen sollte*
	Our order is now 5 days overdue	*Unser Auftrag ist jetzt 5 Tage überfällig*
	The above-mentioned goods are more than a week late	*Die oben erwähnten Güter haben eine Verspätung von über einer Woche*
2	**Request for explanation***	***Bitte um Erklärung****
	We would welcome an explanation for the delay	*Wir würden eine Erklärung für die Verzögerung begrüßen*
	Please give us your reasons for the delay	*Bitte geben Sie uns Ihre Gründe für die Verzögerung an*
	So far we have not been given a reason for the delay	*Bisher haben wir noch keine Begründung für die Verzögerung erhalten*
	We have received no explanation for the delay	*Wir haben keine Erklärung für die Verzögerung bekommen*
	Please let us know why the goods have been delayed	*Bitte lassen Sie uns wissen, warum die Waren verspätet angekommen sind*
3	**Request for delivery by a certain date***	***Bitte um Lieferung bis zu einem bestimmten Datum****
	We must know by return when we can expect the goods	*Wir müssen umgehend wissen, wann wir die Waren erwarten können*
	Please let us know immediately when we will be able to take delivery of the goods	*Bitte teilen Sie uns sofort mit, wann wir mit der Lieferung der Waren rechnen können*
	We must be certain that the consignment will reach our premises by 6 December without fail	*Wir müssen sicher sein, dass die Sendung unsere Geschäftsräume auf jeden Fall bis zum 6. Dezember erreicht*
	Please make sure that we receive the goods within 7 days	*Bitte stellen Sie sicher, dass wir die Waren innerhalb von 7 Tagen erhalten*
4	**Consequences of (further) delay***	***Konsequenzen einer (weiteren) Verzögerung****
	If this deadline is not met, we will have to cancel the order	*Falls dieser Termin nicht eingehalten wird, müssen wir den Auftrag stornieren*

	If this deadline is not kept, we will be obliged to cancel this and all future orders	*Wenn dieser Termin nicht eingehalten wird, sehen wir uns genötigt, diesen und alle weiteren Aufträge zu stornieren*
	We must point out that the goods are needed urgently for our own customers, who might well look elsewhere for their supplies	*Wir müssen darauf hinweisen, dass die Waren dringend für unsere eigenen Kunden benötigt werden, die sich möglicherweise anderweitig nach ihren Lieferungen umsehen*
	... as several customers are now threatening to cancel their orders	*... da mehrere Kunden uns jetzt drohen, ihre Aufträge zu stornieren*
	... since some of our customers have now cancelled their orders	*... da einige unserer Kunden ihre Aufträge jetzt storniert haben*
5	**Polite ending**	***Höfliche Schlussformel***
	Prompt delivery is all that is needed to settle this matter	*Eine prompte Lieferung ist alles, was jetzt nötig ist, um diese Angelegenheit in Ordnung zu bringen*
	We trust that we will be hearing from you in the very near future	*Wir vertrauen darauf, dass wir in nächster Zukunft von Ihnen hören*

B. Making a Complaint

Buyer

1	**Refer to goods**	***Beziehen Sie sich auf die Waren***
	The above-mentioned goods were delivered to us today, 36 hours late	*Die oben erwähnten Güter wurden uns heute mit 36-stündiger Verspätung geliefert*
	The 2,000 mobile phones ordered on 1 February, as per our order no. 74/A, arrived here yesterday as promised	*Die gemäß unserem Auftrag Nr. 74/A am 1. Februar bestellten 2.000 Handys kamen hier gestern wie versprochen an*
	We have just taken delivery of the above-mentioned articles, which arrived 5 days later than expected	*Wir haben soeben die oben erwähnten Artikel erhalten, die 5 Tage später als erwartet ankamen*
2	**Say what is wrong**	***Sagen Sie, was nicht stimmt***
	On examining them we found that one of the desks was badly scratched	*Bei Prüfung der Schreibtische stellten wir fest, dass einer stark zerkratzt ist*
	Upon checking the consignment we discovered that 25 cycles were damaged and therefore unusable	*Bei Prüfung der Sendung fanden wir heraus, dass 25 Fahrräder beschädigt und daher unbrauchbar sind*
	We believe this is the result of rough handling in transit	*Wir glauben, dies ist das Ergebnis unsachgemäßer Behandlung beim Transport*
	We enclose photographs of these items for your information	*Wir fügen Fotos dieser Positionen zu Ihrer Information bei*

	We are of the opinion that this was caused by poor packing (see photographs enclosed)	*Wir sind der Meinung, dass dies durch schlechte Verpackung verursacht wurde (siehe beiliegende Fotos)*
3	**Ask for an explanation***	***Bitten Sie um eine Erklärung****
	We would welcome your explanation of the damage	*Wir würden Ihre Erklärung des Schadens begrüßen*
	Please explain how such a thing could happen	*Bitte erklären Sie, wie so etwas passieren konnte*
4	**Consequences for the buyer and seller***	***Folgen für den Käufer und den Verkäufer****
	You will understand that we cannot sell these items at the normal price	*Sie werden verstehen, dass wir diese Positionen nicht zum normalen Preis verkaufen können*
	You will appreciate that we will not be able to sell such articles at the usual price	*Sie werden Verständnis dafür haben, dass wir nicht in der Lage sein werden, solche Artikel zum üblichen Preis zu verkaufen*
	… and can only keep them if a reduction in price of 25% is granted on the damaged cycles	*… und können sie nur behalten, wenn ein Preisnachlass von 25% auf die beschädigten Fahrräder gewährt wird*
	… if the price is reduced by 25%	*… wenn der Preis um 25% reduziert wird*
	… if you reduce the price of the sub-standard items by 25%	*… wenn Sie den Preis für die minderwertigen Positionen um 25% herabsetzen*
	If they do not arrive here by 15 February, we will have to obtain them elsewhere	*Wenn sie bis 15. Februar nicht hier ankommen, werden wir sie woanders beziehen müssen*
5	**Ask for appropriate action**	***Bitten Sie um geeignete Maßnahmen***
	Whatever the case may be, we need the 250 mobile phones urgently	*Wie dem auch sei, wir benötigen die 250 Handys dringend*
	… and must therefore ask you to send replacements or grant us a considerable reduction in price	*… und müssen Sie deshalb bitten, Ersatz zu schicken oder uns einen erheblichen Preisnachlass zu gewähren*
	We trust you will deal with this matter without delay	*Wir vertrauen darauf, dass Sie sich unverzüglich um diese Angelegenheit kümmern werden*
6	**Polite ending**	***Höfliche Schlussformel***
	We look forward to receiving your comments on this matter in the very near future	*Wir erwarten Ihre Stellungnahme zu dieser Angelegenheit in Kürze*
	We expect to hear from you in the very near future	*Wir erwarten, von Ihnen recht bald zu hören*
7	**Enclosure(s)**	***Anlage(n)***
	Photograph(s)	*Foto(s)*

C. Dealing with a Complaint

Seller

1	**Acknowledge receipt of the buyer's complaint immediately**	***Bestätigen Sie den Erhalt der Beschwerde des Käufers sofort***
	We have just received your e-mail regarding the above-mentioned consignment of office furniture	*Wir haben soeben Ihre E-Mail bezüglich der oben erwähnten Sendung Büromöbel erhalten*
	Your complaint is now being investigated	*Ihre Beschwerde wird jetzt untersucht*
2	**Express regret**	***Drücken Sie Bedauern aus***
	We are sorry to hear the consignment was delayed and that some of the goods are sub-standard	*Es tut uns Leid zu hören, dass die Sendung verzögert eintraf und dass einige der Waren nicht der Qualität entsprachen*
	... and are dismayed to hear that some of the cycles arrived scratched	*... und sind entsetzt zu hören, dass einige der Fahrräder zerkratzt angekommen sind*
3	**Give details of action taken***	***Geben Sie Einzelheiten der unternommenen Schritte an****
	Since hearing from you we have contacted our freight forwarders and are waiting for their report	*Nach Erhalt Ihrer Nachricht haben wir uns an unseren Spediteur gewandt und erwarten nunmehr seinen Bericht*
	As the cycles left our premises in perfect condition, we have got in touch with the shipping company and found out that ...	*Da die Fahrräder unsere Geschäftsräume in einwandfreiem Zustand verlassen haben, sind wir mit der Versandfirma in Kontakt getreten und haben herausgefunden, dass ...*
	... their lorry was involved in an accident in the Netherlands two weeks ago	*... ihr Lkw vor zwei Wochen in den Niederlanden in einen Unfall verwickelt war*
	This explains the delay of 5 days and the damage	*Dies erklärt die Verspätung von 5 Tagen und den Schaden*
4	**Suggest a solution***	***Schlagen Sie eine Lösung vor****
	In the meantime, we are sending you replacements at no extra charge by return	*Zwischenzeitlich schicken wir Ihnen umgehenden Ersatz ohne zusätzliche Kosten für Sie*
	Under the circumstances, we are willing to offer you a replacement consignment or a reduction in price of 25% on the unsatisfactory items	*Unter diesen Umständen sind wir bereit, Ihnen eine Ersatzsendung oder eine Preisreduzierung von 25% für die nicht zufriedenstellenden Positionen anzubieten*
5	**Apologise again**	***Entschuldigen Sie sich erneut***
	In the meantime, please accept our apologies for the inconvenience caused, which was due to circumstances beyond our control	*In der Zwischenzeit nehmen Sie bitte unsere Entschuldigung für die verursachten Unannehmlichkeiten entgegen, die auf Umstände außerhalb unserer Kontrolle zurückzuführen sind*

	Please once again accept our apologies for the inconvenience	*Bitte nehmen Sie erneut unsere Entschuldigung für die Unannehmlichkeiten entgegen*
6	**Polite ending**	***Höfliche Schlussformel***
	We look forward to hearing from you soon	*Wir freuen uns, bald von Ihnen zu hören*
	We hope this suggestion will find your approval	*Wir hoffen, dass dieser Vorschlag Ihre Zustimmung finden wird*
	We look forward to doing further business with you in the future	*Wir freuen uns darauf, zukünftig weitere Geschäfte mit Ihnen zu tätigen*
	We are sure that the matter will be settled to the satisfaction of all parties concerned and will be contacting you again in the very near future	*Wir sind sicher, dass die Angelegenheit zur Zufriedenheit aller betroffenen Parteien geregelt wird, und werden in Kürze wieder mit Ihnen in Verbindung treten*

Exercises

Exercise 1: Jumbled Letters

The sentences below are in the wrong order. Use the letter plans on page 119 to put them in the correct order.

A. Delay in Delivery / Buyer

a. We trust we will be hearing from you in the very near future.

b. Please let us know why the goods have been delayed.

c. We must know immediately when we can expect them

d. On 10 January .. we ordered 100 mobile phones for delivery by 31 January ... Our order is now more than 2 weeks overdue.

e. ... as several customers are now threatening to cancel their orders.

B. Making a Complaint / Buyer

a. On examining them we discovered that 10 of the filters were badly scratched. We enclose photographs of these items for your information.

b. The 50 PureFlow water filters ordered on 10 September .. as per our order no. 44/F were delivered to us today.

c. Photographs

d. Please explain how such a thing could happen.

e. You will appreciate that we cannot sell such articles at the usual price and can only keep them if a reduction of 50% is granted.

f. We must therefore ask you to send replacements or reduce the price.

g. We look forward to receiving your comments on this matter in the very near future.

C. Dealing with a Complaint / Seller

a. … and are sorry to hear that one box of CDs is damaged.

b. We hope this suggestion will find your approval.

c. We have just received the above-mentioned e-mail regarding your order

d. Since hearing from you we have got in touch with our freight forwarders and are waiting for their report.

e. Please accept our apologies for the inconvenience caused.

f. In the meantime, we are sending you replacements at no extra charge by return.

Exercise 2: Instructions I

1. First read through the specimen fax on page 121 from Wirichs Fruchtsäfte KG to Heavytree Natural Fruit Juice Co.
2. Next write the words missing in the fax below on a piece of your own paper. Do this *without* looking at the specimen fax at the same time.

> Dear Mrs Lumley
>
> The 1. ______ ordered over a month ago are now 7 days 2. ______. Please let us have your 3. ______ for the delay.
>
> Whatever the case may be, the 4. ______ must arrive at our factory 5. ______ the end of this month at the 6. ______ because an important customer is 7. ______ to cancel his order.
>
> We will have no choice but to 8. ______ if you cannot meet this 9. ______.
>
> We therefore expect to hear from you by 10. ______ why our order has been 11. ______ and when it will 12. ______.
>
> 13. ______ delivery is all that is needed to 14. ______ this matter.
>
> Yours 1. ______
>
> *Pete Bull*

Exercise 3: Instructions II

1. First read through the specimen letter on page 122 from Ferris Wheel Cycle Stores Ltd to Henkel Fahrradbau GmbH.
2. Next use the ten words in the list and write the words missing in the letter below on a piece of your own paper. Do this *without* looking at the specimen letter at the same time.

List
checking ◆ delivered ◆ enclose ◆ found ◆ granted ◆ keep ◆ look ◆ receiving ◆ sell ◆ were

> Dear Mr Jones
>
> Our Order No. DVD2000 of 3 March .. for 200 Quarz Wrist-watches
>
> The above-mentioned consignment was 1. ____ to us yesterday and when 2. ____ it we 3. ____ that 10 watches 4. ____ damaged. We 5. ____ photographs of the damage for your information.
>
> You will appreciate that we cannot 6. ____ these goods at the normal price and can only 7. ____ them if a considerable reduction is 8. ____.
>
> We 9. ____ forward to 10. ____ your comments.
>
> Yours sincerely
> etc.

Exercise 4: Anagrams

1. First read through the specimen e-mail on page 123 from Marita Henkel to Mr Butcher.
2. The letters of ten of the words have been mixed up. Re-arrange them to make words from the specimen e-mail.

1. dhctrcsae	6. ntcfstsaiaio
2. dlttsee	7. oetrrp
3. eaidymsd	8. rtfeuu
4. eeieoicnnvncn	9. sglpeiooa
5. ieeaothgrfsrdrwrf	10. ssmrpeei

Exercise 5: Crossword

What's wrong with the goods?

Look in the vocabulary list for this unit on pages 141 / 142 and the clues below to find the twelve words (adjectives) in the crossword. Write your answers on the worksheet provided.

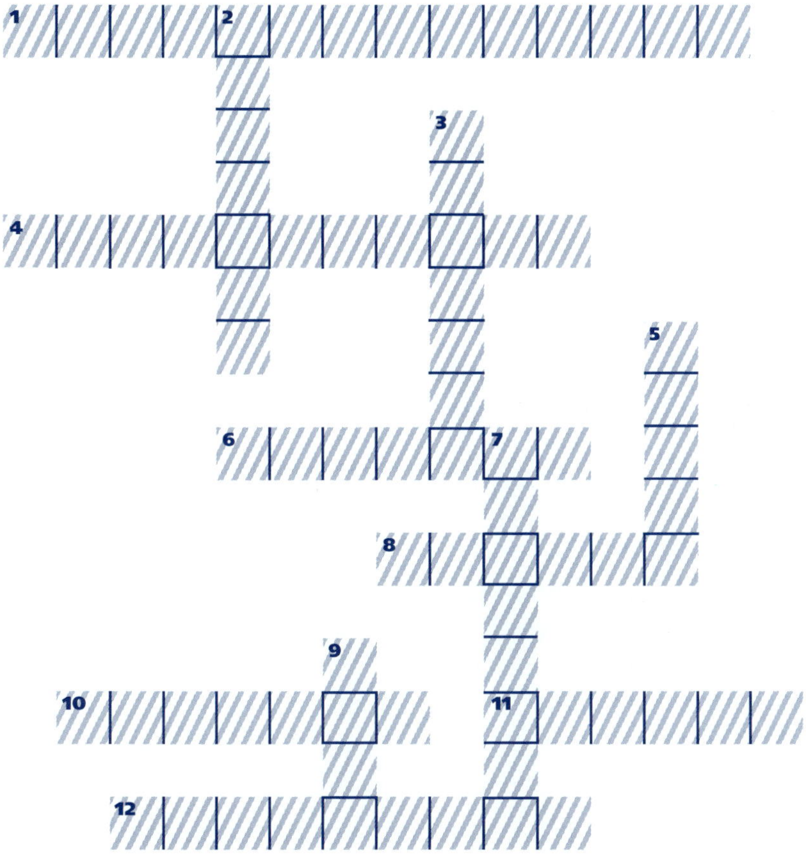

Clues

Across

1. We're not satisfied with the goods. The goods are ______.
4. The standard of the goods is *not high enough* – the goods are ______ (*leave out the hyphen*).
6. The goods are 5 days late – they're 5 days ______.
8. This article has a fault – it's ______.
10. The left-hand edge of the table on page 124 isn't straight – it's ______.
11. I dropped the glass and now it's ______.
12. Bill's car touched a tree while he was parking it and now the car door's ______.

Down

2. The front right-hand leg of the table on page 124 is ______.
3. Someone knocked a cup of coffee over on the sofa and now it's ______.
5. opposite of "clean"
7. If you can't use something it's ______.
9. The back right-hand leg of the table on page 124 is ______.

Aufgaben

1.

Name	Margot (Werner) Meise	Ms Jeannette Francis
Position	Einkauf	Export Sales Director
Firma	Dynamo Paketservice GmbH	Jennifer Green Ltd
Anschrift	Am Brunnen 11, 45133 Essen, Germany	15 Ashburn Gardens, London SW7 4DG, UK
Fax	+49 (2 01) 96 75 43	+44 (1 71) 8 50-39 61
E-Mail	dynamo.paket@firmenshuttle.de	jen.green@compulink.co.uk

Geschäftsfall:
Vor 4 Wochen haben Sie bei der Jennifer Green Ltd mehrere Büroartikel bestellt. Lieferzeit: 3 Wochen. Die Ware ist bisher noch nicht eingetroffen.

Aufgabe:
Schreiben Sie einen Beschwerdebrief unter Berücksichtigung folgender Punkte:
- Bezug auf den o. a. Auftrag und die Verspätung
- Die bestellten Waren werden dringend benötigt, da Ihre Kunden sich möglicherweise anderweitig eindecken werden
- Bitte um Erklärung der Verspätung
- Setzen Sie eine Frist (höchstens 2 Wochen!)
- Sollte die Lieferung bis dahin nicht erfolgt sein, werden Sie diesen und alle weiteren Aufträge stornieren

2.

Name	eigener Name	Ms Sharon Wait
Position	Einkaufsleiter/in	Export Sales Director
Firma	Design Marschall & Co. KG	Kodaphone Ltd
Anschrift	Bruchstr. 11–13, 34130 Kassel, Germany	88 Orwell Parade, Wigan WI7 9HH, England
Fax	+49 (5 61) 30 99 55	+44 (19 42) 2 22 86
E-Mail	design.marschall.kg@aol.com	kodaphone.ltd@firmweb.uk.co

Geschäftsfall:
Sie hatten vor einem Monat mit Auftrag L 28 PR bei Kodaphone Ltd in Wigan, England, 2000 Handys (*mobile phones*) bestellt. Die Handys sind mit Verspätung angekommen und weisen verschiedene Mängel auf.

Aufgabe:
Schreiben Sie eine Beschwerde an Frau Wait, in der Sie folgende Punkte berücksichtigen:

- Der Lkw kam gestern mit einer Verspätung von 36 Stunden an
- Es fehlen 100 Handys (d. h. 2 Kisten)
- 150 der gelieferten Handys sind beschädigt und unbrauchbar (Fotos anbei)
- Sie bitten um eine Erklärung dafür, wie so etwas passieren konnte
- Sie brauchen die 250 Handys bis Ende der Woche, sonst müssen Sie sie von einem anderen Lieferanten beziehen
- Schlusssatz

3.

	Von	An
Name	Rolf (Gabi) Neutzer	Ms Denise Johnson
Position	Exportsachbearbeiter/in	Chefeinkäuferin
Firma	Fitness Baumgartner GmbH	Sports Fashion Ltd
Anschrift	Postfach 10 93 28, 09126 Chemnitz, Germany	Talbot Place, Blackheath, London SE3 OTZ, England
Fax	+49 (3 71) 95 11 03	+44 (1 81) 3 68-87 54
E-Mail	fitness.baumgartner@online.de	sportfash@omnilink.co.uk

Geschäftsfall:
Vor 5 Tagen lieferten Sie an die Sports Fashion Ltd 250 Expander (*expanders*) Marke „Schwarzenegger", die in 10 Kisten verpackt waren. Ihr Kunde teilte Ihnen gestern per Fax mit, dass eine Kiste mit 25 Expandern fehlt und verlangt die sofortige Klärung der Angelegenheit.

Aufgabe:
Schreiben Sie an den Kunden unter Berücksichtigung folgender Punkte:
- Bezug auf Fax
- Bedauern des Vorfalls
- Bieten Sie eine sofortige kostenlose Ersatzlieferung an, während Sie Nachforschungen anstellen
- Nochmaliges Bedauern und Hoffnung auf weitere gute Zusammenarbeit

Vocabulary List

able, to be ~ to	*können*
above-mentioned	*oben erwähnt*
accident	*Unfall*
acknowledge	*zur Kenntnis nehmen*
action, to take ~	*Maßnahmen ergreifen, Schritte unternehmen*
agree	*hier: vereinbaren*
airline	*Fluggesellschaft*
apologies, please accept our ~	*wir bitten um Entschuldigung*
apologise	*sich entschuldigen*
appreciate	*hier: verstehen, dafür Verständnis haben*
appropriate, as ~	*wie geeignet, wie passend*
approval, find your ~	*Ihre Zustimmung finden*
arrow	*Pfeil*
at the latest	*spätestens*
attend to	*sich kümmern um*
believe	*glauben*
bent	*krumm, verbogen*
beyond our control	*außerhalb unserer Macht / unseres Einflussbereichs*
break down	*eine Panne haben*
broken	*kaputt*
business, do further ~	*weitere Geschäfte tätigen*
buyer	*Käufer/in*
by (a certain date)	*bis (zu einem bestimmten Termin)*
by return	*postwendend, umgehend*
cancel	*stornieren*
cause, to ~	*verursachen*
certain	*sicher; bestimmt*
charge, at no extra ~	*ohne zusätzliche Kosten*
checking, on ~ them	*als wir sie kontrollierten*
choice, to have no ~ but to ...	*keine andere Wahl haben, als ...*
comments, your ~	*Ihre Stellungnahme*
common	*häufig*
complain	*sich beschweren*
complaint	*Beschwerde, Reklamation*
concerned, of all parties ~	*aller Beteiligten*
condition, in perfect ~	*einwandfrei, in perfektem Zustand*
consequence(s)	*Folge(n), Konsequenz(en)*
considerable	*beträchtlich*
crash, to ~	*verunglücken, abstürzen*
crooked	*hier: nicht gerade*
cycle	*Fahrrad*
damage, the ~	*hier: Schaden*
damaged	*beschädigt*
deadline	*(letzte) Frist*
deadline, to meet a ~	*eine Frist einhalten*
deal with	*sich befassen mit; fertig werden mit*
delay in delivery	*Lieferverzug*
delivery, to take ~ of	*in Empfang nehmen*
desk	*Schreibtisch*
dirty	*schmutzig, verschmutzt*
discover	*entdecken*
dismayed	*bestürzt, entsetzt*
dissatisfied	*unzufrieden*
due to	*wegen*
elsewhere, look ~ for their goods	*sich anderweitig eindecken*
expect	*erwarten*
explanation	*Erklärung*
express, to ~	*zum Ausdruck bringen*
factory	*Fabrik*
factual	*sachlich*
faulty	*fehlerhaft*
few, too ~	*zu wenig*
for your information	*zu Ihrer Information*
freight forwarder	*Spediteur*
fruit juice	*Fruchtsaft*
furniture	*Möbel*
further	*weitere(r, s)*
grant, to ~	*gewähren*
have to	*müssen*
immediately	*sofort*
important	*wichtig*
in the very near future	*sehr bald*
inconvenience	*Unannehmlichkeit*
insurance company	*Versicherungsgesellschaft*
investigate	*untersuchen, nachforschen*
involved, to be ~ in an accident	*in einen Unfall verwickelt sein*
item	*Artikel*
juice	*Saft*
jumbled	*durcheinander gewürfelt, in der falschen Reihenfolge*

keep, to ~	*behalten*
location	*Ort*
lorry	*Lkw*
managing director	*Geschäftsführer/in*
match, to ~	*hier: zuordnen*
matter, the ~	*hier: Angelegenheit*
meantime, in the ~	*in der Zwischenzeit*
meet (deadline)	*einhalten (Frist)*
missing, to be ~	*fehlen*
mixed up	*durcheinander gewürfelt, in der falschen Reihenfolge*
mobile phone	*Handy*
narrow	*schmal*
necessary	*notwendig*
needed	*benötigt*
Netherlands, the ~	*die Niederlande*
obliged, be ~ to	*gezwungen sein*
obtain	*hier: beziehen*
office furniture	*Büromöbel*
office supplies	*Büroartikel*
overdue	*überfällig*
part-delivery	*Teillieferung*
per, as ~	*gemäß*
place an order	*einen Auftrag erteilen*
point out	*darauf hinweisen*
poor packing	*schlechte Verpackung*
premises	*Geschäftsräume*
promised, as ~	*wie versprochen*
purchasing department	*Einkaufsabteilung*
purchasing director	*Einkaufsleiter/in*
railway company	*Eisenbahngesellschaft*
reach	*erreichen*
re-arrange	*in die richtige Reihenfolge bringen*
reason	*Grund, Ursache*
receipt	*hier: Erhalt*
reduce	*reduzieren*
reduction in price	*Preisnachlass*
reference to	*Bezug auf*
regarding	*bezüglich*
regret, to ~	*bedauern*
replace	*ersetzen*
replacements	*Ersatz (identische Ware)*
reply to, a ~	*Antwort auf*
report, to ~	*hier: berichten*
request for, a ~	*Bitte um*
rough	*rau*
rough handling	*unsachgemäße Behandlung*
sales department	*Verkaufsabteilung*
satisfaction	*Zufriedenheit*
scratched	*zerkratzt*

seller	*Verkäufer/in*
settle, to ~	*hier: erledigen*
several	*mehrere*
shipping company	*Reederei; Transportunternehmen, Versandfirma*
size	*Größe*
solution	*Lösung*
stained	*mit Flecken versehen*
sub-standard	*minderwertig*
suggest	*vorschlagen*
supplier	*Lieferant/in*
supplies	*Lieferungen; Bedarf*
supply, to ~	*liefern*
swivel chair	*Drehstuhl*
therefore	*deshalb*
threaten	*drohen*
touch, get in ~ with	*sich in Verbindung setzen mit*
transit, in ~	*auf dem Transport*
transit, lost in ~	*auf dem Transport verloren gegangen*
trust, to ~	*hier: davon ausgehen, darauf vertrauen*
twisted	*verdreht*
under the circumstances	*unter den Umständen*
unsatisfactory	*unzufriedenstellend*
unusable	*unbenutzbar*
upon examining the …	*als wir die … prüften*
urgently	*dringend*
usual	*üblich*
welcome, to ~	*hier: begrüßen*
whatever the case may be	*wie dem auch sei*
willing, to be ~	*bereit sein*
within	*innerhalb*
without delay	*unverzüglich*
without fail	*auf jeden Fall*
wrist-watch	*Armbanduhr*
wrong, to go ~	*schief gehen*

Secretarial Activities

- Telephoning
- Making Appointments
- Travel Arrangements
- Room Reservations
- Invitations
- Visitors to the Company

Telephoning

When telephoning a large company or organisation in Britain, a caller often first speaks to the switchboard operator and asks to be put through to the person or department he / she wishes to speak to. The switchboard operator puts the caller through, often without asking for the caller's name. When the caller has been put through to the right person he / she introduces himself / herself.

Telephone calls in business are usually friendly and informal. First names are often used.

Starting the call

The switchboard operator answers the phone.

Table 1

Caller Roswitha (Roland) Klein	**Switchboard Operator at Hitech Ltd**
1. *Dials the number*	2. Hitech, good morning (afternoon). Can I help you?
3. Good morning (afternoon). Could I speak to Mr Briant in Exports, please?	4. Certainly, madam (sir). I'll put you through.
5. Thank you.	*(Music)* **Mr John Briant in Exports**
	6. Exports.
7. Good morning (afternoon). Could I speak to Mr Briant, please?	8. Speaking.
9. Hello, John. It's Roswitha (Roland) Klein from Möbel Muckemann in Munich.	10. Hello, Roswitha (Roland). How are you?
11. Fine, thanks. And you?	12. Fine. What can I do for you?
13. The reason I'm calling is to ask you …	

Starting the call

Mr Briant has a direct line.

Table 2

Caller Roswitha (Roland) Klein	**Mr John Briant in Exports**
1. *Dials the number*	2. Exports, good morning (afternoon). Can I help you?
3. Good morning (afternoon). Could I speak to Mr Briant, please?	4. Speaking.
5. Hello, John. It's Roswitha (Roland) Klein from Möbel Muckemann in Munich.	6. Hello, Roswitha (Roland). How are you?
7. Fine, thanks. And you?	8. Fine. What can I do for you?
9. The reason I'm calling is to ask you …	

The reason for calling / Finishing the call

Table 3

Caller Roswitha (Roland) Klein	Mr John Briant in Exports
1a. The reason I'm calling is to ask you …	
1b. I'd like to know …	
1c. Could you tell me …?	**2a.** Just a moment, I'll get the file.
	2b. Just a moment, I'm just accessing it here on the computer.
3. Right.	**4.** Ah yes, here we are … (*gives information*)
5. Well, thanks a lot.	**6.** Anything else I can do for you?
7. No, thanks very much.	**8.** Thanks for calling. Bye.
9. Bye.	

Polite Questions

When making a business phone call, it is often useful to use one of the following polite expressions:

A. The reason I'm calling is to ask you …

B. I'd like to know …

C. Could you tell me …?

Practice

Here are some simple direct questions. First study the examples given and then re-write the sentences on a piece of your own paper in a politer form using structures **A**, **B**, or **C**.

Example 1: "Did you get the goods?"
Polite form A: "The reason I'm calling is to ask you if you got the goods."

Example 2: "When did you get them?"
Polite form B: "I'd like to know when you got them."

Example 3: "Why haven't we got the goods?"
Polite form C: "Could you tell me why we haven't got the goods?"

1. Is Mr Brown in the office?
2. Is he coming back?
3. Can he phone me?
4. Will he come tomorrow?
5. Has he left?
6. Does Mrs Bell work there?
7. Did she work there?
8. When is she coming back?
9. Where was she going?
10. When does she leave?
11. When did she leave?
12. How did she feel?

Mini Telephone Dialogues

Act out the following dialogues with your neighbour. Use the examples in **Tables 1, 2** and **3** and structures **A**, **B** and **C**. You speak to the switchboard operator first.

1.

Walter Warmbier from Knauser Kompressoren in Cologne rings the Lawrence Insurance Company in England to ask Mr John Briant in Exports the question: "Have you received our cheque?" The answer is "Yes." They finish the conversation politely and ring off.

2.

Peter Held from Transworld Software in Berlin rings Priscilla Thorpe in the Sales Department at Amstrad Ltd in England to ask the question: "Will the 2,000 monitors come by the end of the month?" The answer is "Yes". They finish the conversation politely and ring off.

3.

Sabine Schorr from Konrad Elektronik in Essen calls Dallas Instruments in Texas to talk to Clarence W. Goldwater in the Shipping Section. She asks the question: "When did you despatch the 10,000 pocket calculators?". The answer is "Yesterday." They finish the conversation politely and ring off.

1 ## Listening

Telephone Dialogue

Listen to the following dialogue and then write down the words missing in the gaps on a piece of your own paper. There is sometimes more than one word missing.
(*SBO = switchboard operator*)

SBO: Kodaphone, good morning. Can I 1. ___ you?
Roland: Good morning. Could I 2. ___ Susan Sharp in Sales, please?
SBO: 3. ___ sir. 4. ___ put you through.
Roland: Thank you.
– Music –
Susan: Sales Department.
Roland: Good morning. Could I speak to Susan Sharp, please?
Susan: 5. ___.
Roland: Hello Susan. 6. ___ Roland Klein from Möbel Muckemann in Munich.
Susan: Hello, Roland. How are you?
Roland: Fine, thanks. And you?
Susan: Fine. What can I do for you?
Roland: The 7. ___ I'm calling is to ask you if our order is ready.
Susan: Could I have the order number, please?
Roland: Yes, it's 8. ___.
Susan: Just a moment … I'm just 9. ___ it here on the computer.

Roland:	Right.
Susan:	Ah yes, here we are. We 10. ___ the computers yesterday.
Roland:	Good. Did you send them by air or sea?
Susan:	Just a moment ... ah yes, here we are. We sent them by 11. ___ to arrive in Munich tomorrow morning.
Roland:	Oh, 12. ___! That means they'll be here in time for the trade fair.
Susan:	Good. 13. ___ I can do for you?
Roland:	No, 14. ___ very much.
Susan:	Well, thanks for 15. ___. Bye.
Roland:	Bye.

Questions

Answer the following questions in whole sentences (subject + verb).

1. Have Susan Sharp and Roland Klein spoken to each other before or not? Explain your answer.
2. Why is Roland so pleased to hear how the goods will arrive in Munich?

Making Appointments

On the phone

Look at the following dialogue in which Roswitha (Roland) makes an appointment to see Mr John Briant.

Caller Roswitha (Roland) Klein	Mr John Briant in Exports
… *(see "Telephoning" for the beginning)*	… *(see "Telephoning" for the beginning)*
1. I'd like to make an appointment to see you next week.	**2.** Good. I'll just check my diary …. When would you like to come?
3. How about 3 pm on Tuesday?	**4.** Sorry. I've got a meeting then. What about 10 am on Wednesday?
5. I've got an appointment myself then. What about 11 am on Thursday?	**6.** Yes, I'm free then.
7. Good. I'll see you on Thursday then.	**8.** Right, I'll look forward to that. Bye.
9. Bye.	

Now look at how Roswitha (Roland) makes an appointment for her boss, Dr Havekamp, to see Mr John Briant.

Caller Roswitha (Roland) Klein	Mr John Briant in Exports
… *(see "Telephoning" for the beginning)*	… *(see "Telephoning" for the beginning)*
1. I'd like to make an appointment for my boss, Dr Havekamp, to see you next week.	**2.** Good. I'll just check my diary …. When would he like to come?
3. How about 3 pm on Tuesday?	**4.** Sorry. I've got a meeting then. What about 10 am on Wednesday?
5. He's got an appointment himself then. What about 11 am on Thursday?	**6.** Yes, I'm free then.
7. Good. He'll see you on Thursday then.	**8.** Right, I'll look forward to that. Bye.
9. Bye.	

Practice

Mini Telephone Dialogues

Act out the following dialogues with your neighbour.

1.

You are Roswitha (Roland) Klein from SBN Nachrichtentechnik in Munich. You phone John (Joanna) Briant in Exports at Hitech Ltd in England to make an appointment **(a)** for yourself **(b)** for your boss, Dr Havekamp, next week. You suggest 10 am on Monday but he's (she's) at a presentation then. John (Joanna) suggests 2 pm on Tuesday but **(a)** you've got **(b)** your boss has got a meeting then. You finally suggest 11 am on Wednesday and John (Joanna) agrees.

2.

You are Michael(a) Schlohmann from Orange Strom in Essen. You phone Philip(pa) Prentice in Sales at NetPower Ltd in England to make an appointment **(a)** for yourself **(b)** for your boss, Frau Feuerstein, tomorrow. You suggest 9 am but he's (she's) at a working breakfast then. Philip(pa) suggests 10 am but **(a)** you're meeting **(b)** your boss is meeting your/her English agent then. You finally suggest 3 pm and Philip(pa) agrees.

3.

You are Helge (Helga) Reiter from Musikhaus Westernhagen in Cologne. You phone Eric(a) Clayton in Exports at Marshall Sound Ltd to make an appointment **(a)** for yourself **(b)** for your boss, Siggi Partmann, next month. You suggest Monday the 3rd but he's (she's) at a trade fair then. Eric(a) suggests Friday the 7th but **(a)** you're on **(b)** your boss is on a business trip then. You finally suggest Thursday the 13th and Eric(a) agrees.

Standard Expressions

Caller

1	I'd like to I'm phoning to	make an appointment make an appointment for my boss	with to see	... (name)	tomorrow next week next Tuesday on ... (date) some time between ... (date) and ... (date)

3	Right All right

5 a	How about ... (time, day, date, e.g. 2 pm on Tuesday 5 June)? What about ... (time, day, date)?			
5 b	Would ... (time, day, date) be convenient?			
5 c	Are you Is he Is she	free available	at ... (time, e.g. 10 am)	on ... (day, date, e.g. Tuesday 5 June)?

8	Very good Excellent That's marvellous!	I've made a note of that and	I'll/he'll/she'll look forward to seeing you/him/her then

11	Oh, I see	Well, how about Well, what about			... (time, day, date)?
		Are you Is he Is she	free available	on	

13	Very good Excellent That's marvellous	I've made a note of that and	I'll/he'll/she'll look forward to seeing you/him/her then

Other person

2	Just a moment, please	I'll get I'll check	my his her	diary appointments	
4	When would you like to		see me/him/her(?) meet me/him/her(?) come(?) call by(?)		exactly?
6	Just a moment, Now	I'll just check I'm just checking		to see if that's all right	
7	Yes,	that'll be fine			
		I'm he's/she's I'll be/he'll be/she'll be	free available able to see you		then at that time
9	Good, Fine,	I'll he'll she'll	see you	then at … (time) on … (day, date)	
		I've made a note of that Thanks for calling …			
10	No, Oh dear,	I'm sorry (but …)			
		I'm afraid	I'm/he's/she's	busy not available tied up	at … (time) then at that time
			I've got/he's got/ she's got	an appointment a meeting a team meeting an engagement	
	I'm He's She's	meeting … (name of person) having breakfast/lunch/dinner with … visiting our warehouse in … in a meeting with … going to a fashion show going shopping in … (location, e.g. Essen) getting everything ready for Herr Kranz's birthday party			That'll take about … (time, e.g. an hour)
12	Yes,	that'll be fine			
		I'm/he's/she's/I'll be/he'll be/she'll be		free available able to see you	then at that time
14	Good, Fine,	I'll he'll she'll		see you	then at … (time) on … (day, date)
		I've made a note of that Thanks for calling …			

Further Practice

4.

Heike Hensch at Designer Mode GmbH in Essen receives the following e-mail from Diana Dors at TopFit Ltd in Lancaster, England.

e-mail

Mail from:	TopFit@webserve.uk (TopFit Ltd)	**Cc:**	
Subject:	My Visit to Essen	**Attachment:**	

Dear Heike

I'll be in Essen for 3 days from 1–3 of June and I'd like to call in and see you for an hour or so. Please phone me on +44 (15 24) 3 44 87 to arrange an appointment.

Best regards

Diana

Heike phones Diana to make an appointment and both look at their diaries to see when they can meet. Write / Act out Heike's telephone conversation with Diana using the two diaries and the **Standard Expressions: Making Appointments.**

Heike's diary

Montag, 01. Juni

9.00	Team-Sitzung (1 Stunde)
10.00	Gespräch mit Nancy Lux von PowerStyle Inc. (2 Stunden)
12.00	Mittagessen mit Nancy Lux (ca. 2 Stunden)
16.00	Gespräch mit Modelagentur BodyStyle (1 Stunde)
20.00	Abendessen mit Yosira Yakamoto (Japanese Fashion House)

Dienstag, 02. Juni

8.00	Lagerbesichtigung, Düsseldorf (3 Stunden)
14.30	Besprechung mit Außendienst-mitarbeitern (*field workers*) (3 Stunden)

Mittwoch, 03. Juni

10.00	Vorbereitungen für Geburtstagsfeier von Herrn Kranz, Geschäftsführer (1 Stunde)
11.00	Geburtstagsfeier, Herr Kranz (3 Stunden)
14.00	Präsentation Wintermoden (4 Stunden)

Diana's diary

Monday 1st June

8 am	Arrive at Düsseldorf Airport
10 am	Check in at the Sheraton Hotel in Essen
3 pm	Meet Carlos Homberto (1 hour)

Tuesday 2nd June

8.30 am	Meeting with Carl Feldlager to discuss designs (2 hours)
4 pm	Fashion Show at the Holiday Inn in Düsseldorf, Feldlager's winter collection (4 hours)
9 pm	Dinner at Fellini's in Düsseldorf with Carl Feldlager

Wednesday 3rd June

8 am	Working breakfast with fashion designers (2 hours)
2 pm	Meeting with Till Sander to discuss perfumes (1 hour)
4 pm	Shopping in Essen (3 hours)

2 Listening

Telephone Dialogue

Listen to the following dialogue and write down the missing words on a piece of your own paper as you listen. There is sometimes more than one word missing. (*SBO = switchboard operator*)

SBO: Natural Power Ltd, good afternoon. Can I help you?
Nadine: Good afternoon. Could I speak to John Pritchard on 1. ____ 405, please?
SBO: Putting you 2. ____ now, madam.
Nadine: Thank you.
– Music –
John: 3. ____.
Nadine: Hello, could I speak to John Pritchard, please?
John: Speaking.
Nadine: Hello, John. It's Nadine Stickroth from Orange Strom in Essen.
John: Hello, Nadine. How are you?
Nadine: Fine, thanks. And you?
John: Fine. 4. ____ I do for you?
Nadine: My boss, Dr Klein, is coming to London on business and I'd like to make an 5. ____ for him to see you some time between the first and the fifth of next month.
John: Just a moment, I'll get my 6. ____.
Nadine: Right.
John: Now when would he like to see me exactly?
Nadine: Are you 7. ____ at 10 am on Monday the first?
John: Oh dear, I'm afraid I've got a team meeting then.
Nadine: Oh, I see. Well, 8. ____ Tuesday the second at, say, 9 am?
John: I'm sorry, but I'm having a working breakfast with our French agent then. What about 9. ____ for lunch?
Nadine: Yes, that'll be fine.
John: Excellent. I've made a 10. ____ of that and I'll look forward to seeing him then.
Nadine: Good. Bye for now.
John: Thanks for calling. Bye.

Questions

Answer the following questions in whole sentences (subject + verb).

1. Why does Nadine phone John Pritchard?
2. What does John get to see if he's free?
3. When is he free?
4. What does John do after he has told Nadine when he can see her?

Travel Arrangements

3 Listening

Booking Flights

Sonja Wallmann and her boss, Dr Antonia Klar, have flown from Frankfurt to San Francisco, California on business. Now they need to visit a client in San Diego in Southern California, so Sonja calls a travel agency from her hotel room to enquire about flights. Listen to the following dialogue and write down the words missing in the text on a piece of your own paper. There is sometimes more than one word missing.

Travel agent: Cosmos Travel Incorporated. How may I help you?
Sonja: Hello, I'd like to 1. ___ about two return flights to San Diego, please.
TA: Certainly, ma'am. When do you plan to go there?
Sonja: The day after tomorrow.
TA: OK, so we have two adults travelling to San Diego the day after tomorrow. What time of day would you like to 2. ___, ma'am?
Sonja: Oh, early. Let's say about 8 am.
TA: I see … and do you wish to travel first class, 3. ___ class or economy?
Sonja: How long's the flight?
TA: Just over an hour, in fact it 4. ___ an hour and 24 minutes.
Sonja: Well, in that case we'll fly economy.
TA: OK, just give me a moment to check ….Well ma'am, we can offer you a direct flight at 7.45 am or 9 am.
Sonja: And how much would that cost?
TA: Two adult 5. ___ flights will cost you $ 206.
Sonja: Good. In that case I'd like to book two 6. ___ on the 7.45 flight.
TA: And when do you plan to return, ma'am?
Sonja: We'd like to come back the next day and leave at about the same time.
TA: OK, I can get you a direct flight at 10.25 am, arriving at San Francisco Airport at 12 noon.
Sonja: Fine, we'll take that.
TA: If you wish to make a firm 7. ___ now, I'll need your names and a credit card number.
Sonja: My name's Sonja Wallmann – that's S-O-N-J-A and the 8. ___ W-A-L-L-M-A-N-N.
TA: OK.
Sonja: And the other person's Doctor Antonia Klar – that's A-N-T-O-N-I-A and the surname's K-L-A-R.
TA: OK, I've got that. Now I need the number of your credit card.
Sonja: Certainly. It's a Master Card and the number's 9. ___.
TA: 10. ___ date?
Sonja: December of next year.

TA: Right, I have everything I need now. You can call by and 11. ______ the tickets any time from 9 to 6.

Sonja: Thank you. I'll call by tomorrow. Bye.

TA: Thank you too, ma'am. Goodbye and 12. ______.

4 Listening

Buying Train Tickets

Sonja Wallmann and her boss, Dr Antonia Klar, have flown to London from Germany on business. Now they need to visit a client in Manchester, so they go to the ticket office at Euston Station to buy their tickets. Listen to the dialogue and write down the words missing in the text on a piece of your own paper. Sometimes there is more than one word missing.

Ticket clerk: Next, please.

Sonja: I'd like two return tickets to Manchester, please.

TC: 1. ______, madam. Is it for today?

Sonja: No, it's for tomorrow.

TC: What time of day would you like to 2. ______, madam?

Sonja: I want to go in the afternoon.

TC: I see ... and how do you wish to travel – first or second class?

Sonja: Second class, please.

TC: Right, I can give you two 3. ______ on the 3.45 train.

Sonja: And how long does the 4. ______ take?

TC: It takes 2 hours and 53 minutes.

Sonja: Is it direct or do I have to 5. ______?

TC: It's direct.

Sonja: Do I need to 6. ______ seats?

TC: Yes, I would if I were you.

Sonja: In that case I'd like to 7. ______ two seats on the 3.45 train, please.

TC: Right, 8. ______ be £40 please, madam. How would you like to pay?

Sonja: Can I pay by credit card?

TC: Certainly, madam.

Sonja: 9. ______.

TC: Thank you. Would you just 10. ______ here, please?

Sonja: Certainly .... Here you are.

TC: Thank you. And here are your tickets, madam.

Sonja: Thank you.

TC: Next, please ...

Standard Expressions

Traveller

1	I'd like	a/2/3 single ticket(s) a/2/3 return ticket(s) a flight a/2/3 single flight(s) a/2/3 return flight(s)	to … (location)	,please

	I'd like to I'm phoning to	enquire about find out the price of book buy

3	I'd like to	leave travel go	now this morning/afternoon/evening tonight tomorrow on … (day, e.g. Tuesday) on … (date, e.g. January 15[1])
5	I'd like to I'd prefer to I want to	leave travel go arrive there	at about … (time, e.g. 10 am) early first thing in the morning in the morning mid-morning late morning any time after … (time, e.g. 10 am) not before … (time, e.g. 10 am) about mid-day at lunchtime after lunch in the afternoon early afternoon mid-afternoon late afternoon in the evening by … (time, e.g. by 12.30 pm) in good time for … (appointment, e.g. a meeting at 2 pm in the city centre)

7	I'd like to	travel fly	first class business class economy	,please

9 a	How much does it cost? How much would that cost? How much does a single ticket/return ticket cost? How much is a first-class/business-class single ticket? How much is a first-class/business-class return ticket?

1 *This is the American way of saying the date ("on January fifteenth"). The British way is 15 January ("the fifteenth of January").*

Travel Agent

2	Certainly,	sir madam ma'am	Is it for today? When is it for? When do you plan to go there? When do you want to travel? What date(s) would that be, sir / madam / ma'am? Could I have the date(s), please?

4	What time of day would you like to	leave travel go arrive there	sir? madam? ma'am?

6	How do you wish to travel – Would you like to travel Would that be	first class, business class or economy?

8	In that case	I we	can offer you	a seat seats	on the 10.30	train flight
	... arriving at ... (destination, e. g. Leeds, Austin Airport) at ... (time, e. g. 11.33 am)					

10 a	It costs It would cost	... (price, e. g. $ 175 / between $ 170 and $ 200 / about $ 175) $ 200 each way $ 1,000 for a single first-class / business-class ticket $ 2,000 for a first-class / business-class return ticket

9 b	How much does it cost How much will it cost	to travel to go to fly	first class? business class? economy?	
11	How long	does	it the trip the journey the flight	take?
		does it take to get to … (location, e.g. San Diego)?		
13	Is it direct Is it a direct flight	or do I have to change?		
15	Do I need to Is it best to Should I	reserve a seat/seats? book now? make a reservation?		
17	In that case	I'd like to	take that ticket buy two tickets book that seat book a seat/2 seats on that flight/train book a seat/2 seats on the 10.30 train make a reservation (for 1 person/ 2 people) reserve a/2/3 seat(s)	,please
19	I'd like to pay Can I pay	in cash (?) in traveller's cheques (?) by cheque (?) by credit card (?)		
21	Certainly.	It's a Master Card. My name's Sonja Wallmann – that's S-O-N-J-A and the surname's W-A-L-L-M-A-N-N. The card number's 5232 5402 1017 4386 The expiry (expiration) date is December 2005		
23	In that case	I'll I'd like to	leave it	
			take the next available	flight train
			go on … (date, e.g. 16 January)	

10 b	A single economy flight A return economy flight A single business-class flight A return business-class flight A first-class single flight A first-class return flight	costs … (price)	including tax including all taxes		
12	It takes	… (time, e.g. (about) an hour/just over/just under two hours) exactly … (time, e.g. an hour and 24 minutes)			
14	It's direct You have to change once in … (location) on the … (time, e.g. 9.11) flight You have to change twice, once in … and once in … on the … (time) flight				
16	No, you don't need to Yes, it's best to Yes, I would if I were you				
18	Certainly, sir/madam/ma'am Right, In that case	the total price is … that'll be … (price, e.g. €250), please	How would you like to pay?		
20	Certainly,	sir madam ma'am	Could I have your name, credit card number and the expiry (expiration) date, please? Would you just like to sign here, please?		
22 a	OK, I've got that Thanks very much I have everything I need now	You can	have the ticket(s) now, if you'd like call by and collect the ticket(s) … (time) pick up the ticket(s) any time … (time, e.g. this afternoon, tomorrow, after 3 pm)		
22 b	I'm sorry but I'm afraid	we have no more tickets available there are no more seats available the tickets are all sold the seats are all sold the train's fully booked the flight's booked up			
		there's no more room	on that flight	in the	first business economy	class
			on that train	in the first class	
22	Can I book you on Would you like to go on	a later an earlier a different	one? flight? train?		
24 a	That's fine				
24 b	*(See 8 above)*				

Practice

Buying Train Tickets

Sonja (Mark) Wallmann and Dr Antonia Klar are in England on business and now they want to go from London to Leeds by train tomorrow morning. They need to get there in good time to have lunch with a client in the city centre at 12.30 pm, so Sonja goes to King's Cross Station to buy two single tickets for tomorrow. The ticket clerk sells Sonja two first-class tickets, reserves two seats for her and answers her questions using the information on the timetable.

Sonja asks the clerk these questions:
- length of journey?
- change trains?
- pay by credit card?

Look at the timetable to decide which train is best and then act / write out the dialogue between Sonja and the ticket clerk.

Timetable

Journey	Arrival	Departure
London King's Cross York Leeds *Duration: 2:45*	 10:36 11:15	8:30 10:46
London King's Cross Leeds *Duration: 2:23*	 11:33	9:10
London King's Cross York Leeds *Duration: 2:45*	 11:34 12:15	9:30 11:46
London King's Cross Leeds *Duration: 2:25*	 12:35	10:10

First Class	Second Class
Adult Single: £35	Adult Single: £20
Adult Return: £70	Adult Return: £40

All major credit cards accepted

Booking Flights

Sonja (Mark) Wallmann and Dr Antonia Klar are in San Francisco on business. They want to fly to Austin, Texas in exactly a week's time to meet a client for an appointment at 5.30 pm in the city centre, so Sonja calls a travel agent, Cosmos Travel Incorporated, from her hotel room to book two business-class tickets. The travel agent tells her what she wants to know and books two single flights for her using the information in the table. The travel agent also tells Sonja that she can pick up the tickets at the travel agency any time between 9 am and 6 pm Monday – Friday.

While booking the flights Sonja asks the travel agent these questions:

- price of a business class ticket?
- direct flight?
- pay by credit card (VISA, expires in December of next year)?

Look at the table to decide which flight is best and then act / write out the telephone dialogue between Sonja and the travel agent.

San Francisco (SFO) to Austin (AUS) One way

Airline	Depart	Arrive	Stops	Price
American Airlines	**12:15 am** *Dallas, TX* **6:45 am**	*Dallas, TX* **5:31 am** *Austin, TX* **7:41 am**	1	First class: $ 1,018 Business: $ 300 Economy: $ 200
America West	**9:11 am** *Phoenix, AZ* **1:12 pm**	*Phoenix, AZ* **12:10 pm** *Austin, TX* **4:19 pm**	1	First class: $ 1,461 Business: $ 275 Economy: $ 175
United Airlines	**11:00 am**	*Austin, TX* **4:28 pm**	non-stop	First class: $ 1,014 Business: $ 270 Economy: $ 170

All times given are local times. Time difference: e.g. 10 am in Austin / Dallas = 9 am in Phoenix = 8 am in San Francisco.

All major credit cards accepted

Room Reservations

5+6 **Listening**

Choosing the Right Hotel

Silke Schulz works for Zeitgeist Antik Forum in Cologne. Today she has to find out about hotels in Tunbridge Wells, England. Listen to the two dialogues and answer the questions below for **A.** the Waystage Hotel and **B.** the Palace Hotel. Use the worksheet provided.

Reservation:

1. Number of people?
2. Dates (from … to …)?
3. Number of nights?

Hotels: A. Waystage Hotel / B. Palace Hotel

4. Number of stars?
5. How far from the town centre?
6. How far from the railway station?
7. Noisy / quiet?
8. Restaurant?
9. Bar?
10. En-suite bathroom?
11. TV?
12. Telephone?
13. Swimming pool?
14. Gym?
15. Sauna?
16. Basic charge per night for bed and breakfast?
17. Credit cards accepted?

Booking Hotel Rooms

7 Silke Schulz books rooms for a sales meeting at the Palace Hotel in Tunbridge Wells, England. Listen to the dialogue and write down the missing words on a piece of your own paper. Sometimes there is more than one word missing. (*SBO = switchboard operator*)

SBO: Good morning and thank you for calling the Palace Hotel. How may I help you?
Silke: Good morning. I'd like to make a 1 ____, please.
SBO: Certainly, madam. I'll put you through to Reservations.
Silke: Thank you.
– Classical music –
Hotel clerk: Good morning, Reservations. How 2 ____ I help you?
Silke: Good morning, I'd like to make a booking, please.
HC: 3 ____, madam. Could I just have the dates, please?
Silke: Yes, it's from the fifteenth to the twentieth of January next year.
HC: So that's five nights in all .. . Yes, madam we have rooms 4 ____ then. How many rooms do you require?
Silke: Four and a conference room.

HC: That shouldn't be any trouble. Now do you require single, double or family rooms?

Silke: We need three singles for our company directors and a double room for our managing director and his wife. Are the rooms 5. ____?

HC: Yes, madam. All our rooms have their own bathroom or shower. Would that be a double room with a double bed or twin beds, madam?

Silke: Twin beds, please.

HC: So that's three singles and a twin-bedded double for a total of five adults ... Do you require 6. ____, half board or just breakfast, madam?

Silke: We'd like an evening meal on the first day, full board for the next three days and breakfast on the last day, please.

HC: Fine. I've made a note of that. Now you mentioned a 7. ____ room, madam.

Silke: Yes, we'd like to book one for three days, please.

HC: For how many people?

Silke: There will be 20 of us altogether. It's a sales meeting.

HC: I see. Well, we can offer you the Nelson Room, which is for 8. ____ people or the Drake Room, which is for 9. ____ people. Which one would you 10. ____, madam?

Silke: I think the larger room would be better.

HC: Right. I've made a note of that. Is there anything else you 11. ____, madam?

Silke: No, thank you. How much will that cost?

HC: The single rooms with breakfast are £90 per night and the double's £120. The meals will be 12. ____ for separately and the conference room is £50 per day.

Silke: Good, I'd like to book it then.

HC: In that case I now need your name and address, madam.

Silke: Yes, my 13. ____'s Schulz – that's S-C-H-U-L-Z and the first name's Silke, 14. ____ S-I-L-K-E.

HC: Thank you ... and the address and telephone number?

Silke: It's for my company. That's Design 3000 and the address is Nordring 25 – that's N-O-R-D-R-I-N-G 25 in 50765 Cologne, Germany. The telephone number's 15. ____ and our fax number's 16. ____.

HC: OK, I've got that. We require a 20% 17. ____ or a credit card number to make a firm booking, madam.

Silke: That's no problem. I'll pay by VISA.

HC: Right, could I just have the number, please?

Silke: Yes, it's 18. ____.

HC: And the 19. ____ date, please?

Silke: December of next year.

HC: Right, I have everything I need now. We'll fax you 20. ____ of this booking and post you a brochure on our hotel's facilities.

Silke: Thank you very much.

HC: You're welcome, madam, and thank you for calling the Palace Hotel. Goodbye.

Silke: Bye.

Standard Expressions

Caller

1	I'd like to Can I	make a booking, make a reservation, book a room/2 rooms etc.,			please(?)	
3	Yes,	it's from … to … (dates, e.g. the first/second/third/twenty-first/thirty-first of March to the twentieth of April)				
5a	It's for	one person only 2/3 etc. people 2/3 etc. adults			That's one/2/3 adult(s) and one/2/3 child(ren)	
5b	Yes,	that's right				
5c	I We	need	one/2/3	room(s)		
7a	I We	need require 'd like to book		one 2/3 etc.	single room(s), double room(s), family room(s),	please
9b	I We	'd like		(a) double bed(s), twin beds,		please
9a	Are the rooms en suite?					
9b	Does each room have its own bathroom or shower?					
9c	Does each room have a balcony?					
9d	Is there a lift (to every floor)?					
9e	Is there a sauna?					
9f	Is it free? How much does it cost?					
9g	Is there a car park?					
11	Good. I see					
13	I We	'd like	full board half board bed and breakfast an evening meal on … (day/date, e.g. the first day) lunch on … breakfast (only) on …			

Hotel Clerk

2	Certainly,	sir/madam	Could I just have Would you just let me have		the dates, please?
4	So that's … (number, e.g. 2) night(s) in all			Just let me check on the computer, That shouldn't be any trouble,	sir madam
	Yes,	sir madam	we have rooms available then we have a vacancy then	How many	guests is it for? people is it for?
6 a	So that's one single room				
6 b	How many rooms		do you require, would you like to book, would you like to reserve,		sir? madam?
6 c	Would you like Do you require		(a) single, double or family room(s),		sir? madam?
8 a	Certainly Just let me check on the computer That shouldn't be any trouble Could I have your name/the names, please?			Right, I've booked that for you, Right, I can book that for you,	sir madam
8 b	Do you require Would that be Would you like to book			a double room a family room	with (a) double bed(s) or twin beds?
8 c	Could I have your name/the names, please? Right, I've booked that for you, OK, I've made a note of that So that's … (number) single room(s), … double room(s) with a double bed/ with twin beds				sir madam
10 a	Yes, they are,/Most/Some of them are, No, I'm afraid they aren't				sir madam
10 b	Yes, it does,/Most/Some of them do, No, I'm afraid it doesn't,				
10 c	Yes, it does,/Most/Some of them do, No, I'm afraid it doesn't,				
10 d	Yes, there is, There are 2/3 etc. lifts (to every floor), There's a lift to the … (e.g. third) floor, No, I'm afraid there isn't,				
10 e	No, I'm afraid we don't have one Yes, we have a (Swedish, Finnish etc.) sauna				
10 f	It's free for guests It costs … (price, e.g. £5 per hour)				
10 g	Yes, there is. It's free for guests No, I'm afraid there isn't but you can park … (location, e.g. in the station car park)				
12	What meals do you require, Do you require full board, half board or bed and breakfast				sir? madam?
14	Right,	I've made a note of that I've put you down for … (e.g. full board)		Do you require Will you also need Do you wish to book You also mentioned	a conference room (?)

15 a	No, thank you No, we don't need one (now), thank you			
15 b	Yes, we'd like to book one, please That's right. We'll need a conference room for … (number, e. g. three) day(s)			
17	It's for … (number, e. g. 20) people			
19	How much will that cost, How much does that come to, What is the total price for that, How much is a single/double/family room with breakfast/full board/half board per night,			please?
21	Good In that case	I'll take it, I'd like to book it, we'll take that, I'd like to make a firm booking,		please
23 a	Yes, Yes certainly,	my surname's … and my first name's .. . My address is … and my telephone number's …		
23 b	Certainly.	My surname's Schulz – that's S-C-H-U-L-Z and the first name's Silke, spelt S-I-L-K-E		
25 a	I see.	In that case	I'll pay by I'll post you a	cheque
25 b	Right.	In that case	I'll pay by I'd like to pay by	credit card
27	The number's The expiry date's	…		
29	Thanks a lot Thank you very much	Bye Goodbye		

16 a	Oh, I see						
16 b	For how many people? How many people is it for? What size do you need?						
18	Fine. I've made a note of that						
20	It'll cost … in all That will come to … altogether The total price is/would be … A single/double/family room with breakfast/full board/half board comes to … (price) per night The meals will be charged for separately						
22	Fine Good In that case	I now need		your name, address and telephone number			
24 a	Thank you I've got that Would you spell that for me, please?						
24 b	Thank you Right, I've got that	How would you like to pay?					
24 c	We require a 20 % deposit or a credit card number			to make a firm booking, to reserve the room(s),			sir madam
26 a	Certainly,	sir madam		The address of the hotel is …			
26 b	Certainly,	sir madam		What type of card is it, please? Could I have the number and expiry date, please? What is the expiry date, please?			
28	Thank you, I have everything I need now,	sir madam	We'll	fax post send	you	a brochure some information confirmation of your booking	
30	You're welcome,	sir madam		Thank you for calling Goodbye			

Practice

Regency Hotel

Charges	Single Room	Double Room	Family Room (5 max.)
Basic charge per night (bed and breakfast)	£ 80	£ 110	£ 140
Half board per adult per day	£ 12		
Half board per child (under 11) per day	£ 9		
En-suite facilities per day	£ 10	£ 12	£ 15
Extra charge for balcony rooms per day	£ 10		
Conference room per day	£ 40		
Use of sauna per person per hour	£ 5		
Car park	free		

Booking a Single Room on the Phone

Patricia Marcks works for Designer Mode in Essen. Today she phones the Regency Hotel in London to book a room for her boss, Martina Hensch. Martina needs a single, en-suite room from 15 to 20 of next month (5 nights) with half board. She also wants to use the sauna and will be coming by car (car park?). After being told the prices, Patricia gives her company's name, address, telephone and fax numbers (Designer Mode GmbH, Bahnhofstr. 110, 45128 Essen, Germany, tel. +49 (2 01) 99 87 68, fax +49 (2 01) 99 87 69) and pays by VISA (card number: 4524 3643 6534 7768, expiry date: July of next year). The hotel clerk takes the booking using the table showing the Regency Hotel's charges.

Act / Write out the telephone dialogue between Patricia, the switchboard operator and the hotel clerk.

Booking Several Rooms on the Phone

Patricia Marcks works for Designer Mode in Essen. Today she phones the Regency Hotel in London to book rooms for the managing director and his wife, Herr and Frau Feldlager, (double room), two directors, Herr Brandt and Frau Bergmann, and a trainee, Herr Schleier (3 single rooms). They want to be in London from 20 to 24 of next month (4 nights) and they wish to book a conference room for three days. The directors want full board and en-suite rooms with a balcony and will be coming to the hotel by car (car park?). They also want to know how much the sauna is. The trainee will be given the cheapest room with breakfast only.

After being told the prices, Patricia gives her company's name, address, telephone and fax numbers (Designer Mode GmbH, Bahnhofstr. 110, 45128 Essen, Germany, tel. +49 (2 01) 99 87 68, fax +49 (2 01) 99 87 69) and pays by VISA (card number: 4524 3643 6534 7768, expiry date: July of next year). The hotel clerk takes the booking using the table showing the Regency Hotel's charges.

Act / Write out the telephone dialogue between Patricia, the switchboard operator and the hotel clerk.

Booking a Hotel Room in Writing

Look at the following e-mail.

e-mail

Mail to:	royal.park.hotel@hotlink.co.uk	**Cc:**	
Subject:	Single room 1–3 July	**Attachment:**	prices.doc

Dear Sir or Madam

We wish to book a single, en-suite room for the Managing Director of our company, Dr Hubertus. He will require bed and breakfast for 2 nights from 1 to 3 July ...

He will be arriving at approx. 4 pm by car and leaving after breakfast on 3 July ...

Please let us have your confirmation in writing including details of all charges.

Yours faithfully

Patricia Marcks

PA to the Managing Director

Now write an e-mail / fax / letter using the following information.

	Von	An
Name	Patricia Marcks	–
Position	Personal Assistant to the Managing Director	–
Firma	Designer Mode GmbH,	Royal Park Hotel
Anschrift	Bahnhofstr. 110, 45128 Essen, Germany	P.O. Box 48, Birmingham PA3 5UL, England
Fax	+49 (2 01) 99 87 69	+44 (1 21) 64 31 05
E-Mail	designer.mode.gmbh@web.de	royal.park.hotel@hotlink.co.uk

Geschäftsfall:
Sie benötigen eine Hotelunterkunft für vier Ihrer Mitarbeiter/innen (*employees*).

Aufgabe:
Schreiben Sie eine Bestellung an das Royal Park Hotel unter Berücksichtigung folgender Einzelheiten:

- Buchen Sie 2 Einzel- und 1 Doppelzimmer mit Bad / Dusche und WC für die Zeit vom 5. bis 10. ... (Monat u. Jahr angeben) mit Halbpension
- Ihre Kollegen/innen werden voraussichtlich gegen 16.00 Uhr mit dem Auto eintreffen
- Bitten Sie um schriftliche Bestätigung der Buchung mit Angabe des Gesamtpreises

Invitations

8 **Listening**

Invitation to a Trade Fair

Listen to the following dialogue in which Melanie Giese at Allwetter Sport AG in Düsseldorf phones a customer to invite him to her company's stand at a trade fair. Write down the words missing in the text on a piece of your own paper. There is sometimes more than one word missing. (*SBO = switchboard operator*)

SBO: Hiking Ltd, good morning. Can I help you?
Melanie: Good morning, I'd like to 1. ____ John Hoskins in the Purchasing Department, please.
SBO: Certainly, madam. 2. ____ put you through.
– Music –
John: Purchasing Department.
Melanie: Good morning. Could I speak to Mr John Hoskins, please?
John: 3. ____.
Melanie: This is Melanie Giese from Allwetter Sport in Düsseldorf.
John: Hello, Melanie, how are you?
Melanie: Fine thanks, and you?
John: Fine. What can I do for you?
Melanie: The 4. ____ I'm calling is to invite you to our company's stand at the Camping Exhibition in Düsseldorf next month.
John: How kind of you! Just let me check my 5. ____.... What day would that be?
Melanie: Well, the exhibition's from the tenth to the thirteenth and we're 6. ____ a reception at our stand at 4 pm on the twelfth.
John: Now just let me see if I'm 7. ____ that day .... Yes, that'll be fine. I've got no other 8. ____ that afternoon.
Melanie: Good. We'll send you a 9. ____ ticket to the exhibition and directions to our stand in the next few days.
John: Thanks very much, Melanie. I'll look forward to 10. ____ you then.
Melanie: We're pleased you can come. Bye for now.
John: Goodbye and thanks for calling.

Specimen Letter

1.

Neustil Mode GmbH • Franzstr. 48 • 80802 München • Germany

JH/BK
20 July ..

Mr James Ladd
Commission Agent
49 Winchester Park
BRIGHTON
BN2 5JK
England

Dear Mr Ladd

<u>Quarterly Sales Meeting</u>

We would like to invite you to our quarterly sales meeting in Stuttgart at 2 pm on Tuesday 28 August ... Accommodation will be provided at:

Hotel Möwe
Turmstr. 44
71073 Stuttgart
Tel. +49 (7 11) 45 63 87
Fax +49 (7 11) 45 63 88
E-mail: hotel.moewe@t-online.de

The agenda for the meeting is enclosed.

We look forward to seeing you then.

Yours sincerely
Neustil Mode GmbH

Janine Hagemeister

Janine Hagemeister
Export Sales Department

Enc

Specimen Letter

2.

TR/TT
28 February ..

Ms Margaret Miller
Project Director
ShowStar International UK
25 Haymarket
LONDON
SW1 8HJ
England

Neulicht GmbH
Castroper Hellweg 40
44805 Bochum
Germany

Dear Ms Miller

Anniversary Celebration

On 15 June .. it will be our company's 10th anniversary and we take pleasure in inviting you to join us in celebrating this occasion at the Düsseldorf Hilton from 4pm to midnight that day.

Entertainment will be provided by Johnny Red's Big Band and a variety of other performers. Dieter-Thomas Beck will be our master of ceremonies.

Please fax, phone, e-mail or write to us using the enclosed reply card by 31 March .. to let us know whether you will be able to attend.

We look forward to seeing you on 15 June.

Yours sincerely
Neulicht GmbH

Tanja Ronstedt

Tanja Ronstedt
Public Relations Officer

Enc

Standard Expressions

1	I'd like to I would very much like to I am writing to I'm phoning to The reason I'm calling is to	invite you to visit	our stand at our company's stand at	the Do-It-Yourself Exhibition the Office and Technology Fair	in … (location, e.g. Essen)	from … (date) – … (date)
		invite you to invite you and … (name(s), e.g. your wife/husband/colleague(s), Mr/Ms/Miss/Mrs …) to ask if you will be able to come to		my/our Mr/Ms/Miss/Mrs Rademacher's our company's this year's	… (event, e.g. 10th anniversary celebration, birthday party, farewell party, Christmas Party, New Year's Party)	
		invite you to attend ask if you will be able to attend		the next next week's/month's	sales meeting sales conference	
	On … (date)	it will be … (event, e.g. our Managing Director's 60 birthday) we will be celebrating … (event, e.g. our Managing Director's 60th birthday/our company's 25th anniversary)			and we take pleasure in inviting you to join us in celebrating this occasion	
	… at … (address, e.g. Hotel Ambassador) in … (location, e.g. Tübingen) at … (time)/from … (time) – … (time) on … (date)				The address (of the hotel/trade fair site) is as follows:	

2	A(n)/Two/Three etc.	ticket(s) entrance ticket(s) complimentary ticket(s)	(and) directions to our stand (and) a site plan (and) a plan of the area	is/are enclosed will be sent to you shortly	for your convenience
	We'll send you We will be sending you You will be receiving	the agenda of the meeting and directions to our company's premises all the necessary documentation			shortly in the next few days
		a(n)/two/three	ticket(s) entrance ticket(s) complimentary ticket(s)	(and) directions to our stand (and) a site plan (and) a plan of the area	
	We'll send you You will be sent	a complimentary ticket	as soon as you confirm that you will be able to attend		
	I/We (also) enclose directions to I/We will (also) be sending you directions to	… (location, e.g. the concert hall) the hotel our company's premises the exhibition site the trade fair site		(together with) the agenda of the meeting	for your convenience

3	Accommodation will be provided Accommodation has been arranged for you We have arranged accommodation for you	at … (name of hotel, guest-house, e.g. Hotel Möwe)	from … (date) – … (date)	The address of the hotel/guest-house is as follows:

4	Please let us know whether you will be able to come/attend Please let us know if you are unable to come/attend We look forward to receiving your confirmation				
	Please return Please fax, phone, e-mail or write to us using	the enclosed reply	card slip	to let us know	that you can come that you will be able to attend whether you will be able to attend whether you will be able to come or not
				to confirm that you will be attending the meeting/conference	
5	I We	hope to see you look forward to seeing you hope you will be able to join us very much hope you will be able to come very much hope that we will be able to welcome you as one of our guests			then on … (date) there
6	Enc(s) *(If a letter is sent.)*				

Practice

1.

Name	Own name	Ms Samantha Wallis
Position	Head of Sales	Sales Manager
Firm	Kulturkontor GmbH	Culture UK Ltd
Address	Keplerstr. 22, 72074 Tübingen, Germany	45 Regency Square, Brighton BN2 6HZ, England
Tel.	+49 (70 71) 47 62 44	+44 (12 73) 44 38 99
Fax	+49 (70 71) 47 62 45	+44 (12 73) 44 38 00
E-mail	kultur.kontor@t-online.de	culture.uk@bt.co.uk

Background:
You work for Kulturkontor GmbH in Tübingen. Your company is planning a sales conference for all its European agents on the 20th of next month at Hotel Ambassador in Tübingen (Hügelstr. 5, 72072 Tübingen, tel. +49 (70 71) 35 46 77, fax +49 (70 71) 35 46 78, e-mail: hotel.ambassador@hotelnet.de). The meeting will be from 10 am – 6 pm.

Activity:
Contact your English agent, Ms Samantha Wallis, and invite her to come to the conference. Write a letter / fax / e-mail or act out a telephone dialogue with her to include the following details:

- the reason for the invitation
- the location
- the time
- the date
- you enclose / promise to send directions to Hotel Ambassador and an agenda of the meeting
- you have arranged accommodation there from 19 to 21 … (month)
- you ask Samantha to confirm that she can come (fax / phone / e-mail / reply slip)
- polite ending

2.

	From	To
Name	Own name	Mr Howard Johnston
Position	European Sales Director	Head Buyer
Firm	Top Style Damenmoden GmbH	GoGo Fashion Ltd
Address	Chemnitzer Str. 99, 04289 Leipzig, Germany	45 Commercial Road, Newcastle NE4 6HH, England
Tel.	+49 (3 41) 89 84 53	+44 (17 82) 55 48 80
Fax	+49 (3 41) 89 84 56	+44 (17 82) 55 48 81
E-mail	top.style.gmbh@linkall.de	gogo.fashion.ltd@firmweb.co.uk

Background:
Your company markets ladies' fashionwear and will be exhibiting its goods at the Mode Messe Leipzig (*Leipzig Fashion Fair*) from 12 to 14 February next year.

Activity:
Contact Mr Howard Johnston, the Head Buyer at GoGo Fashion Ltd, and invite him to visit your stand at the trade fair. Write a letter / fax / e-mail or act out a telephone dialogue with him to include the following details:

- the reason for the invitation
- the date of the Leipzig Fashion Fair
- the address of the Leipzig Trade Fair site (Leipziger Messe GmbH, Messe-Allee 1, 04007 Leipzig, tel. +49 (3 41) 67 80, fax +49 (3 41) 6 78 87 62, E-Mail: info@leipziger-messe.de)
- you enclose / promise to send a complimentary ticket and directions to your company's stand
- polite ending

Visitors to the Company

9 **Listening**

Dialogue 1

Listen to the following dialogue in which Sarah Kampmann goes to Reception to welcome a visitor to her company. Write down the words missing in the text on a piece of your own paper. There is sometimes more than one word missing.

Sarah: Hello, Mr Green. Sorry to 1. ___ you waiting.
Tony: That's all right.
Sarah: My name's Kampmann, Sarah Kampmann. I'm in Customer Services.
Tony: 2. ___ to meet you, Miss Kampmann. Tony Green's the name. You can call me Tony.
Sarah: Pleased to meet you, Tony. 3. ___ go up to my office, shall we?
– A few moments later –
Sarah: Can I take your coat and umbrella for you, Tony?
Tony: Oh yes, thanks. 4. ___.
Sarah: Would you like to take a seat?
Tony: Thanks.
Sarah: Can I 5. ___ you something to drink – a cup of tea or coffee, perhaps?
Tony: Oh, yes please. I'd like a cup of coffee, please.
Sarah: Milk and sugar?
Tony: Black with two 6. ___ of sugar, please.
Sarah: Here you are.
Tony: Thanks.
Sarah: Would you like a biscuit or a piece of cake, perhaps?
Tony: No, thanks. I had a snack on the plane.
Sarah: What was your flight 7. ___?
Tony: Well, it was quite 8. ___, actually. We went through a bit of 9. ___.
Sarah: Oh, I see. Do you feel all right?
Tony: I'm fine, thanks. It was just a short flight from London to Düsseldorf so I didn't have much time to get ill.
Sarah: Good. Will you have time to do 10. ___ sight-seeing while you're here?
Tony: Well, I've got tomorrow afternoon free, actually. Is there 11. ___ interesting to see around here?
Sarah: There's a lot to do here, actually. We've got some good museums and there's a new 12. ___ of paintings at the art gallery just near your hotel.
Tony: Yes, …
Sarah: We also have a beautiful lake just a few miles away. You could 13. ___ on a boat trip around the lake.
Tony: 14. ___ entertainment?
Sarah: Do you like musicals?
Tony: Oh, yes. That sounds like a good idea for the evening.

Sarah: If you're interested there's a ticket agency just next to the railway station. I'm sure you'd be able to get a ticket for this evening, especially if there's a 15. ______.

Tony: Isn't there a theme park somewhere near here?

Sarah: Oh, yes, I was forgetting. There's a big new one which has just opened. You can go there by 16. ______ from the main railway station.

Tony: That sounds like a good idea for the afternoon. How do I get to the station from here?

Sarah: It's about ten minutes on foot through the 17. ______. You leave this building, turn right, take the second street on the left and it's straight ahead.

Tony: Right, I'll go there after I've talked to Dr Haverkamp.

Sarah: I've got your 18. ______ for tomorrow here. Shall we go through it point by point?

Tony: Yes, please.

Sarah: Your first appointment's tomorrow morning at 9 am. 19. ______ a working breakfast with Dr Haverkamp. After that you're visiting the factory just outside town and then you're having lunch there with Frank Theimann, the Production Manager. Is there anything else you'd like to know about the 20. ______?

Tony: Yes, I do have a question. How long will the visit to the factory last?

Sarah: About two hours, I expect. Oh, look. Here's Dr Haverkamp.

Haverkamp: Hello, Tony! It's nice to see you again.

Tony: Hello, Heribert ...

10 **Dialogue 2**

Listen to the following dialogue in which Sarah Kampmann is sitting in her office when an English visitor arrives to see her boss.

Write down the missing words on a piece of your own paper as you listen. There is sometimes more than one word missing.

Sarah: Herein!

Paul: 1. ___ me, miss. Do you speak English?

Sarah: Yes, can I help you?

Paul: Oh, thank goodness for that! Is this Dr Haverkamp's 2. ___?

Sarah: Yes, that's right. I'm his secretary. What 3. ___?

Paul: I've got an 4. ___ to see Dr Haverkamp at 10 o'clock but I'm a little early. Should I come back later?

Sarah: No, you don't need to do that. Please 5. ___. Could I just have your name please, sir?

Paul: Yes, it's Jones, Paul Jones. Here's my 6. ___.

Sarah: Thanks. Now can I take your 7. ___ and 8. ___ for you?

Paul: Oh, yes, thanks. 9. ___.

Sarah: Would you like to take a 10. ___?

Paul: Thanks.

Sarah: Can I 11. ___ you something to drink – a cup of tea or coffee, perhaps while you're waiting?

Paul: Oh, yes, please. I'd like a white coffee with two 12. ___ of sugar, please.

Sarah: Here you are.

Paul: Thank you.

Sarah: Did you have a good 13. ___?

Paul: Yes, it was fine and it took no time at all.

Sarah: Will you have time to do any 14. ___ while you're here?

Paul: Well, I've got tomorrow evening free. What would you 15. ___?

Sarah: There's a 16. ___ tomorrow evening, actually. I think it's Mozart.

Paul: That sounds good.

Sarah: In that case 17. ___ if I can get you a ticket.

Paul: That's very 18. ___ of you. How do I get to the concert hall?

Sarah: You can walk there. It's about 10 minutes away on foot.

Paul: Oh, good.

Sarah: It's in the "Saalbau". As you leave this building turn right and walk 19. ___ for about half a mile. You'll see it on your left. You can't 20. ___ it. Oh, look. Here's Dr Haverkamp ...

Standard Expressions

1 Greeting the visitor	Hello Good morning/afternoon/evening		Mr Mrs Miss Ms	Green
	Sorry to keep you waiting I hope I didn't keep you waiting (too long)			
3 Introductions	My name's I'm	Silke (Frank) Reimann		
	I'm	in Customer Services in the Sales Department in Accounts in charge of Exports the Export Sales Manager Dr Haverkamp's PA (*personal assistant*)		
5a Making the visitor feel at home	Would you just like to come this way? Would you like to follow me to my/Dr Haverkamp's office? Let's go up/through to my office, shall we?			
5b	Can I take your	hat coat umbrella	for you?	
5c	Would you like to take a seat?			
5d	Can I offer you	some light refreshment? something to drink – a cup of tea or coffee, perhaps? something to eat – a biscuit or a piece of cake, perhaps?		
	Would you like some (whipped) cream on your cake?			
7a Making small-talk – the trip	Did you have a good trip?			
7c	What was the flight like?			
7d	What was the train journey like?			
7e	Did you drive here?			
	What was the drive over like? What were the roads like?			

2	Hello Good morning/afternoon/evening			
	That's all right I haven't been waiting very long			
4a	Pleased to meet you	My name's	Tony Green Green, Tony Green. You can call me Tony	
4b	I'm our company's I'm … 's (name of company, e.g. HiTech's)		agent representative	for Germany for this part of Germany
6a	Yes, certainly			
6b	Oh yes, thanks. Here you are			
6c	Thanks			
6d	Oh yes, please	I'd like	a white/black coffee, a cup of tea with milk and two lumps of sugar, a biscuit, a piece of cake,	please
6f	No, thanks	I've just had something to drink I've just eaten I had a meal/a snack on the plane		
6g	Oh, yes please No, thank you. I'd prefer it without			
8a	Yes, it was fine Yes, it took no time at all			
8b	No, I didn't actually No, there was a bit of a problem	I was delayed at London Airport/at the ferry terminal I got stuck in a traffic jam in … (location, e.g. Brussels, Venlo) The French are on strike		
8c	It was fine/very good/very smooth. We landed (exactly) on time It was a bit bumpy/rough. We went through some turbulence (over the Channel)			
8d	It was fine. There were no delays. We got to … (location, e.g. Essen Main Railway station) on time/on schedule The train was late. We were delayed in … (location, e.g. Calais) I missed my connection in … (location, e.g. Cologne) There was no dining car			
8e	Yes, I did I rented a car … (location, at Düsseldorf Airport, at the ferry terminal in Rotterdam)			
	Not bad at all. The roads were clear all the way I got stuck in a traffic jam in … (location, e.g. Brussels, Venlo) My car broke down in … (location) There was an accident in … (location, e.g. Antwerp) so there was a 5-mile tail-back			

9 – sight-seeing	Will you have time to do any sight-seeing while you're here?				
10	There's a lot to do here				
	There's		an art gallery the … (name of painter, e. g. Picasso) Exhibition a museum a concert tonight/tomorrow etc. a lake a football match. The local team's playing … (team)		
	Do you like		boat trips? musicals? shows? theme parks? guided tours?		
12	In that case		I'll try to get you some information on that I'll see if I can get you a ticket		
14 Giving directions	You can walk there. It's about ten minutes away on foot It's just a few minutes from here As you leave this building, turn left and walk straight ahead for about half a mile. You'll see it on your right. You can't miss it				
	You can go there by		tram bus train	from your hotel from the main railway station from just outside this building	
	You could always get a taxi				
15 Discussing the visitor's schedule	I've got	your schedule for the arrangements for		today tomorrow this afternoon the week	here
	Shall we just go through it, point by point?				
	Your first appointment's		(this afternoon) at 3 pm (tomorrow morning) at 9 am (tomorrow afternoon) at 2 pm		then … next … after that …
	… you're	meeting Dr Havekamp at … (time, e. g. 10 am) seeing the Sales Manager at … having lunch at … going to a board meeting at … going to a presentation at … visiting the factory/plant/warehouse in … (location) at … (time)			
16 Questions about the arrangements	Is there anything else you'd like to know about the arrangements? Do you have any questions about your schedule? Would you like us to change the arrangements for you? Is there anything we've forgotten? Is everything fine with your accommodation?				

9 a	No, I'm afraid I won't. I've got a very full schedule	
9 b	Yes, I've got	some free time a few hours this afternoon / evening tomorrow free tomorrow morning / afternoon / evening free
	Is there anything interesting to see around here? What would you recommend?	
11 a	Oh, good Oh, marvellous	
11 b	Oh, I see That sounds good	How about ... (example of leisure activity, e. g. entertainment)? Is there anything else to do? Isn't there a / an ... (example of leisure activity, e. g. a theme park) around here?
11 c	Yes, that sounds like a good idea No, not particularly	
13	That's very kind of you	How do I get there?
	Oh, I see Oh, good	
16	Oh, good Thanks	
	Yes, please	
	Right, I've got that	
17	No thanks. That's fine Yes, I do have a question. Could you tell me ... (e. g. when the meeting will be over)? Will I have enough time to ... (e. g. meet the Marketing Director)? Would it be possible to ... (get me a different room at the hotel)?	

Practice

Role-plays

1.

You work for Orange Strom GmbH. When Philip(pa) Prentice from NetPower Ltd in England arrives at your company, you go downstairs to Reception to meet him / her. You then go up to your office and talk to him / her for a few minutes before your boss, Frau Feuerstein, arrives.

Using the table of standard expressions and the background information, act out the following role-play with your visitor.

Background Information:

1. Philip(pa) Prentice likes black coffee with four lumps of sugar and Black Forest cherry cake with whipped cream.
2. He / She came over to Germany by car and is late because of an accident in Brussels (10-mile tail-back).
3. He / She will have a free afternoon and evening tomorrow and would like to go to a show (musical?) and on a guided tour of the area. He / She also likes art.
4. You tell him / her that there is a Tourist Information Office at the main railway station and explain that it is ten minutes away on foot, so he / she can walk there.
5. You tell him / her the schedule for tomorrow.

Tomorrow's Schedule:

9 am	*Frau Feuerstein*
10 am	*Board meeting*
11 am	*Presentation of new technology*
1 pm	*Lunch with the Managing Director, Dr Hubertus*
Afternoon	*Free*

6. He / She finally asks how long the presentation of new technology will be tomorrow (two hours).
7. Frau Feuerstein arrives.

2.

You work for Megaware Handelsgesellschaft mbH. When Humphrey Pritchard from Stafford Tableware Ltd in England arrives at your company, you go downstairs to Reception to meet him. You then go up to your office and talk to him for a few minutes before your boss, Frau Schneider, arrives.

Using the table of standard expressions and the background information, act out the following role-play with your visitor.

Background Information:

1. Humphrey Pritchard would like tea with milk and no sugar and a biscuit.
2. He flew to Germany from Birmingham. They went through some turbulence over the Channel but landed at the airport in Germany on time.
3. He will have a free afternoon tomorrow and would like to go to a museum or an art gallery.
4. You tell him there's an art exhibition at a gallery near the town / city centre. You explain he can get there easily by public transport (tram / underground / bus) from his hotel.
5. You tell him his schedule for tomorrow.

Tomorrow's Schedule:

8.30 am	*Working breakfast with Frau Schneider*
10 am	*Visit to Megaware's warehouse*
12.30 pm	*Lunch with Dr Joster, the Managing Director*
Afternoon	*Free*

6. Humphrey asks you how long the visit to the warehouse will take (two hours).
7. Frau Schneider arrives.

Vocabulary List

Telephoning

access, to ~	*hier: die Datei suchen*
certainly	*natürlich, selbstverständlich*
department	*Abteilung*
direct line	*Durchwahl*
expression	*Ausdruck*
introduce yourself	*sich vorstellen*
marvellous	*wunderbar*
pocket calculator	*Taschenrechner*
polite	*höflich*
put through	*durchstellen*
switchboard operator	*Telefonist/in*

Making Appointments

agree	*einverstanden sein*
appointment	*Termin*
arrange an appointment	*einen Termin vereinbaren*
available, to be ~	*zur Verfügung stehen*
busy	*beschäftigt*
check	*kontrollieren*
convenient, to be ~	*passen*
diary	*Kalender*
engagement	*Verpflichtung*
exactly	*genau*
extension (telephone)	*Nebenstelle*
finally	*schließlich*
how about ...?	*wie wär's mit ...?*
note, make a ~ of	*sich notieren*
suggest	*vorschlagen*
tied up	*beschäftigt*
trade fair	*Messe*
warehouse	*Lager*
what about ...?	*wie wär's mit ...?*
working breakfast	*Arbeitsfrühstück*

Travel Arrangements

adult	*Erwachsene/r*
available	*hier: frei*
booked up	*(restlos) ausgebucht*
change, to ~	*hier: umsteigen*
collect	*hier: abholen*
destination	*Reiseziel*
duration	*Dauer*
enquire about	*sich erkundigen nach*
expire	*ablaufen*
expiry (AE: expiration)	*Ablauf*
first thing in the morning	*frühmorgens*
flight	*Flug*
if I were you	*an Ihrer Stelle*
I'm afraid	*hier: leider*
in cash	*in bar*
incorporated	*hier: AG*
length	*hier: Dauer*
location	*Ort*
major	*hier: bekannt*
need, you don't ~ to	*Sie brauchen nicht*
pick up	*abholen*
prefer	*bevorzugen*
return flight	*Rückflug*
return ticket	*Rückfahrkarte*
sign, to ~	*unterschreiben*
ticket office	*Fahrkartenschalter*
timetable	*Fahrplan*
travel agent	*hier: Reisebüro*

Room Reservations

adult	*Erwachsene/r*
approx.	*ca.*
available	*verfügbar*
basic charge	*Grundpreis*
cancellation	*Stornierung*
charge, to ~ for	*berechnen*
charges	*Gebühren*
confirmation	*Bestätigung*
deposit, a ~	*Anzahlung*
double bed	*Doppelbett*
doubtful	*hier: unsicher*
en-suite	*(Zimmer) mit Bad (Hotel)*
expiry (AE: expiration) date	*Ablaufdatum*
facilities	*Einrichtungen*
firm (booking)	*hier: fest(e Buchung)*
full board	*Vollpension*
gym (gymnasium)	*hier: Fitnessraum*
half board	*Halbpension*
I'm afraid	*hier: leider*
jacuzzi	*Whirlpool*
licensed	*hier: hat das Recht, alkoholische Getränke zu verkaufen*
location	*Ort*
managing director	*Geschäftsführer/in*
mention, to ~	*erwähnen*

noisy	*laut*
PA (personal assistant)	*hier: Chefsekretär/in*
public baths	*öffentliche Badeanstalt*
quiet	*ruhig*
require	*benötigen*
separately	*getrennt*
single room	*Einzelzimmer*
size	*Größe*
spell (spelt, spelt)	*buchstabieren*
switchboard operator	*Telefonist/in*
that shouldn't be any trouble	*das dürfte kein Problem sein*
trainee	*Auszubildende/r*
twin beds	*Zweibettzimmer (getrennte Betten)*
vacancy	*hier: freies Zimmer*

Invitations

accommodation	*Unterkunft*
agenda	*Tagesordnung*
anniversary celebration	*Jubiläumsfeier*
commission agent	*Kommissionär/in*
complimentary ticket	*Freikarte*
convenience, for your ~	*zum gefälligen Gebrauch*
directions	*hier: Wegbeschreibung*
entrance ticket	*Eintrittskarte*
exhibition	*Ausstellung*
farewell party	*Abschiedsfeier*
husband	*Ehemann, Gatte*
invitation	*Einladung*
join, to ~	*hier: Gesellschaft leisten*
master of ceremonies	*Zeremonienmeister/in, Gastgeber/in*
necessary	*erforderlich*
occasion	*Anlass*
performer	*Künstler/in*
premises	*Geschäftsräume*
provide	*zur Verfügung stellen*
purchasing department	*Einkaufsabteilung*
quarter	*hier: Quartal*
reply card	*Rückantwortkarte*
reply slip	*Rückantwortschein*
trade fair	*(Handels)messe*
trade fair site	*Messegelände*

Visitors to the Company

accident	*Unfall*
accommodation	*Unterkunft*
Accounts	*Buchhaltungsabteilung*
actually	*eigentlich*
appointment	*Termin*
arrangements	*hier: Programm*
art gallery	*Kunstgalerie*
biscuit	*Keks*
board meeting	*Vorstandssitzung*
break down	*eine Panne haben*
bumpy	*hier: unruhig, turbulent*
Channel	*Ärmelkanal*
charge, to be in ~ of	*zuständig sein für*
connection	*Anschluss*
delayed	*aufgehalten, verspätet*
dining car	*Speisewagen*
factory	*Fabrik*
ferry terminal	*Fährhafen*
guided tour	*Führung*
kind	*nett, freundlich*
lake	*See*
lump of sugar	*Zuckerwürfel*
painting	*Bild, Gemälde*
particularly, not ~	*nicht besonders*
pedestrian precinct	*Fußgängerzone*
recommend	*empfehlen*
refreshment	*Erfrischung*
rent, to ~	*mieten*
representative	*Vertreter/in*
rough	*hier: unruhig, turbulent*
Sales Department	*Verkaufsabteilung*
schedule	*Programm*
schedule, on ~	*pünktlich*
smooth	*hier: ruhig*
straight ahead	*geradeaus*
stuck, to get ~	*steckenbleiben*
tail-back	*Stau*
theme park	*Themenpark, Freizeitpark*
ticket agency	*Vorverkaufsstelle*
Tourist Information Office	*Fremdenverkehrsbüro*
traffic jam	*Verkehrsstau*
tram	*Straßenbahn*
umbrella	*Regenschirm*
warehouse	*Lager*
whipped cream	*Schlagsahne*

Appendix

- Vocabulary List A–Z
- Documents

Vocabulary List A–Z

30 days net	*30 Tage netto*	Unit 3
90-day sight draft	*90-Tage-Sichttratte*	Unit 6

A

a/c (account)	*Konto*	Unit 4
able, to be ~ to	*können*	Units 1, 6, 7, 8
above-mentioned	*oben erwähnt*	Units 1, 6, 8
abroad, at home and ~	*im In- und Ausland*	Unit 3
accept	*akzeptieren*	Unit 6
acceptance	*hier: Akzept*	Unit 7
accident	*Unfall*	Unit 8
account, an ~	*Konto*	Unit 5
account, open ~ terms	*offenes Zahlungsziel*	Unit 3
acknowledge	*zur Kenntnis nehmen*	Unit 8
acknowledgement	*Auftragsbestätigung*	Unit 5
acknowledgement of order	*Auftragsbestätigung*	Unit 4
action, to take ~	*Maßnahmen ergreifen, Schritte unternehmen*	Unit 8
ad (advertisement)	*Anzeige; Reklame*	Unit 2
add	*hinzufügen*	Units 1, 2, 3, 4, 7
addressed, to be ~ (person)	*angeschrieben bzw. angesprochen werden*	Unit 1
advance, in ~	*im Voraus*	Unit 3
advertisement	*Anzeige*	Units 1, 2, 4
advice of despatch	*Versandanzeige*	Units 4, 5, 6
advise	*hier: informieren*	Unit 7
after receipt of our order	*nach Erhalt unseres Auftrags*	Unit 2
agree	*hier: vereinbaren*	Unit 8
agreed, as ~	*wie vereinbart*	Units 4, 5, 6, 7
air conditioning	*Klimaanlage*	Unit 1
air conditioning unit	*Klimaanlage*	Unit 4
AIR MAIL	*Mit Luftpost*	Unit 1
air, by ~	*auf dem Luftweg*	Unit 5
airline	*Fluggesellschaft*	Unit 8
airport	*Flughafen*	Unit 6
all-figure date, an ~	*ein Datum, das nur aus Zahlen besteht*	Unit 1
amount	*Betrag*	Unit 6
apart from	*außer*	Unit 1
apologies, please accept our ~	*wir bitten um Entschuldigung*	Unit 8
apologise	*sich entschuldigen*	Unit 8
apply, to ~ for	*sich bewerben um / auf*	Unit 1
appreciate	*schätzen; dankbar sein für*	Unit 2
appreciate	*hier: verstehen, Verständnis haben*	Unit 8
appropriate, as ~	*wie geeignet, wie passend*	Units 2, 3, 4, 7, 8
approval, find your ~	*Ihre Zustimmung finden*	Unit 8
approx. (approximate[ly])	*ca. (circa), ungefähr*	Units 3, 4, 5, 6
arrange	*hier: bestellen, organisieren*	Unit 1
arrow	*Pfeil*	Unit 8
as	*da*	Unit 2
as per	*gemäß*	Unit 6
as stated	*wie angegeben*	Unit 1

as well as	*sowie*	Unit 3
at the latest	*spätestens*	Unit 8
attached	*beigefügt*	Unit 7
attachment	*Anlage*	Unit 1
attachment, file ~	*Anlage (Datei)*	Unit 3
attend to	*sich kümmern um*	Unit 8
attention	*hier: Erledigung*	Unit 4
attention, for the ~ of	*zu Händen*	Unit 1
available	*erhältlich*	Units 2, 3
avoid	*vermeiden*	Unit 1

B

backpack	*Rucksack*	Unit 4
balance in your favour	*hier: Schuldsaldo*	Unit 7
bank reference	*Bankauskunft*	Unit 3
basis, on the ~ of	*auf der Grundlage von*	Unit 4
bear (risks)	*tragen (Risiko)*	Unit 3
believe	*glauben*	Unit 8
below	*hier: darunter*	Unit 1
bent	*krumm, verbogen*	Unit 8
beyond	*darüber hinaus*	Unit 2
beyond our control	*außerhalb unserer Macht / unseres Einflussbereichs*	Unit 8
bill of exchange	*Wechsel*	Units 6, 7
body of the letter	*Brieftext*	Unit 1
bold type, in ~	*fettgedruckt*	Unit 1
bowl	*Schüssel*	Unit 7
brackets, in ~	*in Klammern*	Unit 1
brass instruments	*Blechblasinstrumente*	Unit 6
break down	*eine Panne haben*	Unit 8
brief	*kurz*	Unit 7
brochure	*Prospekt, Broschüre*	Units 1, 3, 7
broken	*kaputt*	Unit 8
business, family ~	*Familienbetrieb*	Unit 3
business administration clerk	*Industriekaufmann/-frau*	Unit 1
business administration theory	*Betriebswirtschaftslehre*	Unit 1
business park	*Gewerbegebiet*	Unit 7
business, do further ~	*weitere Geschäfte tätigen*	Unit 8
business, to do ~	*Geschäfte tätigen / machen*	Units 3, 6
buyer	*Käufer/in*	Units 6, 7, 8
by (a certain date), e.g. by 30 June	*bis (zu einem bestimmten Termin), z. B. bis 30. Juni*	Units 3, 8
by return	*postwendend, umgehend*	Unit 8
by separate post	*mit getrennter Post*	Unit 3
by, ~ the end of the month	*bis Ende des Monats*	Units 1, 6

C

cancel	*stornieren*	Unit 8
capitalised	*in Großbuchstaben geschrieben*	Unit 1
capitals, in ~	*in Großbuchstaben*	Unit 1
carbon copy	*hier: Verteilervermerk (wörtlich: Durchschlag)*	Unit 1
carriage	*Transport- , Fracht(kosten)*	Unit 3
carrier	*Frachtführer*	Unit 3
case, a ~	*(Latten)Kiste*	Unit 6

case, in the ~ of	*im Falle*	Unit 1
cash discount	*Skonto, Barzahlungsrabatt*	Unit 4
cash with order (CWO)	*Barzahlung bei Auftragserteilung*	Unit 3
catalogue (AE: catalog)	*Katalog*	Unit 3
catering	*Gastronomie, Restauration*	Unit 6
cause, to ~	*verursachen*	Unit 8
certain	*sicher; bestimmt*	Unit 8
chamber of commerce	*Handelskammer*	Units 2, 3
charge, at no extra ~	*ohne zusätzliche Kosten*	Unit 8
check against	*hier: vergleichen mit*	Unit 7
check, to ~	*kontrollieren*	Unit 7
checking, on ~ them	*als wir sie kontrollierten*	Unit 8
chief executive officer	*Vorstandsvorsitzende/r, Generaldirektor/in, Hauptgeschäftsleiter/in*	Unit 1
chocolates	*Pralinen*	Unit 4
choice, to have no ~ but to …	*keine andere Wahl haben, als …*	Unit 8
CIF (cost, insurance, freight)	*Kosten, Versicherung, Fracht*	Units 5, 6
CIP (carriage and insurance paid)	*frachtfrei versichert*	Unit 6
clean	*rein*	Unit 6
clearly	*deutlich*	Unit 1
clothes	*Kleider, Kleidung*	Unit 3
collect	*abholen*	Unit 6
collection, ready for ~	*abholbereit*	Unit 7
colon	*Doppelpunkt*	Unit 1
column	*Spalte*	Unit 4
comments, your ~	*Ihre Stellungnahme*	Unit 8
commercial directory	*Handelsadressbuch*	Unit 2
common	*häufig, weitverbreitet; üblich*	Units 1, 2, 8
complain	*sich beschweren*	Unit 8
complaint	*Beschwerde, Reklamation*	Unit 8
complete, to ~ (form)	*ausfüllen (Formular)*	Unit 1
complimentary close	*Schlussformel*	Unit 1
comprehensive	*umfassend*	Unit 2
computer power unit	*Netzteil*	Unit 4
concerned, of all parties ~	*aller Beteiligten*	Unit 8
condition, in good ~	*in gutem Zustand, wohlbehalten*	Units 1, 4, 6
condition, in perfect ~	*einwandfrei, in perfektem Zustand*	Unit 8
confectionery	*Süßigkeiten*	Units 3, 4
CONFIDENTIAL	*vertraulich*	Unit 1
confirm	*bestätigen*	Units 4, 7
confirmation	*Bestätigung*	Unit 5
confirmation of order	*Auftragsbestätigung*	Unit 4
confirmed	*bestätigt*	Unit 3
consequence(s)	*Folge(n), Konsequenz(en)*	Unit 8
considerable	*beträchtlich*	Unit 8
consignment	*Lieferung*	Units 4, 6, 7
consulate	*Konsulat*	Unit 2
contain	*beinhalten*	Unit 1
contents, the ~	*Inhalt*	Unit 1
Continuation Page(s)	*Folgeseite(n)*	Unit 1
contract of carriage	*Beweisurkunde für den Frachtvertrag*	Unit 6

convenience, at your earliest ~	*so bald wie möglich*	Unit 1
convince	*überzeugen*	Unit 3
Cordially	*Herzliche Grüße*	Unit 1
correspond to	*entsprechen*	Units 2, 7
correspondent bank	*Korrespondenzbank*	Unit 6
crash, to ~	*verunglücken, abstürzen*	Unit 8
crate, a ~	*(Latten)Kiste; Verschlag*	Units 4, 5, 6
crockery	*Geschirr*	Unit 7
crooked	*hier: nicht gerade*	Unit 8
cross-Channel ferry	*Kanalfähre*	Units 5, 6
crystal glass items	*Kristallwaren*	Unit 6
current	*aktuell*	Units 2, 3, 4
currently	*gegenwärtig*	Unit 1
custody	*Obhut*	Unit 3
CV	*Lebenslauf*	Unit 1
CWO (cash with order)	*Barzahlung bei Auftragserteilung*	Unit 5
cycle	*Fahrrad*	Unit 8

D

damage, the ~	*(hier) Schaden*	Unit 8
damaged	*beschädigt*	Unit 8
date of delivery	*Liefertermin*	Units 4, 5
deadline	*(letzte) Frist*	Unit 8
deadline, to meet a ~	*eine Frist einhalten*	Unit 8
deal with	*sich befassen mit; fertig werden mit*	Unit 8
decide	*entscheiden*	Unit 2
decontamination unit	*Dekontaminierungs-, Entgiftungsanlage*	Unit 6
deduct	*abziehen*	Unit 7
delay in delivery	*Lieferverzug*	Unit 8
delay, the ~	*Verzögerung*	Units 1, 5
delighted, we were ~	*wir haben uns gefreut*	Units 3, 5
delivery	*Lieferung*	Units 3, 5
delivery date / period	*Liefertermin, - zeit*	Unit 2
delivery, for ~ ...	*zur Lieferung ...*	Unit 6
delivery, to take ~ of	*in Empfang nehmen*	Unit 8
demand for	*Nachfrage nach*	Unit 3
demonstrate	*vorführen*	Unit 2
departure date	*Abfahrtszeit*	Unit 6
describe	*beschreiben*	Unit 2
description	*Beschreibung*	Units 3, 4
desk	*Schreibtisch*	Unit 8
despatch, the ~	*Versand*	Unit 6
despatch section	*Versandabteilung*	Unit 1
despatch, ready for	*versandbereit*	Units 6, 7
despatch, to ~	*versenden*	Units 6, 7
destination, port of ~	*Bestimmungshafen*	Unit 6
different	*verschieden*	Unit 1
dirty	*schmutzig, verschmutzt*	Unit 8
discount	*Rabatt, Nachlass*	Units 2, 3, 4, 5
discount, cash ~	*Nachlass für Barzahlung*	Unit 7
discount, early payment ~	*Nachlass für sofortige Bezahlung*	Unit 7
discover	*entdecken*	Unit 8
dismayed	*bestürzt, entsetzt*	Unit 8

dissatisfied	*unzufrieden*	Unit 8
distribute	*vertreiben*	Unit 2
distributor	*Vertriebsfirma*	Unit 2
division	*Abteilung*	Unit 1
dock, to ~	*anlegen*	Unit 6
document of title	*Warenwertpapier, Eigentumsurkunde*	Unit 6
documentary credit	*Dokumentenakkreditiv*	Unit 6
draft, a ~	*Tratte*	Units 6, 7
due date, on the ~	*bei Fälligkeit*	Unit 7
due to	*wegen*	Unit 8
due to leave (ship)	*auslaufen sollen (Schiff)*	Unit 6
duly	*ordnungsgemäß*	Unit 1

E

each	*je*	Unit 4
earthenware bowls	*Steingutschüsseln*	Unit 7
economical	*sparsam*	Unit 5
edition	*Ausgabe*	Units 2, 4
elsewhere, look ~ for their goods	*sich anderweitig eindecken*	Unit 8
e-mail subscriber	*E-Mail-Teilnehmer/in*	Unit 1
embassy	*Botschaft*	Unit 2
employ, to ~	*beschäftigen*	Unit 1
enclose	*beifügen*	Units 1, 5
enclosed	*beigefügt*	Unit 6
enclosure(s)	*Anlage(n)*	Units 3, 7
entitled, to be ~ to	*Anspruch haben auf*	Unit 7
entries, an entry	*Eintrag(ungen)*	Unit 1
envelope, window ~	*Fensterumschlag*	Unit 1
environmental convention	*Umwelttagung*	Unit 1
environmental technology consultant	*Berater/in für Umwelttechnik*	Unit 1
equipment	*Ausrüstung, Ausstattung; Geräte*	Units 1, 2, 4, 6
estimate, to ~	*schätzen*	Unit 6
estimated time of arrival (ETA)	*geschätzte Ankunftszeit*	Unit 6
EU	*Europäische Union*	Unit 2
European sales clerk	*Verkaufssachbearbeiter/in für den europäischen Markt*	Unit 1
European sales director	*Verkaufsleiter/in für Europa*	Unit 4
even though	*obwohl*	Unit 1
examine	*hier: prüfen*	Unit 4
except	*außer*	Unit 1
execute	*ausführen*	Unit 6
exercise cycle	*Heimtrainer*	Unit 5
exhibition	*Ausstellung*	Unit 2
expect	*rechnen mit (Waren); davon ausgehen; erwarten*	Units 6, 8
expensive	*teuer*	Unit 3
experience	*Erfahrung*	Unit 3
explanation	*Erklärung*	Unit 8
express, to ~	*zum Ausdruck bringen*	Unit 8
extensive	*ausgedehnt*	Unit 2
extra practice	*zusätzliche Übungen*	Unit 1

F

factory	*Fabrik*	Unit 8
factual	*sachlich*	Unit 8
famous	*berühmt*	Unit 3
fashions	*Mode*	Unit 2
fashionwear	*Modebekleidung*	Unit 3
fast-growing	*schnell wachsend*	Unit 2
faulty	*fehlerhaft*	Unit 8
favour, in your ~	*zu Ihren Gunsten*	Unit 7
favourable	*günstig*	Units 3, 7
ferry	*Fähre*	Unit 5
few, in the next ~ days	*in den nächsten Tagen*	Units 3, 4
few, too ~	*zu wenig*	Unit 8
file, a ~, a data ~	*Datei*	Units 1, 3, 7
firm (adjective)	*fest*	Units 1, 3
first-rate	*erstklassig*	Unit 3
flight	*Flug*	Unit 6
flush-left	*linksbündig*	Unit 1
FOB	*frei an Bord*	Unit 3
follows, as ~	*wie folgt*	Unit 4
for your information	*zu Ihrer Information*	Units 3, 7, 8
foreign trade	*Außenhandel*	Units 5, 6, 7
forward, to ~	*weiterleiten*	Unit 6
forwarding agent(s)	*Spediteur(e)*	Unit 6
franco	*hier: frei*	Unit 4
franco to our premises	*frei zu unseren Geschäftsräumen, frei Haus*	Units 2, 4
franco to your premises	*frei zu Ihren Geschäftsräumen*	Unit 5
freight forwarder	*Spediteur*	Unit 8
freight forwarding agency	*Spedition*	Unit 1
freight, sea ~	*Seefracht*	Unit 6
frequently	*häufig*	Unit 1
from stock	*ab Lager*	Unit 3
fruit juice	*Fruchtsaft*	Unit 8
furniture	*Möbel*	Units 2, 3, 8
further	*weitere(r, s)*	Units 2, 4, 5, 6, 7, 8
future, in the near ~	*bald, in Kürze*	Unit 3

G

grant, to ~	*gewähren*	Units 2, 3, 5, 7, 8
grateful	*dankbar*	Units 2, 4
growing	*wachsend*	Unit 2

H

hand over	*übergeben*	Unit 6
have to	*müssen*	Unit 8
head buyer	*Chefeinkäufer/in*	Unit 2
heading	*Überschrift*	Units 4, 5
heavy (demand)	*hier: erheblich(e Nachfrage)*	Unit 3
hereby	*hiermit*	Unit 5
hesitate	*zögern*	Units 5, 6, 7
hitch, a ~	*Panne*	Unit 1
hold, to ~ (a post)	*(eine Stelle) innehaben*	Unit 1
home draught beer unit	*Bierzapfanlage für zu Hause*	Unit 6

honour, to ~	*hier: einlösen*	Unit 7
human resources officer	*Personalleiter/in*	Unit 1

I

i. e.	*d. h.*	Unit 5
illustrated	*bebildert*	Units 2, 3
immediately	*sofort, umgehend*	Units 3, 5, 8
IMO (international money order)	*internationale Postanweisung*	Unit 4
important	*wichtig*	Units 1, 8
impossible	*unmöglich*	Unit 1
impress	*beeindrucken*	Unit 2
in addition	*darüber hinaus*	Unit 6
in advance	*im Voraus*	Unit 4
in demand	*begehrt; gefragt*	Unit 2
in the top right-hand corner	*hier: oben rechts*	Unit 1
in the very near future	*sehr bald*	Unit 8
include	*einschließen; mit angeben*	Units 2, 4
including	*einschließlich*	Unit 3
inconvenience	*Unannehmlichkeit*	Unit 8
indicate	*angeben*	Unit 2
initial order	*Erstauftrag*	Units 2, 3, 4
inside address	*Empfängeranschrift*	Unit 1
instead	*hier: dafür; statt*	Unit 5
instruct	*anweisen*	Units 6, 7
instructed, as ~	*gemäß Ihren Anweisungen*	Unit 6
instructions	*Anweisungen*	Units 4, 5
insurance	*Versicherung*	Units 3, 4
insurance company	*Versicherungsgesellschaft*	Unit 8
insure	*versichern*	Unit 6
interiors	*hier: Inneneinrichtung*	Unit 1
international access code	*internationale Vorwahlnummer (bei Auslandsgesprächen)*	Unit 1
introductory offer discount	*Angebots-Einführungsrabatt*	Unit 4
investigate	*untersuchen, nachforschen*	Unit 8
invoice	*Rechnung*	Units 4, 5, 6, 7
invoice amount	*Rechnungsbetrag*	Unit 6
involved, to be ~ in an accident	*in einen Unfall verwickelt sein*	Unit 8
irrevocable	*unwiderruflich*	Unit 3
irrevocable letter of credit, by ~	*per unwiderruflichem Akkreditiv*	Unit 4
irrevocable, the opening of an ~ and confirmed letter of credit	*Eröffnung eines unwiderruflichen und bestätigten Akkreditivs*	Unit 3
item	*Posten, Artikel*	Units 4, 5, 8

J

jacuzzi	*Whirlpool*	Unit 5
juice	*Saft*	Unit 8
jumbled	*durcheinander gewürfelt, in der falschen Reihenfolge*	Units 2, 3, 4, 5, 6, 8

K		
keep, to ~	*behalten*	Unit 8
knowledge of English	*Englischkenntnisse*	Unit 1
L		
language	*Sprache*	Unit 1
latest	*neueste(r, s)*	Units 2, 4
latest, at the ~	*spätestens*	Unit 2
lay down, to ~	*festlegen*	Unit 1
leading	*führend*	Units 2, 3
leaflet	*Faltblatt*	Units 1, 3
least favourable	*ungünstigste(r, s)*	Unit 7
letter of credit	*Akkreditiv*	Units 3, 7
letterhead	*Briefkopf*	Unit 1
level, on the same ~	*auf der gleichen Höhe (wie das Datum)*	Unit 1
liar	*Lügner*	Unit 7
liking, to be to your ~	*(Ihnen) zusagen*	Unit 3
link, a ~	*Verbindung*	Unit 1
liquor	*Alkohol; Spirituosen*	Unit 3
list, to ~	*auflisten*	Unit 1
load, to ~	*verladen*	Unit 6
location	*Ort*	Units 2, 5, 6, 8
long-standing	*hier: längjährig*	Unit 2
look, to ~ forward to	*sich freuen auf*	Units 1, 2, 3, 5
lorry	*Lkw*	Unit 8
M		
major	*größere(r, s)*	Units 2, 3
managing director	*Geschäftsführer/in*	Units 1, 2, 6, 8
manufacture, to ~	*herstellen, fertigen, erzeugen*	Units 2, 5
manufacturer	*Hersteller*	Unit 3
margin	*Rand*	Unit 1
marks	*hier: Versandmarkierungen*	Unit 6
match, to ~	*hier: zuordnen*	Unit 8
matter, on this ~	*in dieser Angelegenheit*	Unit 5
matter, the ~	*hier: Angelegenheit*	Unit 8
maturity, at ~	*bei Fälligkeit*	Unit 7
meantime, in the ~	*in der Zwischenzeit*	Unit 8
meet (deadline)	*einhalten (Frist)*	Unit 8
meet our requirements	*unseren Anforderungen entsprechen*	Unit 2
memo	*Memorandum, innerbetriebliche Mitteilung*	Unit 1
message	*Nachricht*	Unit 1
Messrs	*(die) Herren*	Unit 1
missing	*fehlende(r, s)*	Unit 4
missing, to be ~	*fehlen*	Unit 8
misunderstanding	*Missverständnis*	Unit 1
mixed up	*durcheinander gewürfelt, der falschen Reihenfolge*	Units 6, 8
mobile phone	*Handy*	Units 6, 8
mode of delivery	*Versandart*	Unit 5
mode of payment	*Zahlungsweise*	Unit 7
mode of transport	*Versandart*	Unit 6

N

named person, a ~	*eine namentlich genannte Person*	Unit 1
narrow	*schmal*	Unit 8
necessary	*notwendig*	Units 1, 8
need, to ~	*benötigen*	Unit 1
needed	*benötigt*	Unit 8
neither … nor	*weder … noch*	Unit 2
net	*netto*	Unit 3
net, 30 days ~	*30 Tage netto*	Unit 5
Netherlands, the ~	*die Niederlande*	Unit 8
note, please ~ that …	*etwa: Wir möchten Sie darauf hinweisen, dass …*	Unit 7
note, to ~	*feststellen, zur Kenntnis nehmen*	Unit 4

O

obligations	*hier: Pflichten*	Unit 3
obliged, be ~ to	*gezwungen sein*	Unit 8
obtain	*erhalten, bekommen, erwerben, beziehen*	Units 2, 3, 8
of this nature	*dieser Art*	Unit 2
office furniture	*Büromöbel*	Unit 8
office supplies	*Büroartikel*	Unit 8
on board	*an Bord*	Unit 6
on offer	*im Angebot*	Unit 7
on schedule	*pünktlich, planmäßig, termingerecht*	Unit 6
on this matter	*in dieser Angelegenheit*	Unit 5
on-board bill of lading	*Bordkonnossement*	Unit 6
on-screen	*auf dem Bildschirm*	Unit 1
order form	*Bestell-, Auftragsformular*	Units 1, 4
overdue	*überfällig*	Unit 8

P

packing	*Verpackung*	Units 3, 5
pallet	*Palette*	Unit 4
paragraph	*Absatz*	Unit 1
part-delivery	*Teillieferung*	Unit 8
particularly	*insbesondere*	Units 2, 3
payment	*Zahlung*	Unit 6
per, as ~	*gemäß*	Units 6, 7, 8
period	*Zeitraum*	Unit 7
phone call	*Telefonanruf*	Unit 6
place an order	*einen Auftrag erteilen*	Units 2, 3, 4, 5, 8
plant manager	*Werksleiter/in*	Unit 6
pleasantly surprised	*angenehm überrascht*	Unit 3
point of view	*hier: Sicht*	Unit 3
point out	*darauf hinweisen*	Units 3, 5, 7, 8
polite	*höflich*	Unit 2
polite ending	*höfliche Schlussformel*	Unit 7
poor packing	*schlechte Verpackung*	Unit 8
port, sea ~ (e.g. Hamburg)	*(See)Hafen*	Units 3, 6
post, a ~	*hier: Stelle*	Unit 1
postcode	*Postleitzahl (britisch)*	Unit 1
potteries (pottery)	*Töpfereien*	Unit 7
preferred title	*bevorzugte Anrede*	Unit 1

premises	*Geschäftsräume*	Units 2, 4, 5, 6, 8
pre-structured	*vorstrukturiert*	Unit 1
previous correspondence	*vorheriger Schriftverkehr*	Unit 1
process, to ~	*bearbeiten*	Units 1, 5
promised, as ~	*wie versprochen*	Unit 8
prompt attention	*hier: umgehende Erledigung*	Unit 4
provide with, to ~ (a reference)	*erbringen; zukommen lassen; geben (eine Referenz)*	Units 1, 2, 7
publication	*Veröffentlichung*	Unit 4
punctually	*pünktlich*	Units 1, 4, 6
punctuation	*Interpunktion*	Unit 1
purchasing department	*Einkaufsabteilung*	Units 4, 5, 6, 8
purchasing director	*Einkaufsleiter/in*	Units 1, 3, 4, 8
put to good use	*gut einbringen, gut verwerten*	Unit 1
put together	*zusammenstellen*	Unit 3

Q

qualifications	*Befähigungsnachweise*	Unit 1
qualify, to ~ for	*Anspruch haben auf*	Unit 7
quantity discount	*Mengenrabatt*	Unit 4
quarter	*hier: Quartal*	Unit 7
quarterly statement	*Quartalsabrechnung*	Unit 7
query, a ~	*(Rück)Frage*	Units 1, 6
quotation	*Preisangebot*	Units 2, 3, 4
quoted	*hier: angeboten*	Unit 5
quoted, our prices are ~	*unsere Preise verstehen sich*	Unit 3

R

rail, by ~	*per Bahn*	Unit 5
railway company	*Eisenbahngesellschaft*	Unit 8
range	*Palette, Sortiment*	Units 1, 3
rapidly	*schnell, rasch*	Unit 2
reach	*erreichen*	Unit 8
ready for collection	*abholbereit*	Unit 7
ready for despatch	*versandbereit*	Units 6, 7
re-arrange	*in die richtige Reihenfolge bringen*	Units 6, 8
reason	*Grund, Ursache*	Unit 8
reason, for this ~	*aus diesem Grund*	Unit 1
receipt	*hier: Erhalt*	Unit 8
receipt for the goods	*Empfangsbescheinigung für die Waren*	Unit 6
receipt of the goods, on ~	*nach Erhalt der Ware*	Unit 4
receipt, after ~ of order	*nach Erhalt des (Ihres) Auftrags*	Unit 3
receipt, after ~ of invoice	*nach Rechnungserhalt*	Unit 5
receipt, on ~ of our invoice	*bei Erhalt unserer Rechnung*	Unit 3
receive	*erhalten*	Units 1, 3, 5, 6
recent	*letzte(r, s)*	Unit 2
recent letter	*hier: letzter Brief*	Unit 1
recipient	*Empfänger*	Unit 1
recommend	*empfehlen*	Units 1, 3, 5
recommendation	*Empfehlung*	Unit 2
records	*hier: Aufzeichnungen*	Unit 7
reduce	*reduzieren*	Unit 8
reduction in price	*Preisnachlass*	Unit 8

refer to	*sich beziehen auf; zu Rate ziehen*	Unit 3
reference	*hier: Bezug*	Unit 4
reference initials	*Bezugsinitialen*	Unit 1
reference to	*Bezug auf*	Units 3, 5, 6, 7, 8
reference, with ~ to	*mit Bezug auf*	Unit 1
refusal	*Ablehnung*	Unit 5
refuse, to ~	*ablehnen*	Unit 5
regarding	*bezüglich*	Unit 8
Regards	*hier: Grüße*	Unit 1
regards, as ~	*bezüglich*	Unit 3
REGISTERED	*Einschreiben*	Unit 1
regret, to ~	*bedauern*	Units 5, 8
regular(ly)	*regelmäßig*	Unit 3
release, to ~	*aushändigen*	Unit 6
reliable	*zuverlässig*	Unit 5
remit, to ~	*zahlen, z. B. überweisen*	Unit 7
remittance	*Zahlung, z. B. Überweisung*	Unit 7
replace	*ersetzen*	Unit 8
replacements	*Ersatz [identische Ware]*	Unit 8
reply, a ~	*Antwort*	Unit 2
reply to, a ~	*hier: Bericht*	Unit 8
report, to ~	*hier: berichten*	Unit 8
reproduce	*wiedergeben*	Unit 1
reputation	*Ruf*	Unit 3
request, a ~	*Bitte*	Unit 2
request, on ~	*auf Wunsch*	Unit 3
request for payment	*Zahlungsaufforderung*	Unit 6
request, a ~ for	*Bitte um*	Units 5, 8
requested , if ~	*auf Wunsch*	Unit 3
requested, as ~	*wunschgemäß*	Units 3, 4, 5, 6, 7
require	*benötigen, brauchen*	Units 1, 2, 5, 7
required	*benötigt*	Unit 4
return	*hier: zurückschicken*	Unit 7
revise	*revidieren*	Unit 3
rights	*Rechte*	Unit 3
road, by ~	*per Straße*	Unit 5
rough	*rau*	Unit 8
rough handling	*unsachgemäße Behandlung*	Unit 8
row, a ~	*hier: Reihe*	Unit 4
rule, a ~	*Regel*	Unit 1
run out	*zu Ende gehen, erschöpft sein*	Unit 3

S

safely	*wohlbehalten*	Unit 6
sales department	*Verkaufsabteilung*	Unit 8
sales invoice	*Verkaufsrechnung*	Unit 4
sales literature	*Verkaufsliteratur*	Units 3, 4, 5
sales literature / material	*Verkaufsliteratur*	Unit 2
sales manager	*Verkaufsleiter/in*	Unit 1
sales network	*Verkaufsnetz*	Unit 2
salutation	*Anrede*	Unit 1
sample, a ~	*Muster; Probe*	Units 2, 3
satisfaction	*Zufriedenheit*	Unit 8
satisfaction, to your ~	*zu Ihrer Zufriedenheit*	Unit 6
schedule, on ~	*gemäß Zeitplan*	Unit 6

scratched	*zerkratzt*	Unit 8
sea, by ~	*per Schiff*	Unit 5
season	*Saison, Jahreszeit*	Unit 3, 4
selection	*Auswahl*	Unit 3
sell well	*hier: sich gut verkaufen lassen*	Unit 2
seller	*Verkäufer/in*	Units 3, 6, 7, 8
sells well, if this article ~	*wenn dieser Artikel sich gut verkaufen lässt*	Unit 4
separate post, by ~	*mit getrennter Post*	Unit 6
separate, to ~	*trennen*	Unit 1
series	*hier: Reihe*	Unit 7
serve, to ~	*(be)dienen*	Unit 1
set, no ~ layout	*kein festgelegtes Layout*	Unit 1
set out, to ~	*hier: gestalten, formatieren*	Unit 1
settle, to ~	*begleichen; erledigen*	Units 5, 8
several	*mehrere*	Units 7, 8
Severn	*englischer Fluss (the River Severn)*	Unit 7
ship, to ~	*versenden*	Units 4, 5, 6, 7
shipment	*hier: Versand; Lieferung*	Units 4, 6
shipment, port of ~	*Verschiffungshafen*	Unit 6
shipping	*Versand*	Unit 5
shipping charge	*Versandgebühr*	Unit 4
shipping company	*Reederei; Transportunternehmen, Versandfirma*	Unit 8
shortly	*bald, in Kürze*	Units 2, 5
should you ...	*sollten Sie ...*	Units 1, 2
signatory	*Unterzeichner/in*	Unit 1
signature	*Unterschrift*	Unit 1
similar	*ähnlich*	Unit 5
since	*hier: da*	Unit 3
size	*Größe*	Unit 8
sizeable	*größere(r,s)*	Unit 2
solution	*Lösung*	Unit 8
sort code	*Bankleitzahl*	Unit 7
source	*Quelle*	Unit 2
special marking	*besondere Markierung*	Unit 1
special offer	*Sonderangebot*	Unit 1
specialise in	*sich spezialisieren auf*	Unit 2
specimen	*Muster*	Units 2, 5
spirits	*Spirituosen*	Unit 2
stained	*mit Flecken versehen*	Unit 8
state, to ~	*angeben*	Units 2, 4, 5
stated, as ~	*wie angegeben*	Unit 5
statement	*Abrechnung*	Unit 7
stock, from ~	*ab Lager*	Unit 5
stock, in ~	*auf Lager*	Unit 5
stocks, before ~ run out	*hier: solange der Vorrat reicht*	Unit 3
study, to ~	*hier: prüfen*	Unit 4
sturdy	*stabil*	Units 4, 6
subject line	*Betreff*	Unit 1
subject to favourable references	*günstige Referenzen vorausgesetzt, sofern wir günstige Referenzen erhalten*	Unit 3
sub-standard	*minderwertig*	Unit 8

substantial	*beträchtlich*	Unit 2
substitute(s)	*Ersatz(waren)*	Unit 5
substitute, to	*ersetzen*	Unit 5
sub-total	*Zwischensumme*	Unit 4
successful	*erfolgreich*	Units 1, 2
suggest	*vorschlagen*	Unit 5, 8
sum	*Summe*	Unit 6
summarise	*zusammenfassen*	Unit 1
supplier	*Lieferant/in*	Units 2, 6, 8
supplies	*Lieferungen; Bedarf*	Unit 8
supply, to ~	*(be)liefern mit*	Units 2, 3, 5, 8
swivel chair	*Drehstuhl*	Units 5, 8

T

table	*hier: Tabelle*	Units 4, 5
tableware	*Tischgeschirr*	Unit 7
tabular form, in ~	*tabellarisch*	Unit 4
take delivery of, to ~	*in Empfang nehmen*	Units 1, 7
take out	*abschließen*	Unit 4
technicalities	*technische Einzelheiten*	Unit 5
telegraphic transfer	*telegraphische Überweisung*	Unit 7
terms	*Bedingungen*	Units 1, 3, 4
terms of delivery	*Lieferbedingungen*	Units 2, 3, 5
terms of payment	*Zahlungsbedingungen*	Unit 2, 5
terms, on first name ~	*per Du*	Unit 1
terms, on friendly ~	*per Du*	Unit 1
therefore	*deshalb, daher*	Units 5, 7, 8
threaten	*drohen*	Unit 8
throughout ...	*in ganz ...*	Units 2, 3
together with	*zusammen mit*	Unit 3
top-grade	*erstklassig*	Unit 3
total	*gesamt (Betrag)*	Unit 4
total amount	*Gesamtbetrag*	Unit 5
touch, get in ~ with	*sich in Verbindung setzen mit*	Unit 8
trade	*hier: Handel*	Unit 5
trade discount	*Wiederverkäuferrabatt, Handelsrabatt*	Unit 4
trade fair	*Handelsmesse*	Unit 2
trade journal	*Fachzeitschrift*	Unit 2
trade reference	*Handlesreferenz*	Unit 3
transfer, a ~	*Überweisung*	Units 4, 5, 7
transfer, to ~	*überweisen*	Unit 7
transit, in ~	*auf dem Transport*	Unit 8
transit, lost in ~	*auf dem Transport verloren gegangen*	Unit 8
trial order	*Probeauftrag*	Units 2, 3, 4
trombone	*Posaune*	Unit 6
trust, to ~	*zuversichtlich sein; davon ausgehen, dass*	Units 1, 6, 8
twisted	*verdreht*	Unit 8
typist	*Schreibkraft*	Unit 1

U

under the circumstances	*unter den Umständen*	Unit 8
underline	*unterstreichen*	Unit 1

unfortunately	*leider*	Unit 5
unit price	*Stückpreis*	Unit 4
unsatisfactory	*unzufriedenstellend*	Unit 8
until	*bis*	Unit 3
unusable	*unbenutzbar*	Unit 8
upon examining the ...	*als wir die ... prüften*	Unit 8
urgent(ly)	*dringend*	Units 3, 8
use, to ~	*verwenden, gebrauchen*	Units 1, 3, 4
usual	*üblich*	Units 6, 8

V

valid	*gültig*	Unit 3
validity	*Gültigkeit*	Unit 3
vocational training college	*Berufsschule*	Unit 1

W

warehouse	*Lager*	Units 4, 6
welcome, to ~	*hier: begrüßen*	Unit 8
well-established	*gut eingeführt*	Unit 2
whatever the case may be	*wie dem auch sei*	Unit 8
while stocks last	*solange der Vorrat reicht*	Unit 3
wholesaler	*Großhändler/in*	Units 2, 3
widely-used, most ~	*am häufigsten verwendet*	Unit 1
willing, to be ~	*bereit sein*	Units 2, 8
wine-grower	*Winzer/in, Weinbauer/in*	Unit 3
within	*innerhalb, binnen*	Units 1, 3, 4, 5, 7, 8
without delay	*unverzüglich*	Unit 8
without fail	*auf jeden Fall*	Unit 8
wrist-watch	*Armbanduhr*	Unit 8
wrong order, in the ~	*in der falschen Reihenfolge*	Unit 4
wrong, to go ~	*schief gehen*	Unit 8

Z

ZIP code	*Postleitzahl (amerikanisch)*	Unit 1

Shipper

Bill of Lading

for Combined Transport or port to port shipment or through carriage.
Not negotiable unless consigned "to order".

B/L No.

Consignee (if "to Order" so indicate)

New Brunswick Container Line

H. & E. Brunswick
GmbH & Co

Notify address (No claim shall attach for failure to notify)

		Place of receipt
Ocean vessel	Voy No.	Port of loading
Port of discharge		Place of delivery

Marks and numbers;	Number and kind of packages or shipping units	Description of goods said to contain	Gross weight	Measurement

Specimen

Excess Value Declaration: Refer to Clause 6 (4) (B) + (C) on reverse side   Particulars above declared by shipper

Freight and charges

RECEIVED by the Carrier the goods in apparent good order and condition and, as far as ascertained by reasonable means of checking, as specified above unless otherwise stated, to be transported to such place as agreed, authorised or permitted herein and subject to all the terms and conditions appearing on the front and reverse of this Bill of Lading to which the Merchant agrees by accepting this Bill of Lading, any local privileges and customs notwithstanding.

The particulars given above as stated by the shipper and the weight, measure, quantity, condition, contents and value of the Goods are unknown to the Carrier.

One of the Bs/L must be surrendered duly endorsed in exchange for the goods or delivery order.

IN WITNESS whereof the number of original Bills of Lading stated below have been signed, all of this tenor and date, one of which being accomplished, the others to be void.

For the release of goods apply to:

Freight payable at	Place and date of issue
Number of original Bs/L	Signed as carrier H. & E. Brunswick GmbH & Co.

Consignment Note

LETTRE DE VOITURE INTERNATIONALE CMR INTERNATIONAL CONSIGNMENT NOTE

(c) SITPRO, FTA, RHA 1992

COPY 1 SENDER
COPY 2 CONSIGNEE
COPY 3 CARRIER

Sender (name, address, country) Expediteur (nom, adresse, pays) 1	Sender's/agent's reference Reference de l'expediteur/de l'agent 2/3
Consignee (name, address, country) Destinataire (nom,adresse,pays) 4	Carrier (name, address,country) Transporteur (nom, adresse, pays) 5
Place & date of taking over the goods (place,country date) ILieu et date de la prise en charge des marchandises (lieu,pays,date) 6	Successive carriers Transporteurs successifs 7
Place designated for delivery of goods (place, country) Lieu prevu pour la livraison des marchandises (leiu,pays) 8	This carriage is subject, notwithstanding any clause to the contary, to the Convention on the Contract for the international Carriage of Goods by Road (CMR) Ce transport est soumis nonobstant toute clause contaire a la Convention Relative au Contrat de Transport International de Marchandises par Route (CMR)

*NB FOR DANGEROUS GOODS SPECIFY:

1. Substance identification number (if applicable)
2. Substance description.
3. Class.
4. Item number and letter (if any).
5. The initials 'ADR' or 'RID'.
6. Other statements as required by ADR or RID.

Shipping marks; no & kind of packages; description of goods * Marques et nos; no et nature des colis; designation des marchandises* 9	Gross weight (kg) 10 Poids brut (kg)	Volume (m3) 11 Cubage (m3)

Specimen

Carriage charges Prix de transport 12	Senders instruction for customs etc.. Instruction de l'expediteur (optional) 13

Reservations Reserves 14	Document attached Documents annexes (optional) 15 Special agreements Conventions particulieres (optional) 16

Goods received Marchandises recues 17	Signature of carrier Signature du transporteur 18	Company completing this note Societe emettrice 19 Place and date; signature Lieu et date. signature 20

SITPRO Licensee No. 000.

Air Waybill

CSR/ECI

Shipper's Name and Address

Shipper's Account Number

Not Negotiable
Air Waybill
issued by
British Airways London
Member of IATA

BRITISH AIRWAYS

Copies 1, 2 and 3 of this Air Waybill are originals and have the same validity

Consignee's Name and Address

Consignee's Account Number

It is agreed that the goods described herein are accepted in apparent good order and condition (except as noted) for carriage SUBJECT TO THE CONDITIONS OF CONTRACT ON THE REVERSE HEREOF. THE SHIPPER'S ATTENTION IS DRAWN TO THE NOTICE CONCERNING CARRIER'S LIMITATION OF LIABILITY. Shipper may increase such limitation of liability by declaring a higher value for carriage and paying a supplemental charge if required.

ISSUING CARRIER MAINTAINS CARGO ACCIDENT LIABILITY INSURANCE

Issuing Carrier's Agent

Accounting Information

Agent's IATA Code

Account No.

Airport of departure (Addr. of First Carrier) and Requested Routing

To	By First Carrier	Routing and Destination	to	by	to	by	Currency	CHGS Code	WT/VAL PPD	WT/VAL COLL	Other PPD	Other COLL	Declrd Val for Carrg.	Declrd Val for Customs

Airport of Destination

Flight/Date | For Carrier Use Only | Flight/Date

Specimen

Handling Information

No. of Pieces RCP	Gross Weight	kg lb	Rate Class / Commodity Item No.	Chargeable Weight	Rate / Charge	Total	Nature and Quantity of Goods (incl. Dimensions or Volume)

Prepaid | Weight charge | Collect

Other Charges

Valuation Charge

Tax

Total Other Charges Due Agent

Shipper certifies that the particulars on the face hereof are correct and that insofar as any part of the consignment contains dangerous goods, such part is properly described by name and is in proper condition for carriage by air according to the applicable Dangerous Goods Regulations.

Total Other Charges Due Carrier

....
Signature of Shipper or his agent

Total prepaid | Total collect

Currency conversion rates | cc charges in dest. currency

....
Executed on (date) | at (place) | Signature of Issuing Carrier or its agent

For Carrier's Use only at Destination | Charges at Destination | Total Collect Charges

Original 3 - (For Shipper)

Commercial Invoice

INVOICE RECHNUNG FACTURE FACTURA فاتورة

(c) SITPRO 1992

Seller (name, address, VAT reg no.)

SITPRO
The Simpler Trade Procedures Board
151 Buckingham Palace Road, London SW1W 9SS
VAT Reg. No. 241 8235 77

Invoice number
JP-IV2167

Invoice date (tax point)
10.08.94

Seller's reference
JP-IV2167

Buyer's reference
P.O.4123

Other reference

U N I C

Consignee VAT no.
Aikashinko Shibakhoen Inc.
6-1, Honcho
Kanamatsu Cho, Naka-Ku
Kyoto
Japan

Buyer (if not consignee) VAT no.
Aikashinko Group Holdings Inc.
1-11-3 Shiba-Daimon
Kitatoneyama, Toyonaka City
Osaka
Japan

Country of origin of goods
UK (EEC)

Country of destination
Japan

Terms of delivery and payment
DDP - Delivered Duty Paid Kyoto.

Payment via: Bank of Foreign Trade
18-22 Valentine Place, London WC2
Account no. 120 7532 68

Vessel/flight no. and date
Gala Del Mar

Port/airport of loading
Liverpool

Port/airport of discharge
Osaka

Place of delivery
Kyoto

Shipping marks; container number
Aikashinko
P.O.4123
Kyoto
via Osaka
Japan

No. and kind of packages; description of goods
26 Cases
Lamp accessories and
advertising materia

Commodity code

Total gross wt (Kg)
Kilos
82.75

Total net wt (Kg)
75.75

Total cube (m3)

Specimen

Item/packages	Gross/net/cube	Description	Quantity	Unit price	Amount
1) 10 Cases		Cat. E/558W. 3 terminal angle batten lampholder - long skirt	250	1.60 each	400.00
2) 15 Cases		Cat. E/42W. 3 terminal angle batten lampholder - short skirt	400	1.26 each	504.00

					904.00
		1 case of advertising/ promotional literature.			

Invoice total
GBP 904.00

We warrant that the goods described above comply with regulation 4092 of 13 May 1981, and that packaging and labelling are to the specifications laid down in regulation 248 of 11 February 1987.

Name of signatory
B Zbyszewski, Accountant

Place and date of issue
Orpington 10.08.94

Signature
B. Zbyszewski

It is hereby certified that this invoice shows the actual price of the goods described, that no other invoice has been or will be issued, and that all particulars are true and correct.

SITPRO Licensee No. 000.

V5

Pro Forma Invoice

PROFORMA INVOICE

(c) SITPRO 1992

Seller (name, address, VAT reg no.)

Proforma invoice number

Date

Seller's reference

Buyer's reference

Other reference

UNIC

Consignee VAT no.

Buyer (if not consignee) VAT no.

Country of origin of goods

Country of destination

Terms of delivery and payment

Vessel/flight no. and date

Port/airport of loading

Port/airport of discharge

Place of delivery

Shipping marks; container number

No. and kind of packages; description of goods

Commodity code

Total gross wt (Kg)

Total cube (m3)

Specimen

Total net wt (Kg)

Item/packages	Gross/net/cube Description	Quantity	Unit price	Amount

Invoice total

Name of signatory

Place and date of issue

Signature

SITPRO Licensee No. 000.

V5

Insurance Certificate

ORIGINAL

THIS CERTIFICATE REQUIRES ENDORSEMENT IN THE EVENT OF ASSIGNMENT

CLAIMS SETTLEMENT INSTRUCTIONS

1. Lloyd's Settling Agent nearest destination is authorised to adjust and settle on behalf of the Underwriters, and to purchase on behalf of the Corporation of Lloyd's, in accordance with Lloyd's Standing Regulations for the Settlement of Claims Abroad, any claim which may arise on this Certificate.
2. If Lloyd's Agents are not to deal with claims, it should be clearly marked by an 'X' in the adjacent box and claim papers sent to :- A. Short & Co. Ltd., 1 London Road, London EC9 1OC.

Certificate of Insurance No. C 0000/

This is to Certify **that there has been deposited with the Council of Lloyd's a Contract effected by** *A. Short & Co. Ltd.*, **of Lloyd's, acting on behalf of** *Bodgit and Scarpa Ltd.*, **with Underwriters at Lloyd's, for insurances attaching thereto during the period commencing the** *First* **day of** *March, 1997,* **and ending the** *Twenty-eighth* **day of** *February, 1998,* **both days inclusive, and that the said Underwriters have undertaken to issue to** *A. Short & Co. Ltd.*, **Policy/Policies of Insurance at Lloyd's to cover, up to** *US$5,000,000 (or equivalent in other currencies),* **in all by any one** *steamer and/or conveyances, or sending by air and/or post, General Merchandise and/or Goods and/or Equipment of any nature whatsoever including but not limited to Rice, Sugar, Motor Spare Parts, Bicycles, Generator Sets, Raw Jute, Jute Goods,* **from any port or ports, place or places in** *the World,* **to any port or ports, place or places in** *the World, including all transhipments as and when occurring,* **and that** *Bodgit and Scarpa Ltd.*, **are entitled to declare against the said Contract insurances attaching thereto.**

for the Council of Lloyd's.
Dated at Lloyd's, London, 20th May, 1998.

Conveyance **From**

Via/To **To** **INSURED VALUE/Currency**

Marks and Numbers **Interest**

SPECIMEN

We hereby declare for Insurance under the said Contract interest as specified above so valued subject to the special conditions stated below and on the back hereof.

Institute Cargo Clauses (A) or Institute Cargo Clauses (Air) (excluding sendings by Post) as applicable. Excluding rust, oxidisation, discoloration, twisting and bending.
Institute War Clauses (Cargo) or Institute War Clauses (Air Cargo) (excluding sendings by Post) or Institute War Clauses (sendings by Post) as applicable.
Institute Strikes Clauses (Cargo) or Institute Strikes Clauses (Air Cargo) as applicable.
Institute Classification Clause.
Institute Radioactive Contamination Exclusion Clause.
Institute Replacement Clause.

Underwriters agree losses, if any, shall be payable to the order of BODGIT AND SCARPA LTD., on surrender of this Certificate.

In the event of loss or damage which may result in a claim under this Insurance, immediate notice must be given to the Lloyd's Agent at the port or place where the loss or damage is discovered in order that he may examine the goods and issue a survey report. The survey agent will normally be the Agent authorised to adjust and settle claims in accordance with the terms and conditions set forth herein, but where such Agent does not hold the requisite authority, he will be able to supply the name and address of the appropriate Settling Agent.

(Survey fee is customarily paid by claimant and included in valid claim against Underwriters.)

SEE IMPORTANT INSTRUCTIONS ON REVERSE

This Certificate not valid unless the Declaration be signed by
BODGIT AND SCARPA LTD.

Dated

Signed

Brokers : A. Short & Co. Ltd.,
1 London Road, London EC9 1OC.

LLOYD'S

Authorised Signatory

9405CM

Certificate of Origin

1 Consignor	No. DA	ORIGINAL
2 Consignee	EUROPEAN COMMUNITY CERTIFICATE OF ORIGIN	
	3 Country of Origin	
4 Transport details (Optional)	5 Remarks	
6 Item number; marks; numbers; number and kind of packages; description of goods	7 Quantit	

Specimen

8 THE UNDERSIGNED AUTHORITY CERTIFIES THAT THE GOODS DESCRIBED ABOVE ORIGINATE IN THE COUNTRY SHOWN IN BOX 3

Place and date of issue, name, signature and stamp of competent authority

.... 19 ....

DTI/VJ5/5/1

Bill of Exchange

______, the ______
Place and date of issuance

For ______
Amount in figures

At / On ______
Maturity

pay this ______ Bill of Exchange (______ unpaid) to the order of ______

______ the sum of

______
Amount in words

To ______
Drawee

______

at ______

payable at ______
Place

______

with ______
Name and address of the bank

______
to the debit of account No.

Drawer's signature and full address

Specimen

Contract – *The amazing new board game for students of commerce*

Object
The object of the game is to reach the last square without going bankrupt on the way. The first player to reach the last square in this way is a multi-millionaire. The other players then count their capital to see who has come second, third etc.

Rules
1. Each player has € 50,000 capital to start with and keeps a running total of the amount of capital left on a piece of paper which any other player is allowed to see at any time during the game.
2. Each player has a counter which is placed on the **"Start"** square. The player throws the dice and moves the number of squares thrown along the board.
   If the player lands on a **"Situation 1"**, **"Court Case 2"** square, etc., the instructions for this square are read out and followed.
3. Any player who goes bankrupt drops out of the game.
4. The first player to land on the **"Multi-Millionaire"** square (by throwing exactly the right number) wins. The remaining players count their capital to see who has come second, third, etc.

Situation 1
You have made a profit on an export deal. Each player gives you € 5,000. Throw the dice again.

Situation 2
You have made a loss on an export deal. Give each other player € 5,000.

Situation 3
Your insurance premium goes up unexpectedly. Give the player in your group with the longest first name € 20,000.

Situation 4
Your company brings out a successful new product. Each of the other players buys it and gives you € 5,000. Throw the dice again.

Situation 5
Your Chief Accountant is a thief and runs away with your money! You lose € 5,000 to each of the other players.

Activity 1
Spelling test! Throw the dice again and then ask another player to spell an English word with the number of words in the table:

If the other player spells the word right, give him/her € 1,000. If he/she spells it wrong, you receive € 1,000.

If you can't think of a word or spell a word wrong, give the other player € 1,000.

Dice Score	*Number of Letters*
1	4
2	5
3	6
4	7
5	8
6	9

Activity 2
Give the name of an English (American, Canadian, Australian etc.) film with a title of three words or more. For a correct answer you receive € 500 from each other player. For a wrong or no answer give each other player € 500.

Activity 3
Give the English title of a book or play written by one of the following authors:
1. Stephen King
2. Michael Crighton
3. Charles Dickens
4. William Shakespeare

For a correct answer you receive € 500 from each other player. For a wrong or no answer give each other player € 500.

Activity 4
Give the names of the President of the United States and the Prime Minister of the United Kingdom. For two correct answers you receive € 1,000 from each other player. If you cannot give two correct answers, give each of the other players € 500.

Free Fall
It's Black Monday and the Stock Exchange has crashed! Give half of all the capital you have to the player in your group with the shortest first name.

Windfall
The tax laws have been changed. You make a windfall profit of € 5,000. Throw the dice again.

Ransom 1
Thieves break into your offices and steal your hard disk! You pay € 10,000 ransom to get the data back.

Ransom 2
Industrial espionage! There is a break-in at your top secret design plant and the plans for your new product are stolen! You pay € 15,000 ransom to get them back.

Court Case 1
Each of the other players asks you a German → English vocabulary question from the vocabulary list of the Unit you are doing now or did last. You pay € 10,000 to the player for each wrong answer and receive € 10,000 from the player for each right answer.

Court Case 2
Each of the other players asks you two German → English vocabulary questions from the vocabulary list of the Unit you are doing now or did last. You pay € 5,000 to the player for each wrong answer and receive € 5,000 from the player for each right answer.

Joker 1
Congratulations! You've just got married! You get € 5,000 from each of the other players as a wedding present.

Joker 2
Bad luck! You've just got divorced. Give each other player € 5,000.

Joker 3
You inherit € 10,000. Miss a turn while you wait for the money to come through.

Disaster!
Your warehouse burns down and you lose € 25,000! Throw the dice again.

Setback 1
Your premises are robbed and you lose € 10,000! Throw the dice again and go back this number of squares.

Setback 2
Your company's computer network crashes and takes a month to repair. Throw the dice again and go back double the number of squares.

Setback 3
Your telephone system is struck by lightning and takes weeks to repair. Throw the dice again and go back three times the number of squares.